ESSEX PUBLICATIONS THE LIBRARIES SERVICE

Class 920 LAN

Barcode

Location   Received 5.14

Supplier Am2 Price

DYNIX BIB NO.

If we could read the secret history of our enemies, we would find in each person's life sorrow and suffering enough to disarm all hostility.

    Driftwood (1857)
    Henry Wadsworth Longfellow

Proof of Bloodline/Family Tree of Brigitte Langer
J = Jewish, C = Catholic

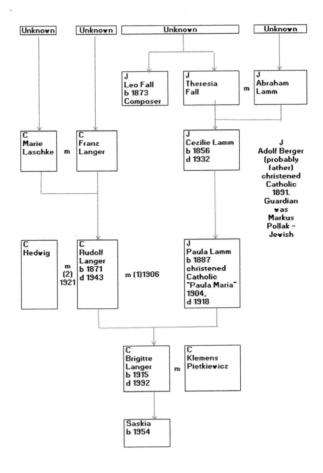

East Dunbartonshire Libraries

3 8060 05579 0190

ED LEISURE+CULTURE
Libraries

BISHOPBRIC
BROOK
CR

SURVIVING BRIGITTE'S SECRETS

A Holocaust Survivor. Her Daughter. Two Traumatic Journeys.

SASKIA TEPE

Published by Author Way Limited
Copyright 2014 Saskia Tepe
All rights reserved

Cover design by Kevin Hickey
kevinthomashickey@gmail.com

This book has been brought to you by -

Discover other Author Way Limited titles at -
http://www.authorway.net

ISBN: 1496073843
ISBN-13:978-1496073846

Map of Modern Europe showing places relevant to Memoir

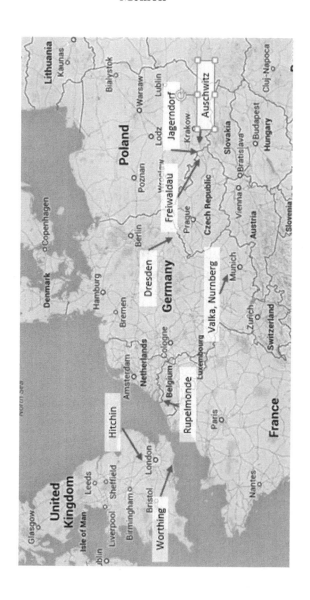

SASKIA TEPE

Introduction

My mother's legacy to me was a box file full of documents, secrets, mixed emotions, and unanswered questions. Her story of survival throughout the Nazi regime, and the documents she left, are part of a social history that continues to interest this generation and the next.

Less well known however, is the story of the children of holocaust survivors. They had to deal with the traumatic discovery of their parent's experiences, and the consequences of the psychological scars that their parents carried. All too often they too suffer an inability to connect with their emotions. This affliction – this emotional handicap – has only been understood by me recently. It has not, to my knowledge, been described in any great detail other than in psychological studies.

I know the day will come when my sons, like me, will feel the need to look for their roots. But I don't want them to be left like I was - with mixed emotions and myriad questions, arising from the gaps left in a mosaic of information, anecdotes, and vague childhood memories.

This book is therefore an attempt to describe the life of a holocaust survivor who had to deal with repressed feelings of guilt, shame and anger, as she struggled for subsistence amongst the thousands of Displaced Persons and Refugees who survived World War II. It is also the story of her daughter, a "second generation holocaust survivor", bequeathed with the psychological wounds of war and its aftermath.

Reviews for Surviving Brigitte's Secrets

Saskia Tepe gently but firmly takes the reader by the hand, and does not let them go until she has shared with them her journey of finding the answers to the troubling questions arising from her mother's hidden history.

During that shared journey, we experience displacement, loss, and family secrets from a tween's and then teenager's viewpoint, put into context by an adult Saskia. She demonstrates their long lasting impact, yet without using these as an excuse to fail in life.

Saskia's story also addresses, in a gentle and matter of fact way, the need for counselling, to help cope with unsettling life experiences. We are guided through her doubts, guilts and her observations on labelling, and ultimately understand how positive life altering counselling support can be.

This book would be ideal for young adults. It uses a voice and perception with which one can easily associate. I think particularly important is the interspersed adult voice that provides balance, and long-term perspective. The strong message is clear: life is a patchwork, it is not a straightforward road to travel, and that this is perfectly acceptable.

Dr Nathalie Sheridan, Lecturer, Learning Development Centre, Glasgow Caledonian University.

Saskia Tepe tells a unique story of how her mother, Brigitte, survived the holocaust and her own experiences as the child of a holocaust survivor in circumstances that will surprise many readers.

This is a hidden story of World War 2 that is at once shocking and intriguing. Brigitte was not Jewish, but was from the contested borders of Sudetenland and, following her ordeal at the hands of Nazis, also suffered at the hands of allied forces.

Brigitte then lived in a displaced persons camp in Germany for years. It was a revelation to me and I suspect to many others, that such camps existed after the war ended. What is more, long after the war formally ended, Saskia was born into refugee life in one of these camps in the mid 1950's.

The account of her mother's life is part biography and part detective story since Brigitte provided only rare and fragmentary insights to her daughter about experiences that were clearly painful, if not impossible to discuss. Saskia describes an unusual and difficult childhood, from being in an orphanage as a baby to life in the displaced persons camp as a young child, relieved during temporary spells with people in other countries - strangers to her who, nonetheless, provided relief from the restrictions of life in a camp and became life-long friends. Eventually mother and daughter moved to the UK as refugees and, in time, could lead more settled lives, but both carried the scars with them.

This is a story well worth the telling, of triumph over adversity by two exceptional women in their private battles to overcome the deep emotional wounds of war and its aftermath and build up their lives in the UK from uncertain and fractured foundations as refugees.

For me, Saskia's story is also an important and timely reminder in today's increasingly cynical world that we should acknowledge the cause of asylum seekers and respect and support them in their journey of recovery from war, conflict or persecution.

Morag Gillespie. Scottish Poverty Information Unit, Institute for Society and Social Justice Research. Glasgow Caledonian University

This is a touching and intriguing memoir about a Sudeten German labeled Mischling during the Holocaust. It sheds light on a relatively unknown dimension of the Holocaust and the postwar years. Sudeten Mischlinge survivors were forced to endure two ordeals, under Nazi and Soviet occupation. It is an amazing survival story, and how that survival created family secrets and a tenuous and mysterious relationship with her daughter. It is also a story of love between mother and daughter and a quest for hidden family history.

Cynthia Southern, author of The Blond Beast of Birkenau and Belsen: The Life and Crimes of Irma Grese

A beautifully written and detailed memoir

Nalini Chetty – Actress and Playwright

PART 1

Chapter 1   Discovery

My mother's confessions one frosty October evening in 1967 exploded like WW2 bombs into my thirteen year old heart, turning my past into a pile of rubble to be sifted through for remnants of truth.

It was the only time she voluntarily shared any of the secrets she had carefully hoarded because of war and its aftermath. The remainder, I had to find out for myself.

I was always an inquisitive child, yet I rarely asked questions. Outwardly I seemed to take what life doled out to me just as hungry children will eat unthinkingly from the plate put down in front of them. But, buried deep within was a 'snooping-around-in-drawers   and   coming-to-my-own-conclusions' type of child. Being able to digest, reflect and reason out the purpose behind whatever I discovered, generally made facing the future much easier.

And so, in my nosy way, I had already stumbled across some clues to my mother's mysterious past just a few days before she revealed the full details.

The sound of Bobby Gentry's Ode to Billie Joe was still ringing in my ears as I walked up the front path. All pleasant thoughts of my visit to my friend Carole's house disappeared as I fumbled in my pocket for the keys. The front door was wrenched open by the old man from upstairs, and I almost jumped in fright. Ugh, how he made me shudder. He was fat and sweaty, and wheezed as he walked. Yet I could never pass him without looking at his face - fascinated and repulsed at the same time, hating myself for doing it, and knowing I would feel the bile rise whenever I saw the hollow gaping socket.

His Glass Eye was in.

I forced my gaze past him down the dimly lit hallway. "Den Dobry" he said in his customary polite way.

"Good day" I replied meekly. Stepping back to let him go out into the cold, I slunk into the house, unlocked the door to our front room and quickly shut it behind me.

Back pressed to the door, anger screaming inside me, hot tears filled my eyes, and the usual thoughts shouted in my head. How I hated this house. How I hated my life. Why couldn't it just have been NORMAL? Why couldn't I have grown up in a nice house, with a TV and a Record Player and another brother or sister; eaten Roast Beef and Yorkshire Pudding every Sunday after church; had parents who loved each other through thick and thin? Why couldn't I have been kissed goodnight in a warm soft bed in a pink bedroom with posters of the Monkees on the wall and a kidney shaped dressing table, and fallen asleep knowing that the friends I had said goodbye to the day before would be the friends I would be seeing the next morning?

After a while I calmed down. Angry as I was, I knew the cause of my unhappiness. And there was nothing that could be done about it. It wasn't as though anything had changed for the worse recently; in fact my newly forged friendship with Carole was my one consolation, which shone like a symbol of hope in the dreary wretchedness of the rest of my life.

Aware that I was shivering, I methodically went through the process of getting the fire lit. After raking out the ashes, I transferred a shovelful of coal from the old metal bucket into the grate, piling the black lumps carefully around the gas poker which would start the coals burning much more quickly than paper and kindling. That poker was the most extravagant appliance my mother had and I was extremely grateful for it.

I was sitting on the floor as close as I could to the hearth trying to heat my chilled bones, contemplating whether to do my homework now or later, when I realised I had not shut the curtains. I knew that the dark evenings allowed passers-by a clear view into people's brightly lit front rooms, and although I liked catching glimpses of other more pleasant lives, I did not wish our shabby little home to be open to scrutiny.

As I turned back from the now safely curtain-covered bay window I spied the case.

It was a square brown attaché case with a carry handle on the top. It was not smooth leather like Carole's father's briefcase, but shiny and patterned like crocodile skin. I hadn't seen it before. It seemed far too fancy and out of place in our Spartan front room. I doubted if my mother could have kept it out of sight previously, because there wasn't any furniture in the small room large enough to house the case, apart from the base of the grey threadbare sofa bed facing me, and I knew it hadn't been in there. The oak desk which leaned against the wall opposite the fireplace was far too small. The carved sandalwood chest below the bay window given to us by Mr Moss was crammed full of material and good linen, and odd pieces of silverware.

My curiosity piqued, I knelt down to examine it, and turned the tiny key. It contained about a dozen envelopes of varying size. I chose one at random. Pulling out a large thick folded piece of paper, I read the title "Statutory Declaration" with the date 25th August 1966 printed in smaller letters underneath. I thought back and realised that I would still have been in Belgium at that time, while my mother would have been studying to be a nurse in Papworth.

Unfolding it, I discovered the "declaration" confirmed who she was: Brigitta Pietkiewicz; where she was born: Stadt Olbersdorf in Czechoslovakia in 1915, who her parents were: Rudolf and Paula Langer, that she had got married to Klemens Pietkiewicz (widower) at the Rathaus in Nuremburg, Germany, on 1st September 1956, and that she had come to England on 29th June 1961. Then there was some convoluted legal wording I didn't understand. It was "Declared" at Cambridge and "Signed before" the Commissioner for Oaths.

I reread it. I could not figure out the point of the document. But what was most intriguing, was that it stated that she had got married in September 1956.

I had photos taken of me and my parents at their church wedding in the Refugee Camp in Germany. It must have been in the winter of 1960, because it had been cold and my mother had worn a fur coat over her best blue suit. My mother had told me that there was a civil wedding before the church wedding. And this was where the maths didn't add up. If the civil ceremony had been in 1956, and I was born in 1954, then that meant I was already two years old when they first got married.

Crimson shame crept up my neck to the tips of my ears as the implication dawned on me. Suddenly I could see headlines spinning towards me, flashing across my cinematic screen of vision: "Refugee Mother Carries Love Child", "Saskia - Born out of Wedlock", "Scandal of Illegitimate Daughter". At the same instant I heard whispering voices, saw pointing fingers. My heart raced, as the blood pumped to my swimming head.

"Oh well." I thought, grappling with and determined to crush the implicit slur. "It's just another label to add to the store." I had been called plenty of names in my thirteen years; one more wouldn't make much difference. Besides, I reminded myself, I had been called loving names, not just cruel ones. And what did it matter if I was illegitimate? The world was changing. It was 1967 after all. It might still be an important issue for religious people, or the upper classes. They also seemed to think that divorce was shameful. A king had been forced to abdicate his throne because he had married a divorcee, for goodness sake. But the historical novels I loved to read seemed to indicate that there were plenty of bastards born outside of marriage, and apart from not being able to inherit tracts of land, they did not seem to be excluded from society.

My thoughts must have continued swirling, trying to assuage the shame, when with sudden clarity, it occurred to me that this was my mother's secret, and I was the only one who had discovered it. No one else need ever know because I would make sure no one else would ever find out.

My heart slowed, my eyes refocused onto the paper in my hand. Having thus rationalised the crisis in my perfectly logical way, I was able to resume looking through the case.

I opened another A4 envelope, thicker than the first, and found that it contained a bundle of what looked like certificates, some with official stamps. There was a wedding certificate dated 13ᵗʰ January 1906, indicating that Rudolf Langer married Paula Lamm, in Lobenstein, Sudetenland. I remembered my grandmother was called Paula. It would have been so much better if I had been called Paula after her, because it would have fitted right in. How more English a name could you get? There was even a song about it - Hey Paula, sung by Paul and Paula - how I had loved that tune.

Suddenly the penny dropped. I recognised my grandfather's surname now, and remembered where I had seen it before.

Picking up my keys, I left the sitting room. I pulled the door shut behind me, quickly took the two steps round the corner and unlocked the door to my bedroom. I opened my wardrobe and retrieved the little black cardboard suitcase that I used for travelling. Now it stored varying yardage of different coloured material that my mother always insisted on buying whenever there was a bargain to be had, intending to transform these into fashionable outfits whenever she could afford to buy a new pattern.

I turned the battered case towards the light and looked at the inside of the lid.

There it was, written in black lettering:

Saskia Rosa ~~Langer~~ **Pietkiewicz**

So it was true! I had been born before my parents married, and had been called by my mother's maiden name! It had stared me in the face every time I had opened my suitcase, but I must simply have been too young to be curious, let alone understand.

My thoughts were interrupted by the lunatic from upstairs. I say lunatic, because he mumbled to himself all the time. He was doing that just now as he walked up the stairs to his room, which was above our dining room. He made my skin crawl.

I put the suitcase back, and when I noticed the time on the alarm clock on the floor beside my bed I scurried back into the front room, quickly replaced the certificates in the order I had found them, and re-locked the case. I managed to put it back

SASKIA TEPE

behind the armchair, sit down, open my school bag and take out a jotter, and was pretending to study it with great intensity when my mother unlocked the sitting room door.

"Hello, Schaeffi." How I wished she would stop calling me that! It's all very well being called a baby lamb when you are younger, but I was nearly fourteen for goodness sake.

The freezing air followed her in and seemed to cling to her coat. My mother was already shorter than me, a mere five foot two inches, with greying hair that she wound into a loose bun and kept in place with numerous pins and a fine hairnet. She carefully took off her mohair beret. Although her round face glowed healthily, I knew it was a false impression caused by walking the half mile from the railway station in the bitter cold. Her normally bright blue eyes looked wan and tired. She unbuttoned her fur lined wool coat, shrugged it off, and folded it carefully over the chair beside the desk.

"Ach, what a day I haf had". My mother's German accent was still strong. She liked to try to use English, but often switched back to German half way through a sentence when she struggled for a word. She sat down on the sofa next to me and took off her shoes, rubbing first the right and then the left of her deformed big toes.

I was never sure whether they were bunions, because although I had heard the word, and knew it had something to do with painful feet, I had never seen anyone else's to compare. My mother had told me the reason her big toes were pushed up and over her second toes was because her stepmother had forced her to wear shoes that were too small for her. Consequently she always bought me sturdy, sensible shoes that would "support" my feet and, much to my embarrassment in front of the eagle eyed- shop assistants, she always insisted on pushing down the tip of each shoe to check that there was plenty of growing room. I looked at the Tuff shoes I currently wore and shuddered. They may have been popular with parents because they were advertised as hardwearing, tough, quality school shoes, but I hated wearing them. Luckily she didn't know I carried my Sunday shoes in my school bag and changed into them as soon as I got out of sight of the house.

My mother winced with pain as she continued rubbing.

"I swear it's a miracle that anything gets produced in that factory the way they take their tea breaks every two minutes and do nothing but gossip!"

I thought that was pretty rich coming from my mother who had a penchant for gossip herself. Maybe she felt the negative vibes emanating from me, because she looked up and paused her foot massaging, before saying "Give me a minute, and I'll go and start making the dinner. Did you have a good day, Schaeffi?"

"Alright" I mumbled.

"Where's Tootsie?" she asked as she carefully slipped her shoes back on.

"I don't know," I replied in an aggravated tone as though I had been accused of something.

I felt my mother's eyes regard me like she had X-ray vision and could peer right into my negative intolerant soul. Goodness knows I could never have told her straight out how irritated by her I sometimes felt, I was far too scared of losing her. She was all I had, after all.

I gathered my books and bag and got up. "I'll put these in my room and give you a hand."

I was desperate to get to my room to reflect on all that I had discovered, but it wasn't until after dinner that I got the chance to sneak off to spend some time on my own. By then I had finished my homework, and my mother had done the dishes, and had gone into the front room to get the sofa bed ready. She would arrange the numerous pillows so she could sit and crochet, with Tootsie acting as an extra hot water bottle, purring on her lap.

We always went to bed early because it saved on the heating bill. During the crisp autumn evenings the kitchen and back room might sometimes have been warmed by the evening sun, but now that winter had truly set in, the only heat source in those rooms was from the gas cooker.

My mother still had the feather filled duvet she had brought with her from Germany, along with her camel-coloured wool coat, both of which had kept her warm during the many cold winters of her past. The fur lining of the coat was torn and patched in several places, but she continued to wear it and use it as an extra layer of bedding whenever the dropping temperatures warranted it.

I still liked to creep under these cozy covers with her on a Sunday morning, when, snugly cocooned together, we would share memories of the lives we had led when we lived apart.

As I got myself ready for bed, I tried to sort through our shared stories to see if there was any indication let slip by my mother, which might confirm that Klemens Pietkiewicz was not my real father.

I started to replay the earliest memories I had. The problem was, I could not be absolutely sure whether they were true, for in certain parts the pictures were so hazy, that I had often wondered whether they were simply stories that my mother had recounted so often in my hearing that I had started to adopt them as memories; like hand me down clothes and pretending the ones you liked best were your very own.

But my mother's bitterness at the way her marriage had turned out seemed to have altered them, so that now the more cherished ones were somehow tainted. For example, I can recall my mother and I at Nurnberg Railway Station, the Hauptbahnhof, saying goodbye to my father. We wave to him as the train steams away into the distance, and suddenly I am walking towards a black man. Then he is hunkered down beside me, laughing, and I can feel his soft springy curls as I run my fingers through his hair.

These images and feelings I am sure of. But whenever my mother told the story she padded out the details, embellishing it so that motives and explanations were added – how I had never seen a black man before and this had caused me to stop him, how embarrassed she felt, for being put into such a delicate situation, and how I had asked her if he could be my new daddy now that my other daddy has gone away? Whenever she recounted this story it was for comic effect, both to make a point about my father being bald; and to describe what a fascination I consequently had for men' hairstyles.

My train of thought had petered out to nothing conclusive at all. It always somehow came back to my mother putting down my father. I sighed.

Then another notion occurred to me. What was the point of trying to sift through memories? Unless I came straight out and asked "is my father my father?" I would never really know. And I knew I could never ask her that question, I could feel the hurt in her eyes just imagining the scene.

Deciding there was nothing for it but to have another look in the box the next day to see if I could find any more clues, I turned off the light.

I suppose I felt a little guilty at my snooping, but curiosity quickly triumphed over any feelings of remorse. I could not wait to get home from school the next day to find out if there were any other secrets in those envelopes.

As soon as the hissing orange flames were licking the coals in the grate, I pulled over the case and planked myself in front of the fire, undid the lock with trembling fingers, and pulled out the large envelope containing the certificates.

I removed the Statutory Declaration and Wedding Certificate I had found the day before and put them face down on the floor. The next document was entitled Confirmation in Lieu of Oath. It was similar in style to the first document I had found, basically a statement of who my father and mother were, and signed by a Public Notary in Nurnberg in 1960.

At the bottom of the Confirmation it stated "Certified Translation"; there was an official stamp, a signature, and something I couldn't make out underneath the words "Translation Specialists".

Attached to this document there was another sheet, which proved more interesting, although I was a little surprised at the poor translation efforts of these specialists.

Curriculum Vitae of the Klemens Pietkiewicz.

I was born in Riga/Latvia on 15 January 1914. I am a Roman Catholic. In 1917 my parents moved to Meyung

District Vilna. Until to the time of drafting to military service, I was employed at parent's farm. In 1939 war broke out and I fought on the Polish side before Lemberg. On 29 September I was taken POW by the Russians in Lemberg. Until November of the year 1940 a Russian Prisoner in the Camp Gawliszczybor. Thereafter discharge. In March 1942 forced deportation to Germany. From April 1942-1945 farmhand at Grossennuhr/Hessen.

After liberation I was in the Camps Fulda and Wildflecken, from May 1947-1949 mining work at Behringen near Hasselt, district Limburg. During this time a double sided inflammation of the lungs. In February 1950 return to Germany into the Camp Hersbruck. After liquidation of the Camp Hersbruck in November 1951 I came into the Valka Camp in Nurnberg and I am there until present day.

From March 1950 – September, Sanatorium Engelthal and from April 26, 1957 – July 1958 Sanatorium Gauting. Since this time unable to work. Since 1 March 1960 I have been working half a day twice a week with permission of the doctor.

On 1 September 1956 I married my wife Brigitte and she brought our daughter Saskia with her.

I reread the last line. OUR daughter. It was the proof I had been looking for. He was indeed my father. They just never got married in time because he had been in the Sanatorium!

Even the dream made sense! I must have been saying goodbye to him at the station when he was going to the Sanatorium in April 1957. I would have been three and a quarter – that would have been old enough to remember saying goodbye to him, wouldn't it?

I slumped with relief. I hadn't realised how rigidly I had been sitting, and how numb my crossed legs were. I also discovered that my left side was rather hot, sitting so close to the fire which had caught nicely, so I turned off the gas poker, and moved away a little, propping my back against the sofa and stretching out my legs.

I understood now that their love affair had been thwarted by his illness. I thought how romantic it was, that she had waited for him to get better, and then married him. I read on:

She is a Roman Catholic, maiden name Langer. She was born at Stadt Olbersdorf CSR as a daughter of a custom official. She attended four years of elementary school, 4 terms secondary school. 2 terms of a Special school for women, half a year care of babies. Then care of babies 1 Jan 1932 – May 1935 Vifa Gyuala, lawyer, Losanc, from June with Madame von Herrman at Szescseny-Kovaci. In 1937 return to the parents. From 1 Jan 1939 an office clerk – bookkeeping.

There followed various dates, employers and places. My interest heightened as I reread the last two and wondered if it was normal for women to work while they were having a baby.

28 Feb 1953 – 1 May 1954 Messrs Stein, Nurnberg
13 June 1955 – 31 Oct 1955 Landeslief and Einkaufsgen.Nbg.
Liquidation.
From 1945-June 1947 Camp Freiwaldau in CSR. 17 June 1947 illegal crossing of border into Germany.

From 1947 until 30 Sept 1951 no employment. Difficulties to get an employment because of younger people is here waiting for work. Marriage on 1 Sept 1956. Since this time housewife. Enclosed a certificate of employment to prove my knowledges. I would like to work in the sheep rising, this is a hobby. My wife is not only a nurse for babies and a bookkeeper, but based on the Woman School in the dressmaking too. We save money since a long time for a sewing machine. If I had to go into the sanatorium again, my wife and child could take care for themselves. We would be very glad if we could find a new home in New Zealand because we do not have good remembrances from here and it's our hope to find a quiet life and to forget all these bad things from here

I checked the date at the top of the previous page, 21 April 1960, and then compared it to my mother's Declaration, where she stated she had emigrated to the UK in June 1961. I concluded that this must have been the paperwork, translated into English, for an earlier, different, application to emigrate to New Zealand. To how many other countries had they attempted to emigrate, I wondered.

I reread it.

It was strange to see my father and mother's lives condensed onto a sheet of paper. They seemed oddly empty, and sad. Fragmented even. But not really surprising.

By my standards, my parents' lives were not abnormal. By the age of twelve I had lived in four countries, been cared for by five "mothers", attended eight schools and called eleven places "home". No, their peripatetic lifestyles did not surprise me at all.

What was abnormal was that they had never really spoken about their lives before the Camp.

Chapter 2   Mixed Up Beginnings

I always believed I was born on a staircase. This conviction was based on a particular memory of mine. I was standing in a dark and imposing hallway, watching my mother stopping half way up the huge flight of steps, turning to me and saying "This is where you were born".

It seemed particularly cruel of her to wait until I was much older to tell me that, although she had indeed said those words, she was referring to the building, not the staircase. But it seems to have been a trait of hers not to correct others' assumptions. I know now it was a form of protection and a means of survival. In my case, ignorance was truly bliss.

The memory which had sparked my childish misinterpretation was born, like me, in a TB Sanatorium in Furth, West Germany. I came into the world on January 31st in 1954, but the memory was probably created four or five years later, during a family visit, the purpose of which was most probably to visit Klemens, or undergo the medical examinations necessary for our application to emigrate.

Nowadays "Refugee Camp" throws up images of tents and corrugated iron roofed shelters made up of flotsam and jetsam gathered in the aftermath of some cataclysmic natural disaster. In fact, the Valka Lager where my family lived consisted of neat rows of large wooden huts.

Located in the Langwasser suburb of Nurnberg in Bavaria, (or as the British call it, Nuremberg), it was originally constructed in 1939 by the Nazis as a prisoner-of-war Camp. In 1945 the Americans converted it into a Displaced Persons (DP) Camp, run by the United Nations Relief and Rehabilitation Administration (UNRRA), and it was used to accommodate those homeless displaced persons, mostly of Latvian and Baltic States' origin, who had been forcibly relocated from their homes during the war for use as slave labour under the Nazi regime. Most of its inhabitants emigrated overseas during the first two post-war years.

When the International Refugee Organisation (IRO) took over the Camp in 1947, it became a major centre for those fleeing from the Soviet regime. Statistics show that in October 1951 the Camp housed 4300 inhabitants from 28 nations, and had the largest number of DPs in Bavaria. Those who lived in these Camps took whatever job opportunity arose to improve their lot in life, but for many the only real means of forging a new life and forgetting the old was emigration.

Men and women were segregated. Single inmates shared rooms and slept in bunks, but married couples with children were allocated rooms as appropriate.

In 1956 a period of rebuilding began and this meant that many of the wooden huts were razed to the ground and replaced by long blocks of concrete single storey accommodation.

Valka Camp wooden huts before being razed to ground (c 1957)

Each block had several entrances leading into a hallway with one flushing toilet and four rooms. As a married couple with a child, my family was allocated a kitchen and bedroom, a shared patch of front and back garden, and an allotment.

I knew nothing of this history when I was a child growing up there. All I knew was that we lived in the very last block, the furthest away from the Catholic Church, but the nearest to the Red Cross hut. Both of these institutions were the lifeblood of the Camp offering spiritual and secular aid to its inmates and I often accompanied my parents to both wooden buildings.

My father communicated with my mother in Polish as his knowledge of German was limited. My mother could speak Polish, German and Czech, as most locals were trilingual where she was born in the north east of present day Czech Republic, near the Polish border,. She could also speak Hungarian and some Russian, and often chatted in one of these languages to the single men who lived in the other two rooms on our hallway, and various other neighbours in adjacent blocks.

My father was a shadowy figure in my younger years and someone with whom a close relationship was impossible, not only because of the language barrier, but also because we were relative strangers to each other. Either he was away recuperating from bouts of TB in the Sanatorium, or I was away being looked after by foster-families. My most vivid memories of Klemens were of him enjoying the company of his compatriots. While the kitchen filled with animated talk and laughter amidst the aroma of my mother's cooking, the steam mingling with cigarette smoke, my father poured beer for his guests from bottles which he would open with a flourish, the rubber and ceramic tops unsealing with a satisfying hiss.

Entertaining friends in the Kitchen Valka Camp 1959

He often worked in the allotment which lay on the other side of the main road leading to our block, and provided my mother with a steady supply of vegetables. I remember her busy cooking at the range which sat diagonally across one corner of the kitchen, opening the little cast iron door to stoke up the fire with firewood brought by my father from the allotment. I helped her beat the rugs on the washing line strung between the posts on the communal land between the blocks.

Klemens in the shared ground between the blocks in Valka Camp 1959

I loved listening to the enthralling fables she recounted while she was sewing at the cloth-covered table, her bent head framed by the tapestry wall-hanging behind her, full of deer, squirrels and other forest animals peeking at each other across stylised fields of grain and flowers. She liked to grow her own herbs and plants in the little square of land which was only accessible through the bedroom window, but most of all she liked sitting on the steps in the entranceway of the opposite block, gossiping with her friend Halina, while I played with the neighbouring children.

Brigitte (bottom right) gossiping with the neighbours - Valka Camp 1959

I had a friend, Roman. He was Hungarian and didn't speak any German, and I didn't understand what his mother said to mine whenever we visited his home, but we didn't need to talk as I swung him around or gave him piggy back rides, and when we fell over and scraped our knees we cried the same tears.

Roman lived two blocks down from us, next door to Caterina, a woman who seemed to be a great object of gossip in the Camp. It was rumoured she had money. I listened wide eyed as my mother told me that Caterina had been a maid to the Tsarina of Russia, and had escaped during the Revolution, with diamonds sewn into her coat lining. She was a very exotic looking woman, rather on the large side, with flame red hair, and her pencilled-in eyebrows looked like black caterpillars. But there was nothing mysterious about her room, which smelled of cabbage, and was rather dark and dank. There wasn't even a table and chairs, just some large cushions and a bed with a red velvet cover which exactly matched the hue of her hair. The only item that indicated she had more money than the rest of us was the mahogany piano shining along one wall, which I often saw her play, fat arms jiggling and red hair quivering, as I walked past her open door.

Caterina was also the first person in the Camp to own a television. On the hot afternoon of its arrival there seemed to be a sudden heightening of the general buzz constantly playing in the background of Camp life, and people suddenly emerged out of doorways like bees out of their hive. My mother took my hand and pulled me along beside her down the path to join a group of our neighbours heading towards Roman's entrance. The doorway was full of people pushing to get into Caterina's room. There was shoving and oohing and aahing and some laughing, and eventually some people moved back and let others in. I managed to push my way through and my eyes took in a group of my kindergarten compatriots sitting on the floor mesmerised by a flickering image in a box. Suddenly I could make out a dark man with very white eyes, dressed in flowing robe and turban, riding past craggy rocks on a basket laden donkey.

"It's Ali Baba", someone cried, "He's going to open sesame – the thief's just gone".

Telling the plot was obviously quite acceptable when it was your first time watching television. I looked round and there sat Caterina on her plush red bed, just like a Tsarina, smiling and surveying the audience, holding court and nodding to those who paid her television homage.

Chapter 3   Foster Families 1957-60

TB was rife amongst DPs. Highly contagious, it was every parent's fear that their children would contract it. As a result there were many programmes run by the Red Cross to foster out children at risk. The Catholic Church also encouraged its parishioners outside Germany to help refugees, and foster young children to help improve their diet and give them a better start than they could get in the Camp. As I was prone to bronchitis, my parents arranged for me to go to Switzerland where the mountain air was sure to help me recuperate. I was three years old and my visa was valid for six months.

I do not recall my host family in any great detail. Photographs indicate a farm run by a couple and their parents, but I also remember two small children.

Switzerland – Saskia in the pig pen 1957

My single vivid memory is of a day bringing in the hay. In the cool of the morning several families gathered to walk alongside a horse-drawn wagon to a field along the valley. The men pulled off their shirts as they sweated under the hot sun, scything in lines across the field, and the women gathered up the cut grass behind them and tied them into bundles, stacking them into pyramid shaped stooks as they followed. The children and I played hide and seek amongst the stooks after eating our picnic lunch, but the highlight of the day came once the bundles had been loaded onto the wagon, and I was lifted and thrown up on to the top of the huge hay pile alongside the other children to ride back to the farm.

On my return to the Camp a second trip was organised through the Catholic Church, to Belgium this time. I have a photo dated June 1958, when I was four, taken in front of the house of Yvonne and Frans Meersman in Rupelmonde, a small village on the banks of the river Schelde, about thirty kilometres south of Antwerp. Their home was a three bedroom, two living apartment with kitchen - end terraced house on two floors. At some point I discovered the strange toilet outside the back door - a tiny room with a raised wooden board which had a round hole cut into it, and a pit somewhere below giving off such a reek that my nose and eyes stung. The stench could be lessened to some degree by slamming the wooden lid over the hole, which I soon learnt to do extremely quickly. Luckily I didn't have to use this toilet at night, as I had my own chamber pot under the enormous bed in which I slept.

The kitchen boasted an ornate hand pump located to the side of a built in stone sink, with an S shaped handle lifted up and down to draw cold water. There was no sink in the kitchen in the Camp, only a tap in the toilet from which my mother would fill pots to boil on the range. In the Camp our dishes were done in an enamelled tin basin, and we washed in the hot water my mother would pour into a galvanised tin bath. In Yvonne and Fran's house, I was washed top to bottom with a face cloth as I stood on a chair beside the kitchen sink. My fascination with the plumbing arrangements of all my future places of residence was most certainly born in Rupelmonde.

Frans' hair had an Elvis style duck's arse at the back and a curl that hung down his forehead. His cigarette always dangled dangerously from the corner of his mouth, and I loved the way he pulled his comb out of his back pocket and slipped it through his greased hair, first one side, then the other. He never touched the top.

He rode off to work every morning on his motorbike, and I would stand at the window to wait and listen for the roar of his arrival while dinner was being prepared for his homecoming.

Mamma Yvonne, as I came to call her, had big kind blue eyes and short curly hair, and was an avid dressmaker. She spent long hours at her foot pedal sewing machine, or sticking pins into material draped over a dummy doll which stood in the corner of the living room like a silently brooding member of the family. I always went home with my suitcase stuffed full of new clothes hand sewn to her own design.

The family was completed by a beautiful German shepherd dog called Rita, the first dog to enter my life. I ate my first French Fries – the Belgian chips that somehow were crispier and more delicious than any others I have tasted since. I loved to help Mama Yvonne peel and chop the potatoes and watch them sizzle in the pan. The chips you could buy from the van parked in the town square were served in white paper cones and doused liberally with great blobs of creamy mayonnaise. For the first time I can recall I also ate ice cream in wafer cones, bought from a man who cycled round the streets with a freezer chest attached to the front of his tricycle. He heralded his presence by ringing a bell which hung from a small canopy suspended over his bike, affording him a little shade as he trundled through the villages.

On weekends we went on picnics with other families, relatives and friends.

Saskia Picnicking with Mama Yvonne and Papa Frans
- Belgium 1958

We rode to these outings on the motorbike, Frans in front, Yvonne on the back, and me, squashed warm and safe in the middle.

We also frequently attended the enormous Catholic Church which dwarfed the town square around the corner from where we lived. It was an imposing building, cool and dark, which resonated thunderously as the congregation pushed and scraped their straw backed wooden chairs to face from back to front, as the worshippers alternately sat and knelt in time with the rituals demanded by the mass.

In fact, my trips to Belgium had a great deal of the Catholic religion in it. I was baptised in that Church the following year, and can even recall the cold water on my head, and being carried out through the huge doorway on Frans' shoulders to a cheering crowd of onlookers. Some were friends and relatives, but many were just members of the congregation for whom the christening of a child was a cause for celebration. It was as though I was truly part of my foster family and their small community.

I knew Yvonne was not well. I soon came to recognise the doctor whenever I was asked to answer the knocking at the door. At some point Yvonne told me that she had a hole in her heart. Once, when I was older, when she was doing some light dusting, she took a hold of my hand and placed it under her left breast and made me feel her hammering heart.

On my second visit to Belgium in May 1959, aged five, there was no Mama Yvonne and Papa Frans to meet me at the station, but a strange woman came and took my hand. I believe my mother had tried to keep the memory of Yvonne alive with pictures, but I must have forgotten all the Flemish I had picked up during my first visit. I couldn't understand what this woman was saying to me. I was put in the back of her car and shrank into the corner of the seat, heart pulsing like a frightened mouse.

On arrival in Rupelmonde I was not taken to Mama Yvonne's house, but to a dark and narrow mid terraced two storey house, which smelled of polish and fish. The woman pointed to herself and said Maria, and then pointed to an older woman, her mother, Godelieve, and then her younger sisters, teenager Paula and ten year old Myriam who were all standing in line, looking at me the way my mother would look at a stray cat slinking into our hallway in the Camp.

As I lay stiffly awake that first night in the bed I was sharing with Myriam, sucking in the hot air pressing down from the eaves, it must have become frighteningly clear to me that I would be staying with these strangers. I eventually managed to rock myself to sleep.

I am sure now that the habit of rocking from side to side prior to sleeping was a coping strategy I developed for feelings of insecurity. I don't know exactly when it began. I daresay I felt the same every other time I had been sent away from the Camp, but I don't remember. It must have been traumatic. If I had been older would it have affected me worse? I cannot say. I must simply have gradually overcome my fear on each occasion, and accepted what happened to me. Perhaps the fact that my foster families were good loving people helped.

Perhaps on this occasion I contented myself with the knowledge that Mama Yvonne was close by, once Maria had taken me to see her - just up the cobbled street and around the corner from the market square which I remembered so clearly from my previous visit.

Gradually I would have got to know Paula and Myriam, playing with them and their friends on the pavement in front of their little house, and started to pick up Flemish all over again. I soon became immersed in this new family and the Flemish way of life.

The main meal of the day is lunch, which is generally a hot meal consisting of soup and a meat course, and the evening meal consists of rolls or bread with cheese and cold meats, of which there is a much greater variety than in the UK. I refused nothing, apart from mussels, a great favourite of my new foster family.

I remember watching with amazement as Godelieve put her back into swishing a bucketful of mussels and a little water around and around with a broom handle for what seemed like hours in order to clean them. After repeatedly changing the water and more swishing, she then scraped them to ensure they were absolutely clean before throwing them into an enormous pot of boiling water.

When they were finally fished out of the pot and ladled onto the family's waiting soup plates, the former inky blue ovals had split open to reveal what looked like a yellowy orange serrated blob with a protruding brown tongue. Nothing could induce me to even try one. I satisfied myself with bread and butter whenever mussels were served.

I loved to watch how the bread was cut. When Mama Yvonne was at the bakers to buy her bread, I watched awestruck as the loaf was placed into a machine, which, once switched on, would roar, rattle and shake the loaf through serrated moving blades into a metal box, only to reappear at the other end, fully sliced, and whooshed into a paper bag, which was then sealed and placed on the counter. Godelieve's table only ever held uncut bread, which she would tuck under her left arm, ask if you wanted butter, slap it on and spread it if you did, and then saw off 1cm thick slabs with an enormous knife. I always held my breath in fear of the knife slipping and slicing her arm or chest.

When I eventually went back to stay with Mama Yvonne

during this visit, she was still recuperating but no longer bedridden. At this point the Catholic influence became obvious. Three nuns took it in turns to come and help Mama Yvonne during the day, bringing food, shopping, cleaning, and keeping an eye on her, and me. I soon discovered that they lived together in the convent situated across the road from Yvonne's house, for as Yvonne improved, we often went there to eat our lunch.

The façade of the building was like any of the other larger village houses bordering the street. However, on entering the regular sized door, the rooms were bizarrely enormous, and there were scores of them. There was even a small chapel, but it was sacrosanct and I was not allowed in. The extensive garden was accessed through the kitchen. It was divided by a cross shaped path into a grassy square, a vegetable patch, an area with flowers, and, to my delight, a cave with a statue of the Virgin Mary, a miniature version of the Grotto in Lourdes. I think I probably desecrated it as I played around it but the nuns were very indulgent. They all wore full black habits and wimples, with plaited string belts from which dangled large dark crosses. The Mother superior was a rather large busted woman, with twinkling eyes and a ready smile. Sister Beatrice was quiet and grumpy and I was a little afraid of her. But Sister Anna, who seemed much younger and wore glasses, sang hymns as she worked around Mama Yvonne's house. I liked her. She would ask me to help her and I followed her around the room with a brush and dustpan or a duster, as she talked about this and that. She was the one who listened to me as I knelt at my bedside, and told me to pray for Mama Yvonne and that God would grant her another baby soon.

Mama Yvonne continued to improve, and the nuns visited less often. We started doing the routine shopping and preparation of the evening meal, visiting friends and family. Life was reassuringly normal. But then suddenly she was back in bed again. She didn't seem to look as white or as weak as before, but she didn't move out of the bed. The nuns were back, Maria visited more often and soon after I moved back along to Maria's house.

It was while I was staying there that I was introduced to Jeff who lived in the neighbouring village of Steendorp, about two miles south along the river Schelde. I found out later that Maria had nursed Jeff's mother throughout her terminal illness, and struck up a friendship with the family. Jeff had been deeply affected by his mother's slow and painful death, and he was initially assigned the task of teaching me my prayers for my forthcoming Christening as a means to divert him from his grief. After my Christening, he was assigned the job of teaching me French.

Belgium is divided into two communities, the Flemish speaking northerners and the French speaking Wallonians in the central and southern part of the country. There has always been disdain between the two, but French was the predominant language as far as job opportunities were concerned. It was thought that Jeff might do me a service by teaching me the language as early as possible. Several times a week I would walk the kilometre along the river bank to his house, carrying my big heavy French picture book, and spending an hour or so with him, repeating the French words for those items he pointed out one at a time.

Saskia's French lessons in front of Jeff's house - Belgium 1959

At first I was scared of him, this quiet man with fingers covered with hair up to the last knuckle.

Jeff lived with his father, sister Maria, and younger brother Roger, though he was not often around the house, being either at work or spending time with his girlfriend. Maria stayed at home and ran the household. Whenever I visited she was washing, cooking or cleaning. Her short dark hair framed her patient face, and she hummed as she worked.

The narrow front of the house hid a large garden enclosed by several barns. One contained rusting farming machinery; another sheltered a wooden cart and an old weighing machine flanked by iron weights of varying sizes. My favourite barn, directly behind the back of the house, had cracked and dusty cobweb covered saddles and bridles hanging along the walls. The farm horse had gone long before, but it had left behind a gigantic pile of dried unused hay, home to about two dozen cats and kittens, who of course became my companions.

Gradually the hours I spent there lengthened, and I stayed for something to eat, and the neighbouring children came to ask me to play. I am not sure when I also started to spend nights there, on this trip or the next; the timing gets hazy.

I now had three families who treated me as one of their own.

On my next visit to Belgium in spring of 1960, I hardly saw Mama Yvonne at all. I stayed with Maria and Godelieve most of the time, occasionally spending a few nights with Jeff and his family, and I started school in Rupelmonde.

On the few occasions that I visited her, Mama Yvonne was still in bed, surrounded by visitors, looking pale, but happy. Her attention and everyone else's was taken up by the baby in the crib beside her. My attention, however, was taken by a large dummy, which was soaking in some red juice in a little bowl on her bedside cabinet. Whenever the baby cried, she grabbed the dummy and popped it in the baby's mouth and it grew quiet.

I wondered what the miracle juice was.

My mother was sure Yvonne spent the whole nine months she was pregnant with her son Chris in bed, just to ensure that she didn't lose her baby again. In later years, whenever we looked through the photos taken during my various trips to Belgium, she swore it was a miracle that Yvonne had delivered a baby and lived through it, given the state of her heart. As it was Chris had to take medication during his childhood years. To me he was simply an excitable child, but whenever he started squeezing his hands together and then grabbing his tummy and going red in the face, Mama Yvonne would give him a pill. She explained that the fits he took were because of all the drugs she had been given when she was pregnant.

I started school in Germany in September of 1960, and further trips to Belgium were no longer organised through the Church, but rather on request of Jeff and Yvonne personally. These later trips were limited to the duration of the summer school holidays and continued until I was thirteen, by which time we had emigrated to England.

At first my mother was not sure that the relationship should continue at all. Yvonne had her longed-for child, and we were living under much improved circumstances. There was certainly no longer any need for me to be fostered.

Years later my mother revealed to me that she had actually harboured doubts over sending me back to Belgium after my initial six month visit in 1958. She had no fears that I was being mistreated, and was grateful for the care and consideration I was given, but what worried her was the question her barely five year old daughter posed her on arrival back in Germany. In a state of confusion I had seemingly asked her "Mama Brigitte, who is my mother? Is it you or is it Mama Yvonne?"

Chapter 4   The Camp

There are several photos of our bedroom in the Valka Camp, and they span three years. I know this because the Christmas tree is different in each photograph, and each tree tells a story in our family's change of fortune.

Every Christmas Eve, this bedroom became the room in which the Christmas tree was erected and decorated by my father, and the room that was off limits to me until baby Jesus had visited and left presents for me. We knew when this had happened because Jesus would ring a bell that hung on the tree specifically for that purpose. I sat with my family in the kitchen and shared a celebratory Christmas Eve meal with visiting uncles while my ears strained for the tinkling bell and excitement bubbled so hard in my stomach it almost hurt.

On my last return from Belgium before starting school in September 1960, this bedroom had been transformed with new, modern furniture - matching bed-stand, dressing table, headboard and wardrobe in a warm golden wood. Beside the double bed there was even a special bed for me, one which could be folded up into a sideboard during the day. The brown and beige patterned bedspread matched the curtains framing the window, through which I could see a window box full of plants nodding their brightly coloured blooms in approval.

Our beautiful bedroom furniture 1960

The density of the Christmas trees reflected my parent's increasing level of prosperity. There is a picture where the tree is very sparse, and my father is standing with two of his friends on either side of the white cloth covered table on which the tree stood. One friend is hunkering down in front, and I can make out a hoopla hoop leaning against the table behind him. In the bottom corner of the photo, I can just see the old bedstead.

Another Christmas photo depicts a somewhat bushier tree, with presents underneath consisting of some Lego, and other parcels. I am a little taller, but the old bedstead is still at the bottom of the picture. And then there is a full colour photo of a luxuriously thick floor-standing tree as tall as my father, its dark green needles contrasting sharply against the beige of the new curtains, drawn shut and hanging to the side of the new wardrobe. This photo has the date 2/1/61 on the back, so would have been taken during our last Christmas celebrations in Germany.

The new bedroom furniture was an indication of the increased comfort my parents lived in – by Camp standards.

My mother was always good with money. Her dressmaking skills allowed her to earn money by sewing for others, and like Mama Yvonne she also had an eye for fashion. Of course I always returned from Belgium with an assortment of new clothing, and it was not unusual for me to stand out from the rest of my playmates, whose scruffy outfits were more in keeping with Camp standards. Whenever I fell out with my sometime friend Gisela, she knew exactly how to get her own back at me. All she needed to do to start me crying was to stamp in puddles to ensure that I went home mud-splattered and worried about what my mother might say.

Being clean was important to my mother. She said that being poor did not mean you needed to be dirty, and anyway, dirt breeds disease. She would polish the kitchen range, wash the linoleum in both rooms, and she was the only one I ever saw who cleaned the shared corridor and toilet. There was no pungent smell of urine as you wandered past our open doorway.

She judged others by their cleanliness too, rarely visiting other women in the Camp whose rooms were not clean and orderly.

Background and education were the other two things that were important to my mother. She knew where everybody hailed from and what social group they had belonged to before their status had been degraded by war and its aftermath. One friend from the block across the way, came from Prague. Her parents had both been doctors and she had been married to a chemist. Another had been a professor at Budapest University. You could tell that one ranked more highly than the other by the tone of voice used by my mother to speak about them: the more miserable the background, the lower the tone.

Gisela's parents did not rate very high on my mother's vocal scale. They had turned one of their rooms at the far end of the opposite block into a barber's shop. The corridor was not particularly clean, and Gisela's older brother and two younger sisters were always squabbling. There was always a lot of noise to contend with while clients waited along one wall, watching nervously as Gisela's dad sharpened the razor on the leather strop hanging from a hook on the wall next to the enormous black greasy leather chair in which his victims sat. But at least the smell of the soap covered the stench of the toilet which had just filled your nostrils on the way in.

Strangely enough, my mother would visit Gisela's mother occasionally, taking along some cake or a parcel containing my outgrown clothing.

There is one particular photograph of my family, resplendent in our Sunday best, taken in the kitchen for purposes of emigration, where I am sitting on Klemens' knee, and he is looking at my mother – an intimate gaze. It confirms to me that on the whole my parents were happy together in Germany as their good fortune improved and the prospect of emigration drew closer. But I was a child and for me, the Camp was a place to play in between school times, and visits to other countries. What did I know of the subtle horrors of daily life endured by a cross section of European homeless languishing in close proximity with each other? Regretting their pasts, trying to create a safe and secure future for themselves and their families, wishing they were somewhere better.

Photo of the model Catholic family applying for emigration - Brigitte, Klemens, and Saskia (1958)

On reflection, one incident indicates very clearly to me that perhaps my parent's luck was a reason for envy amongst those of our neighbours, whose prayers to emigrate were still not answered, and who did not have the means to save for fancy furniture.

I don't know how long the argument had been raging in the hallway, but I could hear my mother's voice above the rest as I pushed my way past the neighbours who had gathered outside our entrance.

I couldn't understand what my mother was saying, but she was agitated and shaking her finger at one of the men who lived in our hallway. He was turning away and trying to go back into his room. But she kept hurling a stream of words at him and he kept turning back to let them wash over him, looking as startled as if he had been hit by a rush of cold water. One of the neighbours behind me whispered to me to get my father. Luckily I knew where he was, for I had seen him chopping wood at our allotment as I walked up the road.

I started shouting to him as I ran, but he must have seen me coming, for he stopped his axe in mid swing, and began walking towards me.

"Was ist los?" What's the matter?

"Mutti! Komm schnell!" Mummy, come quickly.

He followed me, quickening his step as he saw the crowd in the distance, overtaking me as he neared the entrance way. Heads turned and the murmuring crowd fell back as he deliberately swung his axe up and onto his shoulder. Time seemed to slow as we watched the scene in front of us. Our neighbour, this timid shuffling man who rarely said a word to anyone, was in the act of tipping the contents of his chamber pot over my mother!

My mother stood frozen in time as everyone sucked in their breath at once. Then she turned on her heel, shamed and dripping, and staggered like a drunk into her kitchen, slamming the door behind her. My father turned round and barked something at the crowd and the spectators melted away. My neighbour disappeared into his room as Halina took my hand, and led me away with her out of the hallway. She hurried me to her room in the opposite block, but I managed to overhear a spectator saying something about people who got too big for their boots, while nodding meaningfully towards our kitchen window.

I never found out what happened next, or what had happened to cause the incident; I could not bring myself to ask, but I was aware that my father had been ready to defend my mother with an axe.

Chapter 5   My First Lie

The first day of school in Germany is marked by parents presenting their six year old children with large multi-coloured cones of paper filled with sweets. Despite the sweets there was little to reassure me that I was going to like this school. It was not the small friendly place I had been used to in Rupelmonde. This building was massive. Instead of the convivial pews that I had been used to, this classroom had individual desks, the windows that lined one wall were too high to be able to see out of, and the children were somehow more confident, pristine and threatening than the children in the Camp. Moreover, on being introduced to my class teacher, Frau Muller, I was taken aback by her short fair hair and masculine features. Frau meant Mrs, but, to me, she looked like a Mr.

Saskia (second from left in back row) with classmates & Frau Muller 1960

Although I didn't cry on my first day at school in September 1960 in Germany, I remember I did not want to get up the next morning to start the daily routine of walking with my mother down the long road to be lifted up on to the high steps of the quarter past seven bus where I was wedged between several other boisterous pupils, then lifted and squeezed off the bus at the school gates, just before the eight o'clock ring of the bell.

Frau Muller sat me at the back of the class, behind a pasty faced asthmatic looking girl whose hair always looked like an attempt a crow might have made at building its first nest. I had to dodge either side as she moved her head in order to get a decent view of the blackboard.

I have always enjoyed learning, but two incidents occurred that tarnished my experience of school in Germany. The first occurred one cold winter morning.

Frau Muller had a passion for making her own stained glass pictures, often bringing in her handiwork to show us, and would lean her pieces on the high window sill so that she could point out how the light shining through made the colours more vivid. This particular morning, shortly after having placed her latest effort on the high ledge, she was called out of the room. She had not been gone long when someone shouted that it was snowing. All eyes turned to gaze at the soft white flakes drifting past the panes. Like little ants the whole class instinctively swarmed towards the window wall, lifting chairs and scraping them into position. We took turns standing on tip toe on the chairs and craning necks to look beyond the window sill to the white scene below. I was entranced by the snow twisting in a white whirlwind by the bicycle shed. The thought of playing in those drifts beckoned like an ice cream on a hot summer day.

"Frau Muller's coming back!" There was an intake of breath, a scurry and scrape to get back to desks. Someone knocked against my chair, and as I reached out for the sill in panic, I knocked the stained glass tableau, just a fraction, but enough to send it floor-ward, crashing and cracking into myriad splinters of blues, reds and purples.

There was no time to escape. I was left standing on the chair, the guilty party, looking aghast at the evidence of the crime around me, as Frau Muller appeared at the classroom door. Her eyes cut from the scene on the floor to me and sliced through me.

"What have you done?" she cried as she ran into the room, bent over her shattered mosaic, took a deep breath and control of herself. She looked at the other children frozen like so many statues trying to get back to their desks.

"Get back everyone. Keep away from the glass. YOU" she looked at me, as she put her hands on her hips, "get OFF the chair and come here. YOU will clean up this MESS." She turned to one of the cupboards but I had already stepped down and started picking up the ruins of her handiwork before she got out the broom and shovel. The tears in my eyes made it difficult to see the little shards that crunched underfoot, and I drew back at the sharpness to look at the blood starting to appear on my fingertips.

"STOP, you stupid girl. Not with your HANDS. Here take this."

She handed me the broom, and I grappled with the too-long handle to clumsily sweep up the particles which were being ground ever finer as my boots trampled over the remaining pieces.

"Not like that! Ach, get away!"

I cried, not at the discomfort of my throbbing fingertips, but at the shame of Frau Muller's anger, and later, at home, I cried with disappointment at not being able to go out to play in the snow now that my fingers were covered in bandages. My mother sat me on her lap, hugged me to her warmth, and wiped away my tears with her apron. Then she made me sit at the table, placed one of my favourite meals - creamed spinach, mashed potatoes and fried egg - in front of me, and slowly fed me.

I did not go to school for a few days, but I was confined to the kitchen. By the time the bandages came off, the snow had gone.

The second incident occurred when the promise of snow had disappeared and the days were growing longer and milder.

Once again, Frau Muller was called away from the

classroom. She told us to carry on copying the letters on the blackboard. The class became restless. Some of the boys got up and stood around Gerhard's desk at the front. I did not leave my seat in her absence; I had learnt my lesson well. But the noise of the class got louder and louder until eventually Frau Muller stormed back in and shouted above the din:

"What sort of behaviour do you call this? I can't leave you for a few minutes to talk to the Principal? What do you think he thought when he walked back along the corridor and heard this racket? That I can't leave my children because they are so badly behaved? Well, you will all learn a lesson from this. You will practise reading the next TWO chapters of your reading books and you will also do exercises five, six and seven in your mathematics books, by tomorrow. And woe betide you if I find out you haven't done your homework!"

My heart plummeted. Even though we were only in the first grade, it was not unusual for us to be given homework. Although school finishes at 1.00 pm in Germany, there is an expectation that work continues to be done at home in the afternoon. But the sun was shining, and I had wanted to go and play with Gisela that afternoon.

I sat in front of my books at the kitchen table, struggling with the additions and subtractions, intermittently watching the lengthening shadows beneath the tree which grew in the little patch of communal grass outside my kitchen window.

When my mother walked in and asked what was taking me so long I finally burst into tears of frustration. "Frau Muller gave me these exercises to do as a punishment, and I don't know why. I didn't do anything bad. She hates me. Ever since I broke her stupid mosaic she's been picking on me!" It felt good to vent my anger at her.

"What did she give you to do?"

I showed her the half page I had done, and the page that remained. I never told her that the rest of the class had the same amount to do. She never asked. I didn't lie.

"You can stop now. You can go out to play if you want."

"But if I haven't finished it Frau Muller will punish me more."

"I'll go and see the Principal tomorrow and get this sorted out."

As I sat in class the next morning, tremors of apprehension gripping at my stomach, imagining Frau Muller's reaction when she found out that I hadn't finished the exercises, I was relieved to see a member of staff appear at the classroom door and ask Frau Muller to step outside. When she reappeared her face was as red as Gisela's the time she had nearly missed the school bus.

"Saskia, please go to the Principal's office".

My mother was sitting in front of the Principal's desk, dressed in her best blue suit, the one she had got married in, and was looking at me, her expression solemn. The Principal told me to come in and sit down. I shrunk into the mammoth chair. My clasped hands became moist, but my mouth felt dry.

"Saskia, tell the principal what you told me yesterday."

"Frau Muller gave me some exercises to do as a punishment, and I don't know why." I stuttered nervously.

"Did she give the exercises to anyone else to do?" The Principal gently asked.

My mother leaned towards me, expectation shone in her blue eyes. I didn't know what she wanted me to say.

"No, just me."

I chose the lie because I knew that she would never have let me have the afternoon off if she had known that Frau Muller hadn't just singled me out. It was the lie I had avoided the previous day by simply skirting around the truth.

Her eyes flickered for a millisecond. She leaned back, took a deep breath and said "Can Saskia go and wait outside please?"

She sat rigid and quiet on the bus back to the Camp, her eyes avoiding me. Even though I was sitting next to her she felt farther away from me than all those times she had been in Germany and I in Belgium. Of all the mothers I had had, this one had the ability to turn off her love, leaving me shivering as her coldness flooded my heart.

I vowed I would never tell a lie again. I vowed that I

would never do anything that would make her withdraw from me like that again.

Chapter 6   Emigration Process

I have a memory that is etched into my mind like a fairy tale. The first part is a little vague; being awakened in the middle of the night, drifting in and out of sleep as I was dressed, bundled into a blanket and carried outside into the bitter cold by my father, lifted into the back of a van, and laid onto something hard. I must have been rocked back to sleep by the lulling motion of the vehicle.

When I awoke properly it was daylight and my mother was sitting beside me. I sat up on my makeshift bed and unfolded the layers of cocooning blanket. I could see my father sitting beside the driver, a stranger. Out of the front window I saw the cobbled streets and looming buildings of a city.

"Are we in Nurnberg?" I asked.

"No, Munich" my mother said smiling. She looked beautiful. Her bright blue eyes sparkled and I could see that she had finger waved her medium length dark hair, and had put on red lipstick, like she did on a Sunday when we went to church.

We eventually stopped outside a building and as I scrambled out of the back of the van I noticed my father pulling out the black suitcase I used for my trips to Belgium. A man came down the steps and shook my father's hand. Motioning to us to follow, he led us into the building, along a dark corridor and then up several flights of stairs, to a long room filled with rows of wooden bunk beds. Some had their blankets rumpled as though people had just got out of bed, and some had suitcases lying on them, guarding the bunks for their absent owners. The solitary window was barred and cast a gloomy light into the unwelcoming room.

The man pointed to two empty beds, and my father hefted my suitcase onto the bottom bunk. He took out a towel and a wash cloth rolled around some soap, and my mother said

"Komm, Schaeffi, let's get you washed."

Clean and with combed hair, we rejoined my father and sat in silence, squashed on our allotted bottom bunk until the man reappeared.

We followed him down the stairs and into a small bare walled room. It was lit by a solitary light bulb and two barred windows, but it was just as gloomy as the bedroom. In a corner sat a desk with a metal machine of sorts covered in buttons, a pile of clean white paper on one side, and on the other side there was a little box full of pencils. He motioned for us to sit at the wooden table in the middle of the room and left. We waited yet again, my parents taut and unspeaking, while I traced the spindly tracks of the uneven grain on the table-top with my fingers.

Eventually another man came into the room. He glanced briefly at the papers my father pulled out of the envelope, shook his head, and started talking in quiet patient sounding tones, like a teacher correcting a slow pupil.

I lost interest and started daydreaming, but my reverie was interrupted when the man got up and walked over to the desk. He took a piece of paper from the pile and inserted it into the black machine with one hand, then with his other hand held onto something I couldn't make out, but which made a clicking noise. He sat down in front of it and I could see him moving his arms like Caterina playing the piano, although they weren't jiggling or as fat as hers, and the sound that came out was different, a click clack click, rather than a plink plonk plank..

I couldn't restrain myself. "What's he doing, Mutti?"

"Typewriting" she whispered, pressing her finger to her lips in a shushing motion.

And sure enough, when he had finished playing the same dull notes for what seemed forever, he stopped and pulled out the paper with a zipping sound. To my astonishment it wasn't ripped as I had thought, for in the next instant it was lying on the table in front of us, whole and rectangular, magically transformed from plain paper to paper covered with the neatest writing I had ever seen

My father read it, let my mother read it, and then he signed it. My parents seemed to breathe as one with relief as they all stood up and shook hands.

"Can we go home now?" I asked.

"No, this is just the beginning of the process, Schaeffi. We just wrote down the reasons why we want to emigrate to England. Now they'll look at the papers and decide. But it's wonderful that we have got this far. You know you must continue to be on your best behaviour, because they won't let naughty girls emigrate."

I sat as still as a mouse through the interminable hours, as my parents were interviewed several times that day, the only relief a stretching of legs as we moved from one room to another. I had acquired the ability to sit quietly for given lengths of time in the company of adults. I simply got lost in a world of rambling thoughts, asking questions and supplying my own answers. I knew that "Emigration" meant that people left the Refugee Camp. They obviously started living in another place, like I had left the Camp and started living with Mama Yvonne, or left Mama Yvonne and starting living with Uncle Jeff, in a different house, in a different town. England, where is England? Near Rupelmonde? Would we be able to take the bedroom furniture with us? No, silly, how can you get a bed onto the train? Where would our new bedroom furniture go? Perhaps mummy will give it to Halina like she gave the old wardrobe away?

It was not until the evening that my patience was rewarded. I have no recollection of how we got there or back, it was just another journey for me, but the sights that met me as we entered through the wrought iron gates of a large park let me know I was somewhere magical.

I stared entranced at the sparkling lights on the Ferris Wheel and at the little cars that zoomed round and round in all directions and bumped each other so hard that the screaming and gleeful passengers were thrown this way and that. My mouth watered at the spicy meaty aroma of the bratwurst and roast potatoes which were put into little paper bowls for us to eat. The rich cinnamon whiff that rose from the glass of Gluh

Wein my mother drank was nearly as mouth-watering as the ice cream I was presented with. I was filled with a glow of happiness and forgot the hours of trancelike waiting that I had endured that day.

My delight peaked when we walked into the beer tent, and I was faced with a moving mass that extended as far as I could see. Bodies in multicoloured outfits, weaving backwards and forwards, arms intertwined, red faced, singing at the tops of their voices to the oompah beat of the music that reverberated around me. We found some space at the end of a bench that ran the length of a table stretching from where I now sat to the near side of the band stand. In front of the band stood a ruddy faced man dressed in Lederhosen and a red shirt, which matched not only his face but also the feather sticking out of his green trilby. He was waving his arms in time to the music and encouraging the singing.

A busty, curly haired woman carrying so many condensation covered glass Steins that the front of her white bodice dress was soaking wet, spoke to my father as she squeezed past him, almost drenching him in beer, but then turned and set down the glasses three at a time in front of the people further down the table to us. She was back soon after with some beer for my father, but I hardly noticed as she placed a glass of Coca-Cola each in front of me and my mother, I was so entranced with the conductor and the colour and convivial atmosphere of the place. When my mother eventually called my attention to my drink, and I sipped the sweet liquid through the straw, I noticed for the first time the number of American GIs sitting at the table along from us, incongruously sober and starchy in their green uniforms. However, the next time I looked, their ties seemed a little looser, their faces a little more flushed, their smiles a little more relaxed. By the time I was standing on the bench, conducting the rocking and the singing of those on either side of me just like the man in the Lederhosen, they had started to lift their steins and were trying to sing wordlessly along with the rousing ballads. I was so encouraged by this that it felt only natural for me to step onto the table and take a few steps in their direction and include them in my audience as I conducted ever more energetically. My mother was holding on to me in case I fell, but I was oblivious.

Their smiles and laughter spurred me on. The next thing I knew I was off the table, on the floor, dancing with curtsies to and fro, delighted at being able to release some pent up energy and be the centre of so much attention after a day of being totally ignored. I was such a thunderous success amongst the GIs that one of them asked my mother if he could give me a little brooch, something he had won at the shooting gallery no doubt, a little hand painted wooden boy and girl joined together by their toes, bellies and lips. He sat me on his knee and pinned it on my dress, and as he wiped tears from his eyes, my mother said it was probably because I reminded him of his own little girl so far away in America.

That night as I lay next to my mother in the bunk too excited to sleep, playing the evening over in my head, I fervently wished we were trying to emigrate to America or even to Munich.

After the round of interviews the following day, we were picked up by the same van that had brought us. I must have fallen asleep during the journey, for when I woke up I was in my own bed.

During the winter months that followed, as I sat in the back of my class room not listening to Frau Muller, re-running the faces, smells, sounds and colours of that night through my head, I wondered time and again whether I had simply day-dreamed it all.

But one day, when my mother was getting ready for church and asked me to get her amber necklace from the little jewellery box on the dressing table, I came across the brooch wrapped in a little piece of tissue paper. I said nothing, merely smiled to myself, knowing it be true, and glad that it had not been an imagined thing.

Months later, on a day when I arrived home from school and noticed that the scraggly tree outside our kitchen window had just started sprouting lime green leaves, my mother excitedly told me to sit down at the table before I had even taken off my coat. She sat down carefully beside me. I could tell she had something important to tell me by the way she paused, hands clasped together in front of her on the table, dinner bubbling away unattended on the stove behind her.

"Our emigrations papers are through!"

"What does that mean?" I asked.

"It means we are going to leave this awful place and fly to England on a real airplane" she said, her eyes sparkling, her smile as big as mine must have been in that beer tent all those months before.

Chapter 7   Immigrants

In June 1961 my father, mother and I flew from Munich to Heathrow airport.   My excitement was overshadowed by my mother screaming when the plane hit some turbulence. We were bussed to Worthing in Sussex to the reception establishment run by the British Council for Aid to Refugees, also known as the BCAR.   A woman called Marika ran the place.   I was never sure of her origins, but she could speak various eastern European languages.   The people who helped her keep the house running – the cooks and administrators who found host sponsors, jobs and homes for the immigrants - were also former refugees who had already passed through the same process we were about to undergo.

For three months we shared one furnished room and were immersed in learning the language and about English customs. We sat in a makeshift classroom located on the first floor of the building that was our first home in England, and were taught the basics of survival in a foreign country – the value of Sterling, how to shop for vegetables, groceries and meat, how to use a telephone box, how to ask for tickets on a train or bus. Finally our family was resettled to Hitchin in Hertfordshire at the beginning of the school year, and then it seemed to me we were left to fend pretty much for ourselves.

My father had been found a job as a gardener with Harkness Roses and we were housed in a furnished end terraced two bed roomed red brick house.   We gazed in wonder at its red exterior, and felt growing delight as we walked through the front door into a tiny front room with a sofa and an armchair in it, then through a hallway with steep staircase, on to a sitting room with another sofa, a table, three chairs and a coal fire.   From this room, through a door and down a step we arrived in a kitchen, complete with sink, Formica-topped table and glass fronted sideboard, and from there we went outside to view the toilet at the back of the kitchen, and see the narrow garden stretching into the distance. No more need to traipse to an allotment to weed, water, and pull up vegetables. Upstairs, there was a bedroom to the front and one to the rear; and a bathroom complete with another toilet. A bathroom and inside toilet! What luxury…chamber pots were no longer required.

And as if all this was not enough to fill our hearts with gratitude at the charity we were being gifted, the piece de resistance was a small black and white television in the downstairs sitting room! This was pure heaven - our very own television. And what a great learning tool it proved to be for my mother, who continued going to English lessons in the evenings, and diligently watched Cliff Michelmore every week because her teacher had told her he had "Received Pronunciation" and spoke the best English. My favourite programme was The White Heather Club, with tartan clad highland dancers spinning around the room and Andy Stewart singing and swinging his kilt to a clapping happy audience. I became very adept at copying his Scottish accent.

My father discovered that there was a large Polish community in the area and soon made friends among his ex-compatriots. I suppose it was easier to mix with his own kind for he was struggling to learn English just as he had struggled to learn German.

My mother however, ventured out more into the English speaking community, specifically to the shops on a daily basis. Her biggest frustration was that she could not ask the butcher for the cuts of meat she was used to and she often grumbled at the quality of the meat she was given.

She kept at her lessons and tried to strike up conversations with locals whom she met in the shops in order to practise. She took great delight in reusing any new vocabulary that she had learnt, unconsciously stressing it so that it struck the listener as more important than the rest of the sentence. But her greatest struggle in grasping the English language was the use of colloquialisms.

For example, she had been waiting in the queue for a bus, (queuing was something new she also had to learn), and when it finally arrived the two people in front of her got on. But as she attempted to step up onto the bus, the conductor barred her way, saying: "Sorry love, I'm full up."

She attempted to climb on board again. "I must go to shops," she uttered.

"You'll 'ave to wait for the next one, love, I'm full up!"

"I don't care if you haf had gut dinner," she spat out.

The penny must have dropped because he laughed. "No love, the bus is full up – see?"

She soon became acquainted with the local shop owners, and, ever the entrepreneur, started sewing and making alterations on commission for a local haberdashery. She also became fast friends with Bummi, a lively, laughing German woman, who worked in a shop selling knick knacks and fancy goods. I loved to visit her with my mother, to browse the shelves filled with dainty figurines and hand-painted glassware, always heeding my mother's warning "Schaeffi, don't touch!" I never forgot my previous encounter with painted glass.

I started at the local Catholic primary school where there were a few other immigrants, mostly Polish. My mother arranged for me to have piano lessons at a Polish woman's house, and I even started Polish lessons on a Saturday morning along with the children of a new friend of my father's who began visiting us regularly at the house.

My first encounter of physical punishment occurred within that first winter. Not from my parents, but from my class teacher. She was not a nun, but a middle aged stick-like woman who was very fond of smacking inattentive pupils over the palm or knuckles with a ruler. I was very quiet and rarely caught her eye, but once or twice, when I was late from the toilet or playtime, she accosted me. Her punishment was particularly painful for me that first winter in England, because my hands were covered in chilblains.

It was strange, that I should have been afflicted with chilblains, because the weather was not nearly as cold as in Germany or Belgium, where snow fell regularly and the temperature was well below freezing for long spells throughout the winter. I had suffered fingers numbed with cold before, but it must have been a different kind of cold, which seeped into my poor fingers and toes, turning them blue, then yellow and numb within minutes of playing outside. When I got back into the warmth of the house, they turned hot and red, as they adjusted to the ambient temperature. I probably exacerbated the condition by running my hands under warm water or holding them too near the fire. Patches became itchy and enflamed and it got so bad my mother took me to the doctor to get some salve to rub on which smelt to high heaven. At night she insisted not only on putting socks over the salve on my feet but also over my hands to stop me scratching. Once the chilblain healed, the skin peeled off, and I spent many a happy hour peeling my fingers and toes. Most charming. However, most painful when getting rapped by a ruler.

When I eventually told my mother what the teacher had done she was outraged and arranged to see the teacher and the priest. When I came home from school that same day she was extremely angry. Pacing the sitting room, she raged at me:

"That's it; I am never going back to that church. You are never going back either, and you are definitely not going back to that school. I'm going to move you – you can go to the Protestant school that that nice Mr. Price is headmaster of!" Mr Price was one of the people who had been something to do with the Teachers' Association that had sponsored our family's emigration. He came to visit our family shortly after we had arrived in Hitchin to see how we were settling in.

"But what happened?" I couldn't understand why she was so angry. I had only complained about the teacher hitting me after all. What had I started?

"That priest! How dare he speak to me like that? Two faced hypocrite!" I didn't understand what she was saying, but her face tightened and she wouldn't say any more, and when she looked like that I knew not to ask.

When my father came home from work later that afternoon, there was an argument. I didn't like it when my parents argued, something I had never been aware of in

Germany, but which had started and was becoming more frequent over the last few months. It began in the kitchen where my mother was cooking. I could pick out the same words over and over during these quarrels, and one of them was "Curva". From the way my father shouted it I knew that this was not a pleasant word. The yelling got louder and more unsettling until I couldn't stand it anymore and went fearfully into the kitchen to try to stop them.

What I saw next made my heart stop. My father was walking towards my mother with his hand raised as though he was going to hit her, when she quickly reached out and grabbed the knife on the table beside her and pointed it at him.

"Don't touch me" she growled.

I must have screamed. He glanced at me and lowered his hand. Time seemed to slow as she very deliberately put the knife down, holding his gaze as though she was still challenging him to make a move. The tension hung in the air until she came towards me and herded me out of the kitchen. She sat down on the sofa and held me as I shook and sobbed. My father came into the living room, but he merely got his jacket off the back of the chair and walked back out. I heard the slamming of the back door and felt my mother's taut body relax.

Drying my tears with her hankie before she ushered me back into the kitchen, I stood in silence as she started cooking, not knowing what to say. She took some potatoes and carrots out of the string bag in which the vegetables were kept. I loved the way her hand would work its way round each potato, the knife dislodging the peel into one long curly tendril, but today her hand shook and she stopped several times. I could see her face in the kitchen window, the darkness outside reflecting a blank stare. As she stopped and started, stopped and started, her expression became calmer, although her lips still seemed a little too tightly pressed together.

The potatoes were bubbling on the gas cooker when she finally began talking about other things. I had just seen a trait of my mother's which I witnessed repeatedly in later years. Whatever feelings of fear or anger my mother experienced in the face of violence or threat, she resolved her struggles internally. She never discussed what thoughts were rambling in her head, even when I was older and she might have been able to unburden herself.

I was not aware of how the quarrel was resolved between my parents, but my church going days were over for the time being, and I did move school.

Hitchin Primary school was different to the Catholic school in that I was the only foreigner there. I was placed in a year below my age group to allow for my lack of English, but within a few months I was moved to another class with others of my own age.

Learning was fun for me. I enjoyed school lessons, and my written and spoken English improved daily. However, I came across a word that I didn't understand and could not find in the old well-thumbed dictionary that my mother had at home, and to which we both referred as we improved our vocabulary. This particular word was used not in the classroom, but in the playground. It seemed related to the British winning a war, and the games the boys played. Then it became a word that was directed at me.

The incident occurred during lunch time. I was standing alongside the gym wall, watching the boys playing football, when one boy kicked the ball and it hit me hard in the face. Tears came to my eyes but I bit them back with anger. I caught the ball as it bounced off me to the wall and back. The culprit tried to grab it but I held on tight, determined that he would not kick the ball at me again. It became a tug of wills as he kept pulling at the ball, and I eventually gave in. I could see the glee of triumph in his eyes, so I wasn't prepared for his next move – a punch to the stomach that made my breath explode out of my mouth like a bullet.

Blind with fury and pain I did what came naturally, and retaliated with a kick, which, because of his height, landed squarely in his crotch. He doubled up and I felt some satisfaction in seeing that I also had hurt him. His face twisted in hatred and he spat out the words "Nazi Pig".

The next thing I knew a crowd had gathered and a chant had started. "Nazi Pig! Nazi Pig!" I was ready to defend myself with more kicking at crotches if anyone came any closer, but they kept their distance.

A teacher came over to see what was going on and of course the boy, Michael, was in tears and clutching between his legs, and the chant changed to "she kicked him". Another teacher came over and we were both escorted into the building. Michael was taken in the direction of the staff room, while I was taken to Mr Price's office.

By now I was scared, realising that I was going to be punished. Mr Price looked at me in disbelief when he heard that I had kicked a boy between the legs, though I took some reassurance from the calm way he asked me what had happened. He left the room, presumably to talk to Michael and get his side of the story, and when he came back he accompanied me back to the classroom. All eyes were on me as I made my way quietly to my desk. The class waited expectantly for Mr Price to begin. Very solemnly he stated that he did not want to hear the word Nazi used ever again in the classroom, in the playground, or anywhere where he would hear of it.

I realised that saying the word was obviously a much worse crime than my kicking Michael so hard that he had to be sent home. I heard later during afternoon playtime, that he had been bleeding "down below". One of the girls said pointedly, in a tone of voice so obviously an imitation of her mother's, "It is very dangerous to kick a boy between his legs. It can stop him having babies."

However, she had told me a week previously that babies came out of your belly button, and I knew that wasn't true because my mother had told me that the stork brings babies, so I didn't take her comment to heart. Besides, I had only kicked out straight; I hadn't aimed for between his legs. It wasn't my fault that the kick had landed there. I supposed that my continental style leather boots were sturdier than the plimsolls worn by the school children in England. Perhaps this was what had caused the damage.

When I got home I told my mother what had happened. I asked her if she knew what a Nazi was. I was surprised to see the hurt that clouded her eyes.

"The Nazis started the second world war. Hitler, their leader, was a very bad man; he caused the murder of many innocent people and destroyed so many lives, so many homes, so many countries. The British fought for six years and lost thousands of good men fighting the Nazis, and there is still a lot of hatred felt for the Germans. People don't forgive easily. But not all Germans were Nazis, and not all Germans are evil." She sighed. She seemed sad but there was anger in the way she clenched her teeth as she continued speaking. "Whenever you're called a Nazi by spiteful children, or even adults, you must realise that they don't always understand this."

When Michael came back to school a few days later, I kept a wary eye on him. I was prepared to stand my ground when he came up to me with a group of boys during playtime a few days later.

"Do you want to play with us?" he asked.

I was dumbstruck. Then I became suspicious. "What are you playing?"

"Spies. We thought you could be the German spy." He stressed the German ever so slightly.

"George is going to play the part of John Wayne when he..."

He talked on and I gathered he was talking about some war film he had watched with his dad and he was trying to explain the plot.

I joined in the game, acting out the scene he had described, which ended with me getting shot. I was soon part of the gang, and many play times were spent enacting scenes from films that the boys had seen at the previous Saturday Matinee in the local cinema, with me always taking the role of the German or Russian spy, and of course always getting found out by the hero whom Michael usually portrayed, and being shot by him at the end.

When we played cowboys and Indians I always ended up being an Indian, and the same scenario was performed. Another boy, a dark haired thin boy, who sat two desks down from me, Paul Cross, often got the same villainous roles. I wasn't sure whether he had kicked Michael between the legs, but we soon became friends, united in our ability to be the baddies. It also helped that he lived near me and we walked to school together.

Every morning when I left the house, Paul would be waiting at the end of the road and we would stop at the sweet shop at the next corner. The store's windows were so crammed with goods that the interior was rather dark and cave like. But, unlike Aladdin's grey cave shown on Katerina's television, this cave was overflowing with jars stuffed with coloured multi-shaped treasure. Paul would point to a row and ask for exotically named delights such as gob stoppers, pineapple cubes, cola bottles, or bull's eyes, and the chubby-cheeked proprietor would reach up, grab a jar, and carefully tip a small number of the contents into a shiny silver bowl cradled on one side of a scale. Our mouths watered as we watched him weigh one or two ounce quantities, and then carefully pour them into small white paper bags. But for me the best part was the entrancing way the owner caught the bags at the top two corners and swung the heavier end round and round several times, placing the final product, a neat little package with two flat ears, onto the large coloured ashtray-like dish on the counter in front of him.

I had never seen anything like it. All I could remember in Germany was pretzel sticks which were bought occasionally as a special treat from the single shop in the Camp, whenever I accompanied my father there to buy some bottled beer.

I discovered that the sixpence Paul had for spending in the sweetshop was called his "pocket money" and that his mother gave it him every day. He also told me he didn't always spend his sixpence, but that he would put some of his money into a "piggy bank".

When I told my mother about this extravagant habit, she decided that we would have to become like the English and do the same. Sixpence was a little beyond her means, but she did give me a penny every day, and when I got any money from the uncles that came to visit my father, she encouraged me to put that money into a jar she kept in my bedroom wardrobe.

We tried to adopt English habits even though, of course, we were like fish out of water. Just before our second Christmas in England I learnt from Paul that presents were placed under the tree and opened on the 25th, not the 24th of December, and that Santa Claus visited the house during the night and left pillow cases full of toys on the bed.

Santa Claus had obviously not heard that my family had moved to England, because he never left any presents in a pillow case on my bed. But baby Jesus still knew where I lived because more Lego appeared miraculously under the Christmas tree in our front room on our first and second Christmas Eves in Ickleford Road.

It was the following year, 1963, before Santa Claus found his way to our house and it was that same year we were so anglicised that I got a part in the school play which was put on just before Christmas. My mother helped with the costume making and on the night of the show, she was at the school, getting the main characters ready amidst a hubbub of excitement. My mother was even photographed by the local paper as she was applying lipstick to Shirley, while Michael and I waited in line.

Someone must have given a little background information to the journalist to explain the reason for the unusual names of the mother and daughter in the photograph. Of course, like any normal local paper, the facts and grammar were a little incorrect. The headlines read:

The Pictorial   Friday December 20 1963

Sazkia Knew No English – Now A School Star

One of the Children taking part in the St Andrew's, Hitchin, Primary Schools Christmas Concert, last Thursday and Friday evenings, was nine-year-old Sazkia Pietkiewicz, a little girl from West Germany who just over a year ago could not speak a word of English. Sazkia's family were housed during World Refugee Year by North Herts Teachers' Association and her mother was at St Andrew's last week to help with the make-up. Saskia was one of the stars of "The Invisible Man", a colourful and lively adaptation of an old tale. It was produced by Mrs. V Foley, and featured 36 members of the school's Class 9.

My mother cut out and kept the clipping in a cream coloured folder along with other newspaper clippings which she found of particular interest.

Article in Hitchin Pictorial December 1963

Chapter 8   Separation

Whilst I settled in and became happier at school, my mother became less happy at home. My father spent more and more time socializing at the Polish club. His increased drinking annoyed her, not just because of the regularity with which he came home drunk, but also because he often invited friends round and my mother would have to be hospitable or even eke out our dinner to include whoever arrived at the door. His income from the garden labourer's job was not enough to cover the amount that was spent on his social pastimes, and this was the cause of a lot of the arguments that increasingly raged in the house.

One particular argument was, however, caused by me and somehow I have always felt that it was probably the straw that broke the back of my parents' marriage.

Paul was going to be nine years old and was having a birthday party, my first ever such experience. As I recall, birthdays were not really celebrated on the continent. In countries where the Catholic faith was the main religion, those named after saints sometimes got presents on the particular saint's day.

I gathered there would be balloons and jelly and ice-cream and a cake with candles, and those invited had to dress in their best clothes and bring a present. After some discussion with my mother I decided to buy Paul a matchbox car. It cost two shillings and three pence and I knew that I had enough saved in my "piggy bank" jam jar to be able to afford it. However, when I went upstairs to get the money from the wardrobe where it was kept, it contained only a few halfpennies. I knew that there had been five shillings and nine pence saved since the day my mother had dropped my first penny into the jar over a year ago, and I knew who had taken the money as surely as I knew how much had been in the jar. I sat on the bed and wailed like a dog in pain at my father's betrayal. My mother came upstairs to see the reason for the strange noise. When she saw the jar in my hand and the look on my face, she also knew.

The row that night was one of the worst. I heard the raised voices as I sat guiltily upstairs in my room. I did not want my mother to have to defend my right to my money to him, to have to justify that what he had done was wrong. But I knew how she would have shamed me if I had done the same to anyone else. The argument raged on. I tried to shut out the rising and ebbing storm below me, but then I heard something crash, and my mother scream and the abrupt silence that followed filled me with fear.

Heart thumping, I ran down the stairs and on pushing open the living room door, was met with the sight of my father holding my mother by the hair, keeping her at arms length to avoid her flailing fists, and using his superior height to push her downwards and towards the fire. I may have screamed. I ran towards him and started kicking and punching him. He must have let go of her hair for she grabbed me to her, trying to protect me. When my father stepped back, I realised that he had been drinking again. I could smell the stale alcohol fumes expelled with each rasping breath, and could see the slowness in his reaction, a dazed expression on his ruddy face. As he came to his senses, he dropped his hands to his sides and walked out of the room.

This time it was me who comforted my mother, pulled her away from the heat of the fire, sat her on the sofa, set right the shovel and brush on the hearth. She cried. It was not the first time he had raised a hand to her but I had never seen my mother cry. I had heard her scream in pain and howl in frustration, but I had never seen her cry. She had always seemed a strong person to me, a person in control, a little hard perhaps, but nevertheless a rock, a warm place to go to for comfort and sensible advice, and somehow, to see her sitting there crying, unsure and vulnerable, upset me more than seeing him hit her or trying to push her into the fire.

An overwhelming need to protect her overcame me, and without rationally thinking how I could possibly do it, I told her that I would never let him hit her again.

She slept in my single bed that night, and I lay in their room, falling asleep despite my resolve to stay awake. I was woken by his stumbling up the stairs, and sat up when he switched on the light, to let him see that it was me on the bed, not knowing whether he would put up with me or cause a scene. He registered I was there, asked "Brigitte?", and when I pointed to the other room, nodded, removed his jacket, and switched off the light. I felt the mattress move as he sat on it to take off his shoes, heard him grunt as he fumbled with the laces. He flopped down suddenly and within seconds his snoring filled the room. I lay awake for hours, breathing the fumes that emanated from him, unforgiving and detached.

I went to the party, wearing a red tartan pinafore dress my mother had sewn for the occasion, with matching ribbons in my hair, a four ounce bag of Cola Cubes, and a kilo of embarrassment as I handed over my paltry present, all eyes on me.

At home, the atmosphere was icy cold even though the summer was just around the corner. I noticed that my father occasionally did not come home from work and stayed out overnight, and was glad because it meant fewer arguments. My mother took on more sewing, working late into the evenings, grumbling that it was the only way to put food on the table. However, one day my mother announced that we, she and I, would be moving out of Ickleford Road, as she had been able to get a full time job to make some more money to pay bills.

Bummi, her German friend, had a sister who had been working in a stately home a few miles out of town but was leaving to go back to Germany and her position had become available. My mother would need to "live in" to do the job, as the hours of work meant that she could not travel there and back to Hitchin every day. I would go and live with her, and she would come back on her days off to cook and wash for my father, and keep the house clean.

In the late spring of 1964, my mother packed what she could, and arranged the move to Kings Walden, where she became housekeeper to Colonel and Lady Harrison. I started taking a 40 minute school bus ride from the village to school in Hitchin, and, to my utmost satisfaction, I never had to witness my father's drunken cruelty again.

As arranged, my mother did go back to the house to cook and clean, but only for a few weeks. One day when I came home from school, I found her in the sitting room, pacing the floor, extremely agitated.

"He locked me out! He changed the lock – I couldn't get in! Can you believe it? Luckily I had a witness." Witness? Witness to what, I wondered in some trepidation.

"The next door neighbour heard me banging on the door and came to see what the matter was. She noticed that the kitchen window was slightly open and helped me climb up and I managed to get in. She saw everything! I only took what I could get into the wicker basket."

I noticed the basket on the floor behind her, stuffed with bedding and her fur lined coat.

Sitting on the sofa she pulled me down next to her, and put her arm around me. Was she expecting me to be upset? I felt nothing, neither surprise nor anger.

"So what if he changed the lock. I never wanted to go back anyway!"

She looked surprised. "I didn't know you felt that way! Didn't you like him?"

No I didn't like him. He never played with me. He stole my money. He always smelt of beer. He never even spoke to me! "No, I didn't. He always called you Curva. I don't know what it means but I think it's a bad word. Like Nazi."

Tears sprung to her eyes. Instantly I felt remorseful for having caused her pain, I should never have been so outspoken.

"Yes", she nodded, "It's a bad word. It means a bad woman… a woman who has had many men." I didn't understand the implication of this explanation; I just understood that he had no right to call her a bad woman, because he was a bad man himself for hitting her.

"It's not easy for a woman on her own. But we'll

manage, Schaeffi. You can help me here in the evenings with the evening jobs; you can help me speak English when I don't know the words. We are "in service" now. Colonel and Lady Harrison are good people – they understand our situation, they'll look out for us."

I still have no idea whether our move to the Bury was supposed to be a temporary measure to pay off debts, or simply a suitably respectable way of arranging to live apart from Klemens. Neither open separation nor divorce were common in 1964, in fact the whole idea of a "broken marriage" was rather shameful for women, for it implied some kind of failure in their marital duty. In the divorce papers issued several years later, the cause was cited as desertion, but of course in those days neither mental and physical cruelty nor irreconcilable differences were valid justification.

But to this day I am unsure whether my parents' separation occurred because my mother moved out to get work, or as a result of Klemens locking her out of the marital home. When Klemens filed for divorce, my mother was most incensed that her "witness" was unable to put the record straight. It was almost a point of honour with her, that she had not defaulted on her marriage vows. It took me until after her death to discover the reason why.

Chapter 9   The Bury, Kings Walden 1964

Kings Walden was a small village in Hertfordshire many of whose cottages were leased out to tenant farmers by Lt.-Col. John Fenwick Harrison and his wife. There was no escaping the pride in my mother's voice when she told me that Lady Harrison was the daughter of the Third Baron Burnham, and if I was ever to speak to them I would have to address them as Sir and Ma'am. They resided in the Bury, a manor house of modest proportions which, if I had been older I might have recognised as the sort of house that one of Jane Austen's heroines could have lived in before she married into real money. To my nine year old eyes it was a veritable palace.

The Bury was a building of two halves. The main part was solid and square shaped, two storeys high with a flat roof, and covered in rambling ivy. I recall at least five Georgian-style windows along the length of the western and southern walls, the ground floor ones taller and more imposing than those on the first floor, with a low pillared wall running along the top hiding the windows of the second floor rooms which were set into the roof, one of which was mine. If I stood on a stool at my bedroom window I could see over that wall and watch people approaching down the tree-lined drive towards the grand front door below me. On one side of the drive cows chewed their slow way round a large field, on the other side a park full of mature trees sheltered a large herd of fallow deer.

A series of modern extensions added onto the eastern side of the original, made up the other half of the Bury. Their high pitched roofs gave the Bury an oddly disproportional look. The house sat in large grounds, and as I slowly explored the various gardens, I felt like Alice in Wonderland.

St Mary's Parish church bells pealed every Sunday, calling the members of the household for morning service. Colonel and Lady Harrison and any of their eight daughters who might be staying for the weekend would sit in the family pew, and the remainder of the tenants and servants sat in the pews tradition had allocated them. I was unaware of it then, but the inhabitants of this estate still followed the customs that the squire and his tenants had practised since the twenties, when he had first acquired the Bury.

Those who lived in the house accessed the church through a gate in the graveyard and I used this short cut on a daily basis to make my way to the bus stop on the single road through the village to catch my school bus. When I eventually dared to venture through the rose-covered pergolas bordering the left hand side of the path between graveyard and house, I discovered a secret garden, in three terraces, the lowest of which contained a swimming pool. To the right, a view of fields dotted with sheep and cattle, trees and hedges, and the occasional house, stretched for miles.

To the rear of the house there were several French doors which opened onto a large paved area, fronted by a huge stone staircase leading down to a manicured lawn, the centre piece of which was a striking weeping willow. To the left of this lawn was an impressive rock garden of about an acre in size surrounding a pond fed by a small waterfall which was sourced from a lake to the east.

As I walked along tree, brush and bamboo-lined paths leading through the rockery to some hidden outhouses which once were the stables and now housed the Colonel's cars, I sometimes met Lady Harrison walking her dogs. She was very elegant in her tweed suits, and her soft white hair was always immaculately styled. She would invite me to walk with her and enquire politely about my day at school. Her two Pekinese dogs followed at her heels and were very protective of her, always barking at anyone who approached. At first I thought it was just because I was unknown to them, but when I learnt that they barked at all the servants and gardeners, I figured they were just a bad tempered breed.

There were not a great many servants, but there was a certain pecking order that I became aware of. The cook, Mr O'Keefe, his wife and son had their own quarters on the ground floor of the newer part of the Bury, housing the servants' quarters and the kitchens. The Butler and occasional footman lived offsite in the village. Coxie, who helped my mother, lived on the far side of the deer park.

My mother, as housekeeper, had her own sitting room on the first floor of the servants' quarters. It was conventionally furnished, with chintz curtains and sofa, Victorian fireplace, burred walnut sideboard teeming with knick knacks, and probably gave my mother her introduction to English antiques. In fact the traditional aspect of this genteel way of life suited my mother extremely well. She embraced it for its Englishness, and in later years it seemed to me she gave herself certain airs and graces because she had once lived "the upper class way", albeit as a servant.

There was little love lost between my mother and the O'Keefe's. I occasionally saw Mr O'Keefe when I was watching the only television, located in the shared staff room along the corridor from the kitchens. We did not eat in this room along with the rest of the staff; my mother brought our food up to our sitting room instead.

I think that one of the reasons she kept herself apart from the others was that she did not understand everything that was said, and got embarrassed at my having to translate in front of everyone. My mother's English was certainly increasingly fluent, although she still had a very strong German accent. She tried to speak in English to me as much as possible, and still took time daily to read books or articles in magazines and note and look up any new words in her well thumbed dictionary, which constantly lay at the ready on the coffee table in our sitting room.

Certainly I had difficulty myself understanding the O'Keefes, because they spoke with a strong Irish accent. However my mother insisted that the reason she did not like them was because she thought they stole food and drink from their "benefactors". I never really understood the reason for this antipathy on my mother's part, but I did notice that none of the dogs liked Mr O'Keefe.

There were three dogs in the household. Lady Harrison's two Pekinese, Ming and Lotus-Flower, and Colonel Harrison's gun dog, a black Labrador called Wally. My mother explained to me that gun dogs are highly trained to do exactly as they are told. Their job was to search for and fetch the birds that had been shot during "bird stalking hunts" and give up the birds to their masters without tearing their flesh.

Wally was my favourite. Whenever the Colonel was "away on business" or at "Ascot", Wally was abandoned to O'Keefe's care, and like two lost orphans we adopted each other. He slept at the foot of my bed; he played with me and followed me about the gardens and the house. He even came to meet me off the school bus. I would start to look out for him in the fields about a mile before the village, and once he saw the bus he would bark and run after it. As I walked along the path from the bus stop to the house, he would come tearing across the field at top speed, to jump and dance and lick me joyfully. I had never been loved like that.

But Wally was a very different dog when he was with me compared to when his master was home. On his master's return Wally ran dutifully to his side. The Colonel's legs were stiff and he sometimes walked awkwardly with sticks, but mostly he was wheelchair-bound. Most of his time at home was spent in the large sitting room. I often hid behind the balustrade at the top of the open staircase and looked down at Wally being gently petted as the Colonel read. Wally knew I was there but his first loyalty was to his master. I knew I was only his friend.

It was the cook's job to feed Wally when the Colonel was away. Whenever the Colonel oversaw the feeding process, with Mr O'Keefe preparing the mixture of bone meal and tinned dog meat, Wally was watchful and quiet. I took this as a measure of his docile nature and good training. But the times that the Colonel was away, and I was present at feeding time in the pantry, I noticed that Wally's demeanour was different. The look in his eyes was wary as he kept his head down. He would not eat the food that was prepared for him by the cook. He sniffed it, but he wouldn't touch the bowl. Mr O'Keefe grumbled at the dog to eat but eventually went off to do something else, huffing "I doan't have de toime to weight till dat bluddy animal has aiten".

I waited for Wally to eat. He looked at me pleadingly with his soft brown eyes. Only when I jumped off the counter and scooped the food out of the bowl with my bare hand and held it out to him would he eat it.

When I told my mother she recounted stories of dogs that pined for their masters when they were away, and even gave up on life once their owners had died. But the Colonel was there more often than not, so I figured that as long as Wally would feed out of my hand, he would not suffer. It was not until I was older, that she told me of her suspicion that the cook maltreated the dog.

Now that my drunken father was removed from our daily lives my mother seemed much happier. She worked long hours, but, because I helped her in the evenings, we spent much more time together and were able to form a new bond of closeness.

I learned to swim. My mother walked along the side of the pool giving me instructions, while I swam from one side to the other wrapped in an inflated rubber ring, trying to perfect my strokes. My biggest fear was of swallowing the variety of beetles and other bugs that floated on top of the water, so I concentrated more on avoiding the debris around me than I did on my stroke, and consequently I never became a strong swimmer.

In the evenings, after she had taken our supper tray back down to the kitchen, I helped my mother fill hot water bottles, ran baths for the Harrisons in their separate bathrooms, and turned down the beds in their separate bedrooms. I came to realise that bedding in England was different to the feather quilts we had been used to and brought with us from Germany. In the morning stiff white sheets were carefully tucked in at the corners of the bed, folded back no more than one spread hand-width onto layered scratchy blankets and then covered with a bedspread for decoration. In the evenings the bedspread was folded back halfway, a hot water bottle placed between the sheets, and a corner of the bedding was folded back in a triangle to allow easy access.

Whenever Lady Diana, the Harrisons' daughter, came for the weekend with her friends I would watch the butler polish the silver in the silver room and help him set the table in the dining room. I helped my mother and Coxie clean the main bedrooms on the first floor, make the beds, and change the towels. Once the green curtains had been drawn I could sit at the dressing table in the Emerald room, as Lady Diana's bedroom was called, and play with the silver mirror, brush and comb set lying on her dressing table. I could open and smell the pots of creams, watch my mother smoothing over the green bedspread in the reflection of the hand-held mirror, and I could look at myself and comb my hair and imagine that I was like Cinderella once she had got the slipper to fit and my servant was attending to my every whim while I waited for Prince Charming to appear at the door.

It was a fairytale world for me. And in some ways it was for my mother also. It certainly became even more exciting for both of us, when my mother announced that Coxie was going to have to come in to work extra days and hire some more help for the next few weeks in preparation for the "Luton Hoo".

"The Luton Who! What on earth is that?" I asked wide eyed.

"Why, that's when the daughters of the "aristocracy" who have "come of age" are presented to "court"."

She still had that habit of enouncing new English words. It probably stemmed from our conversations - a mixture of German and English, with newly acquired words given pride of place.

"They are "debutantes", it's a ball and they dress in their finest clothes. It's truly "wondrous" to see, and we are going to make sure that all the people who are coming to stay here as Lady and Colonel Harrison's guests have the best time and that all the dresses are pressed and..." she stopped in mid-breath and grabbed my hands and danced around the sitting room with me. Then she scrabbled about on the coffee table in front of the sofa, found a copy of The Lady magazine, and showed me the article she had been reading. She was so excited you might have thought she was going to the ball herself.

I recently discovered that the Luton Hoo was in fact the name of a stately home in the vicinity of Luton, which the queen visited once a year. To my knowledge, there was never any Debutantes' Ball called the Luton Hoo. It was more likely that my mother had misinterpreted the article in The Lady and made the assumption that the ball, presumably held in the Hoo, was to celebrate some debutantes "coming out".

I don't know if she was prepared for the amount of work that was involved. The house was to be full of guests, and my mother worked long into the night weeks before the guests were due, preparing not just the named rooms – Emerald, Ruby, Turquoise, Garnet, Sapphire, which were always kept in a state of near readiness for family visits, but also the rooms on the third floor where I slept, which had not had their doors opened in a long time. She and Coxie scrubbed and polished, beat carpets, and washed and starched curtains and linens. I was even moved out of my bedroom to sleep on the sitting room sofa a few days before the guests were due to visit.

The household buzzed with activity. I discovered that there was to be a "banquet" on the first night the guests were due to arrive. I was banned from the kitchen – not that I went in there very often anyway. Mr O'Keefe shouted at his wife and son a lot, so I was quite happy to keep away. I did try to help the Butler polish the long dining room table which had lengthened even more somehow, although my arm soon tired of the constant pressure that was required to do the job properly. I didn't stay to help too long, but when I returned a while later it was polished so highly that I could see my face reflected in it.

I had never seen so much silver. The butler and footman grumbled at the numerous tarnished tureens, salvers, and candelabra that required polishing. More crockery and glasses of varying size and shape than I could count came out of the previously locked room at the back of the scullery, as did large boxes that opened to show layers and layers of spoons, knives and forks lying in pretty patterns on green baize.

As soon as I got home from school on the Friday afternoon the guests were due to arrive, I ran down the back staircase and twisting corridor used by the servants to get from the kitchen to the dining room. My breath stayed in my mouth as I saw how the room had been transformed.

The normally austere dark wood-panelled room sparkled with glass and silver. There were more settings than I had ever seen before, when Lady Diana and her friends had come to stay. The room seemed filled with chairs, and yet there was still ample room for the butler, the footman and the O'Keefe's son, all smartly dressed in black and white, to walk around. There was even an extra sideboard brought in from the drawing room whose sole purpose was to display an enormous flower arrangement which matched perfectly in colour and shape the two smaller arrangements which had been placed at either end of the laden table. Gleaming silver candelabra waited proudly for the butler to light their myriad candles. I imagined how their flickering glimmer would add that final enchanting radiance to this changed room. It was stunningly beautiful.

I ran back upstairs bursting to tell my mother but my excitement was soon quashed as I heard her exclaim:

"Schaeffi, you must not run around so much now. You must calm down, and stay in the sitting room. You are "Off Limits". Lady Harrison doesn't want the guests to see you in the corridors."

"Can I still help you with running the baths?" I pleaded, noticing the crisp white apron she was wearing.

"No my darling, Coxie and her cousin are helping me."

Suddenly realising I would not, as I had imagined, be able to see the wonderful dresses that my mother was going to hang up in the wardrobes, or look at the sparkling jewellery in their lovely jewel boxes, left me crushed with disappointment.

Even though I craned my neck from the sitting room window I could not see anything through the few gaps in the leaf covered trees, although I could hear cars driving up to the front of the house, sometimes screeching to a halt, and the sound of muffled voices. I dared not even run up the back stairs to my bedroom which overlooked the driveway to get a glimpse of the guests.

Lying miserably on the sofa during that never-ending evening, I had to be content with the descriptions my mother gave me of the guests and their activities whenever she popped into the sitting room.

Initially she was astonished to find out that the majority of the visitors were the same age as the Harrisons and that there was only one "deb". During her next visit she told me the deb was sleeping in the garnet room, like a guest of honour.

When she next returned she told me in a very disapproving tone of voice that the deb's mother and father had arrived in a mud-splattered old Landrover an hour after their deb daughter had driven up the drive in a smart green sports car.

In between visits I would lie and imagine what she had seen, guessing the details. Had my mother been standing at my bedroom window herself to witness these arrivals, or had she been standing waiting in the hallway for the guests to arrive in order to show them up to their room?

The next time she came in she made her way over to her sewing box which she kept at the end of the sofa, and started rummaging around in it.

"She (the deb) has a beautiful sky blue silk dress, with tiny pearls on the bodice, and I will need to get a needle and thread to it while I can, because she showed me where a few of them had come loose. I am going to try to do it while they are all having drinks before they go into the dining room, and once they are in there I will have to go round the rooms and unpack the clothes of the ones that came late, and put down the bed covers while they are all eating…"

She bustled out of the room.

And so it went on for the whole weekend that the guests were there, I hardly saw her, or anyone else, as I stayed cooped up in the sitting room. The only time I was allowed to roam was on the Saturday night after all the guests had left for the ball. And of course then there was nothing of any real significance for me to see as they were all wearing their very best finery.

On Sunday evening, finally sitting down with a cup of tea after the last guest had left, my weary mother tried to console me with more tales of what she had seen and done.

Her face was incredulous as she told me about the behaviour of the deb's mother.

"You know, Schaeffi, she had forgotten her fur coat. You should have heard her! Gott im Himmel! The bad words that came out of her mouth."

She laughed delightedly, holding her cheeks with embarrassment at the memory.

"She ended up wearing the old camel coat she arrived in. I had to brush the dog hairs off of it. Her husband had on a "deerstalker" as though he was just home from the hunt, and they drove away to the ball in that awful jeep! That poor girl, with parents like that! But you know she didn't seem to care that they were like tramps and she in her beautiful dress on the most important day of her life. Nah, only the rich can behave like that and get away with it!"

After the "Hoo", life settled down again to a more normal routine. I moved back into my bedroom, and with the summer holidays looming my mother started making arrangements with Jeff for my annual visit to Belgium.

The Harrison's daughter and son in law, Lady and Lord Pilkington, (of Pilkington Glass my mother would add significantly whenever mentioning the name to anyone in later years) moved in to one of the larger houses on the estate. It sat on the farthest side of the Rose Garden and I often went over to play with their daughter. She was no more than a toddler, but it was company for me and I overheard Lady Pilkington say to my mother that she was very happy for me to play with her little girl after school until tea-time.

It was arranged that Jeff would come to The Bury to pick me up on the Thursday before school broke up for the holidays. He would of course have to stay overnight. My mother asked permission of the Colonel and he agreed.

However, he was "away on business" with Lady Harrison when Jeff was due to arrive.

I collected Jeff from Hitchin Station. We took the bus back to Kings Walden and my mother arranged for us to eat some supper in the sitting room. We had an early night as we had a long day's travel ahead of us. Jeff spent the night in my bedroom and I slept on the sofa in the sitting room. Early the next morning I was awoken by a commotion outside. Suddenly my mother walked in followed by Lord Pilkington and Jeff, and in the shadows of the corridor I could see Mr O'Keefe.

"Bridget, I am not happy about what has happened here. It is not seemly that a strange man stays the night in the Colonel's House without asking prior permission." He was a tall man, blond, with a haughty appearance, who towered over my mother.

"I did ask permission, sir" she replied quietly.

"Yes well, the Colonel is not here to corroborate that, is he? I want this man out of this house as soon as possible. And I do not want to ever have to be put into this position again!"

Standing behind my mother I could see her neck turn red with shame as she assured him she was sorry. He left the room and as she turned after shutting the door behind him, her expression was livid. I was shocked that she had been spoken to in such a way, neither the Colonel or Lady Harrison had ever raised their voices like that.

My mother asked me to apologise to Jeff for the shouting and asked that we set off as soon as possible to catch the bus to Hitchin. I did not dare to ask her what had happened to cause Lord Pilkington to shout at her like that. Jeff did not say anything about it either, but he must have been highly embarrassed.

I can only guess at how mortified my mother felt at O'Keefe's interference and the unspoken but obvious sexual inference made by Lord Pilkington in front of O'Keefe. This would most certainly have shamed my mother more than standing accused of not having followed protocol.

When I came back from Belgium in September, my mother met me at Dover, so there was no need for Jeff to stay the night again. Within a month we left King's Walden for my mother to take up a new position as housekeeper in Hitchin. She never told me and, being a child I never dreamed of asking the reason for the change of job. But I can't help but wonder whether she simply found the situation with the O'Keefes untenable.

Chapter 10   Elmside, Hitchin 1964-65

Elmside was the home of Mr Hubert Moss, whose grocery store "W B Moss and Sons Ltd", located in Hitchin High Street, made him a small fortune over the half century it had been doing business. The shop was still flourishing, but was now run by his nephew Godfrey, since Mr Moss was in his nineties, and bedridden. His son William employed my mother to be Mr Moss' housekeeper, cook and carer, but it was William's wife who was most involved in advising my mother of her daily duties.

Although smaller than The Bury, Elmside was still a substantial house set in its own gardens. It was surrounded by a brick wall that was so high you could walk past without realising the house was there at all, yet it lay only about a quarter of a mile away from the town centre and was within easy walking distance to school.

The house had a number of rooms that were never used. I looked in them out of curiosity, but the furniture was covered in white sheets. The lived-in parts of the house were the rooms nearest to Mr Moss' bedroom. In the first few weeks I mostly spent my time in the kitchen, which was enormous. It had built-in white painted cupboards that reached from the floor to the ceiling with a large wooden table in the centre that could easily have seated ten people. My mother loved working in it. There was a transistor radio on the kitchen window and she discovered the delights of the Light Programme, and soon became a fan of The Archers.

I could watch television in the drawing room, and would watch Blue Peter or Heidi when I got home from school and Top of the Form at 7.30 after dinner. My mother would sometimes join me for Steptoe and Son and Double your Money, but she never missed the Frank Ifield Show, which was her favourite. On Saturdays, I watched Juke Box Jury and Dr Who, although I closed my eyes when it got too scary. We both liked to watch the Dick Van Dyke Show, and the Billy Cotton Band Show, and on a Sunday the London Palladium, to get a glimpse of the middle of the road pop stars like The Springfields, or Peter and Gordon and Peter Paul and Mary, whose songs were more acceptable to the older generation.

My favourite programme by far was Top of the Pops, which was aimed at "teenagers". I had watched it every week in King's Walden, and I still looked forward to Thursdays so I could get a glimpse of the rock-and-roll stars of that year - good looking Billy J Kramer badly miming "Little Children", Gerry bouncing like a frog in front of the Pacemakers, and of course the Beatles, Rolling Stones, and the Kinks, who by 1965 constituted the more dangerous face of a pop culture which was increasingly shocking the older generation. I loved to watch the young, hip studio audience dancing nonchalantly around the various bands. I took in the details of their outfits, and I would copy their moves as I gyrated in front of the television.

To my utmost disgust, on Thursday, January 30th 1965, the day before my 11th birthday, Top of the Pops was cancelled and the only pictures that filled the screen that particular evening were of someone called Churchill and his funeral cortege. I knew nothing about, and was not in the least interested in, the fact that he had led Britain to victory during the last world war.

Most of my time, however, was spent in my bedroom. It was on a half landing, to the front of the house, while my mother's room was up another short flight of stairs, next to Mr Moss' bedroom, so that she could hear him through the night and attend to him if needed.

I had always liked singing and listening to the radio; now it became my main interest. "Santa" bought me my very own transistor radio for Christmas and it became my bedroom companion. I would stand in front of the full length mirror stuck to the outside of the wardrobe and mime to the songs, mimicking the singers I had seen on television. I would sweep my fringe over my forehead and sing along to Wayne Fontana, or draw my eyebrows down and scowl at the mirror in an attempt to look as moody as Dave Berry as I sang along to "The Crying Game". Or I would just do the dance that was linked to the music, the Twist, the Mashed Potato, or the Hippy Hippy Shake. The latter always caused my mother to laugh out loud as my whole body shook and my long hair flew all over the place. She said I looked like a "lunatic".

Sometimes my mother would call up the stairs to me to turn down the radio, as the noise disturbed her (not Mr Moss, as he was very hard of hearing), but mostly I lived uninterrupted in my little world.

My other source of entertainment was books. Mrs Moss gave me Annuals containing stories of girls' escapades in boarding schools, and after I had read those, I started reading proper books, like Robert Louis Stevenson's Treasure Island, Daniel Defoe's Robinson Crusoe, and Charles Dickens's Oliver Twist, which I found in the fusty smelling library next to the dining room.

I often went into Mr Moss' room. I had never seen anyone as old before. He was very thin and frail, with pure white wispy hair that stuck out and had to be patted down with a wet comb. At first I was shocked at the transparent skin on his hands, which were also covered in brown spots and dark bruises. He had very shaky hands and had to be helped to eat and drink. In fact he was capable of very little independent activity.

Sometimes I helped my mother. I might hold the bowl of warm water while she shaved his white stubble; get his special tray with fold down legs set up over his lap, so that she could place the plate with his mashed up lunch on it; fetch and hand her towels or bowls as required; or help her get him out of his bed and over to his red armchair, which had a special rubber ring on it covered by a tartan blanket to make it softer to sit on. Sometimes I would sit in this same chair and read very loudly a chapter or two to Mr Moss (or Grandfather Moss as my mother told me to call him).

Unaware as a child, I now know that he was still quite active mentally. He read with the help of a lamp and a variety of carved bone handled magnifying glasses. He liked me to tell him what I had learnt at school, and sometimes I would read articles from the newspaper for him. I had to talk very loudly, which was a bit tiresome, and when he spoke he always had to clear his throat which was rather repulsive to listen to at first, but I got used to it. And then when he did speak he was so breathless that his voice was very weak, so you had to listen carefully to make out what he was saying.

Despite careful repetition, or how loudly I shouted it at him, he was never able to make out my name, and finally I settled on Sandie, which he kept repeating, as being an acceptable alternative. The name actually rather appealed to me, as it reminded me of Sandie Shaw who often appeared on Top of the Pops. Her trademark was singing without any shoes on and as I liked to walk barefoot around the house, it seemed quite apt to adopt Sandie as my English nickname.

It wasn't easy to get the girls at school to call me by my new name though. My friendship with Paul Cross had fizzled out since I had stopped walking to school with him. Once the novelty of having a real German to act as the spy in their games had worn off, the boys turned their backs on me and I gradually formed tentative friendships with a few of the girls.

There was Helen, a pretty girl with enormous blue eyes, who was diagnosed with Diabetes. She often had to leave the classroom to get injections, and sometimes she came back crying. Once she showed me the red marks where the needles had pierced her thigh. She was allowed to eat a biscuit in the classroom at certain times of the day, but even though the rest of the class watched enviously as she ate, I did not think that made up for her pain.

There was also Patricia, with whom I probably got on best after Helen stopped attending school. But I was only able to play with Patricia during school because she had to get a bus home. And finally there was Shirley, whom I tolerated more than liked, because she always had to have the first and last say in everything.

One day we were told that there was going to be an extended playtime for the boys, but the girls were only allowed ten minutes instead of the usual fifteen to go to the toilet and then were to come straight back to the classroom.

Unfortunately the teacher hadn't considered the queue in the toilets and therefore I was the last back to the classroom. Consequently I only heard the tail end of the teacher's instructions which had something to do with towels and an incinerator.

I asked Helen, what the announcement had been about, but she wouldn't tell me as the boys were coming back into the classroom by then. At lunch time, once we were finished with our canteen meal and had gone outside to the playground we stood in a corner along with Patricia and Shirley.

Shirley always had to be first: "My mother told me about them already. You have to have them so that you can have babies."

"Well I don't want them. I don't want to have to wear a towel, it'll be like wearing a nappy", said Helen, who had just got a baby brother. "You'll see the lumps through your dress."

"Silly, you can't decide not to have them. And anyway you don't wear a towel like the one you dry your hands with. There are special towels you get made from cotton wool that clip on to an elastic belt, my mummy already told me and showed me" said Patricia, ever the sensible one.

I couldn't figure out what they were on about, but I guessed from what I heard that this was to do with growing up, getting bosoms, wearing bras, sex and babies. We talked about it often enough.

"So what is an incinerator? I asked. They looked at me blankly.

"Well, isn't that what Miss said, we had to put them in a special bin ready for the incinerator"?

I could see by their faces that no one knew the answer, but I knew Shirley wouldn't leave it at that.

"Oh, that'll be a grown up word for the janitor."

When I got home I couldn't wait to tell my mother and ask her what it was that you needed a towel for that was worn like a nappy on a belt.

She was in the kitchen, preparing dinner, humming. I

could tell she was in a good mood. She told me that the towels were used to soak up blood that comes out of your bottom once a month. I was stunned.

"Does it hurt?"

"No, sometimes you get a little tummy ache, but it doesn't hurt. You'll get used to it." She probably knew what I was going to ask next and pre-empted it. "It's part of growing up, becoming a woman, and being able to have babies."

Perhaps she wasn't prepared for my next question, because she blushed before answering. "Sex? Ahem…, sex is when the man pokes about in the woman's bottom".

It didn't sound worth growing up for.

Grandfather Moss was intrigued by my mother's cooking, which of course was not English but continental, with gravy that had never been thickened with Bisto and vegetables cooked in sauces rather than just boiled in water. The gravy and sauces were useful for mashing up the food so that it could be easily eaten by a 90 year old. He was a bit picky at first, but my mother was encouraged when he liked a particular meal she had made, and she liked to spend time trying out new recipes in her lovely big kitchen to entice him to eat. She even read cookery books and tried out traditional English dishes like Shepherds' Pie and Irish Stew.

In February, Grandfather Moss became increasingly weak, and at the end of the month I was farmed out to spend a few days with a friend of the family, a stranger to me. When I returned I understood that the reason was that Mr Moss had died and that my mother did not want me in the house during the days before and after the funeral.

We were allowed to stay a short while in the house, until, sometime in March 1965, we moved once again.

It wasn't as though the two moves since we left Klemens had caused us much upheaval. We had nothing to pack but our clothing and some bedding, after all. However, moving became more complicated because we were encumbered with Grandfather Moss's bequests – furniture that my mother had to arrange to have transported or placed into storage as we roamed from one address to the next over the following five years. We were now the proud owners of grandfather Moss' red armchair, a carved Sandalwood chest that contained a few pieces of silverware, an oak desk, his bone handled magnifying glass, and a painting that had hung in his bedroom.

I was kept totally unaware of all this until the afternoon that we moved. My mother met me at the school gate, and she told me what was happening as we walked the long road to our new address.

Chapter 11   Lavender Croft, Hitchin 1965-66

The house called Lavender Croft in Wymondley Road belonged to the British Council for Aid to Refugees (BCAR). It housed several refugees and ran an in-house workshop. My mother started her new job here, cutting templates out of leather, then machine sewing them together and finally stuffing the leather with straw to create various animals of differing sizes. The leather was treated with special wax which turned the colour from tan to smudgy brown, prior to being packed for exportation to South America. Luckily I loved the smell, which permeated the whole house.

We were the only tenants who had rooms on the ground floor, next to the workshops; the others lived on the first and second floors. We had three rooms, a kitchen and living room which were accessed separately from the main hallway, and a bedroom with two single beds that was reached through the living room. So for the first time since moving from the Refugee Camp, we had to lock the kitchen door if we were both in the living area and vice versa. The only advantage to this home was that the bedroom was south facing and had an enormous bay window which made the room bright and warm on cold sunny winter days, and therefore saved on heating costs.

It was a long walk for me to reach school, and I hated the last term of primary school for that reason. I think it might have been during the previous school year, that the Education Department in Hertfordshire did away with the 11+ test, the national exam used to identify and stream children according to academic ability. I certainly have no recollection of taking that particular test. Instead of a formal test, those who were in the top twenty percent of my class were deemed clever enough to go to Grammar school. This gave them access to a more academic education and therefore the opportunity for professional futures. The remainder were considered to benefit more from the education provided by the secondary modern schools, which were geared towards producing skilled and unskilled labour.

My mother was therefore delighted when she learnt that I had passed the class tests that replaced the 11+, and was ninth in my year group, and therefore eligible for a place at the Hitchin Grammar School for Girls. As I had been walking past the Grammar School on my way to primary school for the last few months, I was particularly delighted when I realised that I would not have to walk as far to school in the mornings.

Needless to say I spent the school holidays in Belgium. I passed most of the time at Mama Yvonne's house this time, playing with Chris, but the highlight of the trip was attending Jeff's sister Maria's wedding to Gerard. I really was treated like a guest of honour in Jeff's family. Mama Yvonne had spent the first half of the holiday sewing the dress that I was to wear, made out of a stiff taffeta tartan and decorated with an enormous bow tied in front. She also took me to the hairdresser to get my hair cut and styled as I was to be included in the formal wedding photograph. I was excited at my first visit to a proper hairdresser, but to my dismay all my long ringlets were cut off, and my straightened shoulder length hair looked very severe. My sombre, unhappy face did not do the wedding couple's expensive photographs much justice.

But I cheered up at the party that was held in Maria's father's house, where I had spent so many previous visits, for there was music and dancing.

I was the centre of attention once more as I danced for the guests, pretending I was Pavlova, improvising the dying swan scene, going up on tip toe, as I had practised so often in my bedroom in Elmside. Jeff was so impressed he asked me later if I was taking ballet lessons.

Saskia at Maria and Gerard's wedding (bottom row), Josephine and fiancé Jeff (right middle row) – Belgium 1964

When I came back from Belgium, my mother had got a job as a nursing auxiliary in Pinewood Hospital, in Hitchin, working shifts which meant spending a lot of the time on my own in the house, before and after school. She liked my shorter hair as she no longer had the time to comb and plait it in the mornings.

My mother arranged for me to get violin lessons, deciding that my love of music should find a suitable outlet. She had learnt to play the piano and organ as a child, and was determined that I should learn an instrument. I did not particularly care for the screeching sounds that I managed to produce, and practised very little in her absence.

My radio became my best friend. When Radio One started broadcasting on Saturday 30th September I tuned in to listen at seven in the morning to Tony Blackburn play his introductory signature tune followed by Flowers in the Rain by the Move. Unfortunately it took a few years for Radio One to be broadcast all day, so I still had to listen to Radio Luxembourg or Radio Caroline in the evenings, but the reception was sometimes very poor. When I found out that

Radio Caroline was broadcast from a ship, I figured that the ship's rocking to and fro in stormy weather would explain why the music weaved in and out of hearing.

On the whole I liked my new school. Unlike Primary school, we wore uniform, navy gym slips, white shirts, and a stripy tie. My pet hate was the musty smelling communal changing rooms, where we rushed to undress for PE, and later as we showered naked, all studiously avoided looking at each others' budding bodies in fear of seeing any proof that we might be unnaturally deformed.

There was a different teacher for every subject, and my favourite was the history teacher who was young and energetic, entering the classroom like a whirlwind, banging the chalk against the blackboard when she started writing. She moved around the room like she was a caged animal desperate to get out.

It took the first term for us girls to get to know each other well enough to form friendships. I had started getting to know two girls in particular. Fiona, who had very flaky skin, was the first person in the class to wear nylon stockings; everyone else still wore socks. My other friend was by far the tallest in the class, heavy boned with rather unattractive features and was nicknamed "The Griffin", but she didn't seem to mind and was very good humoured, which made her popular despite her physical shortcomings. I got friendly with her as a result of a drama class in which we were told to pair up and act out a word. The teacher allocated the partners and the words to be enacted by writing them on pieces of paper placed in a box. The Griffin pulled out my name and the word "hilarious".

I didn't know the meaning of the word but she did. After a while we agreed that it's the hardest thing in the world to act out being funny. You either are or you are not, or you get a script to read that is funny, like Peter Sellers and Harry Secombe reading the Goons on the radio.

We thought of all the jokes we knew. We decided we didn't know any that were funny enough, and any way I wasn't sure that telling jokes would count as acting.

I said "Clowns are funny, they don't speak, they do silly

actions that embarrass people, like knocking them over, throwing water over them, tripping them up. What can we do to each other that will make people laugh?"

She looked at me and smiled. "I know what to do. I did this at home with my brother at Christmas and it made my whole family laugh. But we can't practise it or it'll give it away, and then it won't be funny anymore. I'll tell you what we'll do when it's time to do it for the class, but you must promise to keep a straight face and not smile the whole time we're doing it."

I was both surprised and intrigued, but I didn't know whether to trust her or not. I thought about how embarrassing it would be to be totally unprepared in front of the class and just stand there like a fool. Reluctantly I nodded agreement.

We had to sit and watch some of the others enact their word before it was our turn. As we got up, she whispered, "Just pretend you are my dancing partner and stand on my feet and let me do the work. And act serious."

I looked at her feet - the most enormous I had ever seen. I was embarrassed about the size of mine, but hers must have been two or three sizes bigger, and they were twice as wide. She faced me and I gingerly put my right foot on her left foot and awkwardly held on to her as she grabbed my left arm and put her right arm around my waist. Finally, as I stood atop her feet, I thought of Fred Astaire and Ginger Rodgers, put on the serious but rapt expression I had seen on Ginger's face, and pretended in my head that we were dancing round the room.

The Griffin didn't dance like Fred Astaire though. She moved her feet like Frankenstein, like they were two rigid blocks of cement, and slowly turned round and round.

There was total silence.

Suddenly, there was a titter from one of the girls, then some choked laughter, and eventually the whole class was laughing at us. No-one guessed what the word was, probably because hilarious was not that common a word for our age group. But we were funny, and it felt wonderful to be laughed at for trying to be funny, and not just for being.

Christmas 1965 was the first Christmas I remember which my mother and I celebrated without a tree or decorations, but she insisted we would follow the English tradition, and I woke up on Christmas day to what looked like a bulky pillow case lying on the floor beside my bed. As soon as my mother realised I was awake, she got out of her bed over the other side of the room where she had been crocheting, and encouraged me to open my presents. "Go ahead! See what "Santa" got you!" I realised that she was almost as excited as I was.

Although of course I knew that Santa didn't exist, it was thrilling to be faced with a pillow case full of presents. I soon realised that it was actually one of the covers for the featherbed. I reached inside and pulled out the sleeve of a Navy gabardine school winter coat. It in turn was wrapped around something long and heavy. I finally discovered a wooden tennis racquet complete with press, and a hockey stick with a blue towelling handle. They must have cost a fortune.

I saw expectation on my mother's face. I could only guess what it must have cost her to save up for these pieces of sport equipment necessary for school, and I knew they had probably cost her more than anything I had ever received before, but they were not something that I could cherish like the radio I had found under the tree in the dining room in Elmside the previous Christmas.

I did my best acting ever. I smiled my best smile and stood up and hugged her hard, thanking her for the wonderful presents, and I hoped I had sufficiently hidden my disappointment.

At least the coat was warm.

Anna, one of the refugee women in the house was Polish and was always very friendly to my mother and said hello whenever she passed me in the corridor. My mother didn't have much time for her, stating that she seemed to have a lot of "gentlemen callers", and I could tell by the tone of her voice that this was not a thing she approved of.

So both my mother and I were shocked one Spring Saturday morning as we were walking in the direction of the town centre, to see Anna and my father walking towards us.

I think I must have recognised him first, for it was a few seconds later that I heard my mother catch her breath. I realised that this could become an awkward incident. She had told me that he had written to her in King's Walden asking her to come back to him. I wondered if he would stop and create a scene or, worse still, ask her again, and what she would say now, given how things had turned out for us since.

Anticipating the worst I looked everywhere but at him and Anna. Every step that I took towards him seemed heavier than the first as I steeled myself for the confrontation. As I saw his feet come towards us I looked up.

He walked right past. Perhaps there was the briefest of glances in our direction, or maybe I imagined it. My mother said nothing until we turned the next corner, out of sight and hearing. Then she stopped, turned to me, and burst out laughing. She laughed so long and so hard, she had tears in her eyes.

"Oh Schaeffi," she said, in answer to my puzzled expression, "don't you see? Now he has to go to her for his comfort! He's not the big man now!"

I didn't understand. I was just glad that there had been no shouting. But I did wonder later, when I found out about my mother's intention to move again, whether her decision had anything to do with the fact that he was possibly coming to the house to visit Anna.

Either way, in April, I was told that my mother had been accepted into a nursing course at a hospital in Papworth Everard near Cambridge, and that we were going for a visit to see if she could find me somewhere to live, because I would not be able to board with her in the nurses' accommodation.

During the Easter school holidays we took the train to Cambridge and then a half hour bus journey to Papworth, as it was more commonly called. The town was strung out along a main road, but the hospital was set back behind housing, in large grounds dotted with splashes of colour from early flowering shrubs. I could sense the pride that my mother felt in having been accepted for the nursing course because she talked at length about how this hospital was linked with Addenbrookes Hospital, where research was being done on heart transplants, the first successful one having just been carried out in South Africa.

It didn't mean much to me. I was more concerned with where I was going to be living.

It is strange sometimes how things happen in life. There we were walking aimlessly through the grounds, when a helmet clad woman on a scooter drove past and suddenly came to a halt, then backed up towards us. We stopped guiltily, as though she had caught us trespassing.

"Can I help? Are you lost?" She enquired.

"No, well, actually, yes, I need to find out where the nurses' accommodation is, thank you?" replied my mother.

"Oh, are you starting training? I work in the hospital, you see," she added, as though that would excuse her nosiness.

"Yes, I am starting in May, but I need to find some accommodations for my daughter."

The woman looked me up and down. "How old is she?"

"Twelve."

"Oh, she's tall for twelve. I would have thought she was older."

"I have got her a place in the Girls Grammar School in Cambridge. She is a good clever girl. It is a problem for me to find her accommodations. Is there a boarding house near the nurses' accommodations?"

"No, there isn't anything like that in Papworth. I can see you're going to have a hard time finding somewhere for her. You can ask at St Peter's, but maybe I can help. I've got a spare room; she could lodge with me until you find somewhere more suitable. Here, I'll give you my address, and you can write to me, if you can't find anything else before you move in."

She pulled a handbag from the basket on the front of her scooter, delved inside for a pen and a piece of paper, wrote her name and address, gave directions to St Peter's Nurses Home, and, after my mother had thanked her profusely, she scooted off.

By the first week of May, my mother had placed all our furniture in storage; we had taken our final journey out of Hitchin; she had moved into St Peter's Nurses Home; and I had moved in with the Shoebridges, who lived about a mile and half away at the far end of Papworth.

I had not seen my friends since school had broken up for Easter. I never got a chance to say goodbye or tell them where I was going. My only consolation was that my violin lessons came to an end.

Chapter 12   Papworth 1966

When Mrs Shoebridge was de-helmeted and off her scooter you could see that she was short, rather on the plump side with red-dyed hair, although her grey roots were visible more often than not.

Mr Shoebridge looked positively waif like beside her, but his easy smile below crinkly dark eyes and thinning grey hair belied any trace of being hen-pecked. They lived in a semi-detached council house in an estate where all the houses looked the same.

They had a Chihuahua dog called Zack who wasn't even the size of a full grown cat, but he was the most stubborn dog I had ever encountered. I adored him. When I took him for walks his little legs, no longer than my middle finger, had to move at the speed of light to keep up with me, and once Zack got tired, he refused to move. I would pull his lead, and I could drag him along on his hind quarters for all he cared, he totally refused to budge. There was no alternative but to pick him up. I finally understood why old ladies transported their miniature dogs in shopping trolleys.

The Shoebridges kindly let me treat their house like it was mine. I had the second bedroom upstairs, across the landing from theirs, but most of my time was spent with them in the kitchen and living room. For the next six months I lived a normal everyday working class English life, first hand.

Mondays to Fridays I walked down the hill to the main road to get the school bus into Cambridge. I saw my mother on a Saturday afternoon, and on Sunday mornings, I attended church with the Shoebridges, their daughter, her husband, and their two children, and in the afternoons we had Sunday dinner. Roast beef or lamb; parsnips or carrots; roast potatoes and mashed; Bisto gravy, and my favourite of all, Yorkshire puddings. Then we would sit down and watch television for the rest of the day or if the weather was good and there was a cricket match playing in the afternoon, the whole family might go for a walk to the field and watch while the children played behind the seating area.

I loved it. I loved the regularity, the security, the freedom. I felt like a normal English child. Within the first few weeks I made friends with neighbouring children and at school. I fancied the boy next door and wrote little notes to him during class but was too scared to give any to him. I hung out with a girl from up the road when I wasn't at school. I could go to her house, or we could go for a walk, or I could invite her into the house if I wanted to, because there was nothing to be ashamed of.

As the weather got warmer, we hung about outside, congregating with others in little groups, sitting on garden walls or strolling through cornfields, talking about the latest hit records, smoking, flirting. At the age of twelve I was able to attend my first pop concert in Cambridge, because I had the freedom to do so.

It was a triple bill extravaganza. As I screamed and jumped up and down in a frenzy of excitement I watched Dave Dee miss hitting, Dozy, Beaky, Mick and Titch with his whip as they played "Xanadu". I saw Reg Pressley of the Troggs do his trademark neck kinking in time to "Wild Thing", but I didn't see anything of Scott Walker or his brothers because everyone stood up as soon as they came on stage, and we had to leave after the first song to catch the last bus home.

This empowering sense of freedom made me a little more forward with my mother. One Saturday I even harangued her into buying me a pair of modern T bar tan suede shoes, with an inch and a half heel. She grumbled that they were totally unsuitable for school but in my eyes they were the most fabulous shoes I had ever owned, and I held my head up high as I paraded in them in front of my school-friends the following Monday.

Two weeks later I wore them in the rain, and left them to dry on the wood burning stove in the kitchen overnight. When I came downstairs in the morning I found them curled up, the suede cracked and loosened from the soles because of the heat.

I had to wear them to school like that, and get Mrs Shoebridge to contact my mother and arrange for her to meet me after school to buy a new pair of shoes. She raged at me as she dragged me from one shoe shop to another, closing her hears to my pleading and insisting that she had been right all along. With ten minutes to go until closing time, I finally had to give in to her choice of suitably drab sensible school shoes.

The next day at school my friends smirked. I finally understood the meaning of the proverb 'pride comes before a fall'.

During the summer holidays I went over to Belgium, and this year I spent more time living with Maria, Jeff's sister, who was no longer staying with her father and Jeff at the farm by the river Schelde, but in their new house which Gerard had just finished building. I was struck by Maria's softened features. Marriage and pregnancy had made her bloom.

Jeff's younger brother Roger and his wife Josephine lived about a kilometre away. They had recently bought a television, and we spent several evenings there during that hot summer, playing cards and watching the world cup, which was won by England that year.

In August, Jeff married Florentine, a girl whom he had met at the factory where he worked, and to whom I had first been introduced at Maria's wedding the previous year. I was dressed up for the occasion, but this time not in a dress made by Yvonne, but a short cream dress which Florentine had bought for me. I had my hair cut again, and now it was bouffant, in short layers. The wedding was less formal than Maria's – Josephine did not wear a long white dress, but a cream suit and hat, and the party was at Florentine's parents' house in Bornem, a village on the other bank of the river Schelde. During the celebrations Maria, by now uncomfortably pregnant, became unwell and we had to leave early. For the first time ever I was disagreeable and petulant at missing out on something I had looked forward to for so long.

No one spoke during the ride home in the taxi. Maria sat cold-faced, no doubt troubled at the extraordinarily harsh words I had let fly at her as we were leaving. I became increasingly ashamed of my display of bad temper. My conscience reminded me that these people had always been so kind to me – how could I have been so inconsiderate.

There was no doubt that all the freedom I had recently enjoyed was turning me into a more selfish and demanding child who found it much easier to disregard other people's feelings than in the past. I was no longer willing to be weighed down with the responsibility of always having to be good and fit in with other people's wishes.

I apologised the following day, because I knew that it was the right thing to do, but from then on I remained torn emotionally between having to conform and the burgeoning need to put myself first, for a change. I suppose these mixed emotions were the first sign that I was entering the ambivalent state of adolescence.

The journey back to England was also a little anxious for me, as I missed my mother at Victoria Station where I was supposed to meet her off the Dover train. I sat on my case and waited under the departure board as agreed, and finally, after several hours, I decided that I would have to go home alone. I went to the ticket desk and was advised I had to cross London in a taxi, to catch a train to Cambridge from Kings Cross station, and by the time I got back to Papworth it was late evening so I headed to the Shoebridges' house with my suitcase. The next morning I went to St Peter's Nurses Home to find my mother, only to discover from the Supervisor that she had set off for London earlier that morning. There must have been a mix up in the date confirmed for my return in the letters between Jeff and my mother.

It wasn't until the following morning, as I was brushing my teeth, that my mother appeared at the back door of the Shoebridge's house, and I rushed into her arms. Through tears of relief I heard her relate how the Supervisor had had the sense to contact Victoria Station, and how she had nearly fainted when she heard her name announced over the loudspeaker, with a message to go to the information desk.

Two months later my mother fell ill. By the time she recovered she had missed too much of her course to enable her to keep attending that year. With nowhere else to go, my mother had no alternative but to turn once more to the British Council for Aid to Refugees for help.

By the time I was informed arrangements had already been made for us to move back to their reception house in Worthing, while the wheels were set in motion to help my mother convalesce, find her a new job and one of their flats for us to rent. Returning to Hitchin was not an option she would consider.

Chapter 13   Pavilion Road 1967-68

We were back where we had started, waiting, like those other refugees who had just arrived, for what life would throw at them in their new country of adoption.

While we waited for a new flat to become available to rent, we stayed in a room in BCAR headquarters in Thorn Road. I started at Worthing High School for Girls after the Christmas holidays but within three weeks became ill with appendicitis. I spent my 13th birthday in hospital, and after I had spent four weeks recuperating in a convalescent home, I finally moved into our new home.

We rented the bottom floor of a red brick terraced house. We had a front room, my bedroom, a small dining room and kitchen. The three rooms upstairs were occupied by three single people, two men and a woman. The woman was about the same age as my mother, in her late forties, with blond curly hair, and seemed more stylish and much less strange looking than our male neighbours who were both Polish. The one with the glass eye was in his fifties, rounder and older than his neighbour Franz, who was skinny with short spiky hair, and always dressed in black. What made them scary was that one was disfigured and the other spoke to himself. Franz's room was above our dining room, and we could often hear him droning on. Occasionally he became so loud it sounded as though he was shouting at some imaginary demon, and both my mother and I would stop what we were doing. The look she gave me said "Ignore it; it won't be long until we're out of here."

It was because of Franz that I didn't go upstairs to the bathroom which was ostensibly shared by all the tenants. We preferred to wash at the kitchen sink and luckily we had an outside toilet. But at night time we reverted back to chamber pots.

There were at least two similar other houses owned by the

BCAR along Pavilion Road and rented out by the room. Some refugees had arrived years before and never ventured further than Worthing. Some integrated easily into their adopted community. Like Doddy, the Czech widower with three children, who had managed to land a skilled job in Beechams, one of the largest employers in the Worthing area. His improved fortune allowed him to afford a bubble car – a small yellow three wheel front opening monstrosity. The steering wheel was part of the door and once everyone had squeezed onto the single seat, the door was pulled shut. They looked so odd, Doddy and his bright eyed children staring like goldfish out of that bulbous yellow tin can.

Some refugees never integrated. Like Zolly. I understood why he couldn't find a job, for if I had been an employer I would never have hired him. My mother said he was a poor soul, had something wrong with him, a curvature of the spine which meant that his head was always tilted forward so that he was looking down at the ground. His protruding belly left him S shaped, and he made a strange figure shuffling along the pavement, which seemed to be his sole occupation. But, despite his bent head, which might have given the impression of meekness, he always managed to stare sidelong at any female form that passed by. I could feel his bold eyes on me whenever I passed him. He gave me the creeps.

My mother was aware I didn't like this place, the men upstairs, the locking of doors, the feeling of being unsafe. Unable for the time being to improve our living conditions, she bribed me with a kitten to be patient with her and our circumstances.

My delight was sincere though, I loved my little Tootsie. She did keep me company. She made me laugh as she scrabbled up and down the curtains, she made my heart ache when she got lost and then fill with joy when she was found hours later in-between the bedcovers stored in the base of my mother's sofa bed. As she grew, her coat became thicker, softer and longer, and my mother swore that she must be of Persian stock. I brushed her coat, collected the fur gathered in the bristles, and then threw the fur ball for her to chase and bring back to me to throw again, and I swore that she had been a dog in her previous life. She often slept with me, her comforting presence making me feel a little less alone and vulnerable at nights.

Conditions at my new school improved. I got to know a girl who joined my class not long after me, and our isolation brought us together. Carole had moved to Worthing from Scotland, and so was also a foreigner of sorts. She was obviously from a well-heeled family, because on her first day she was wearing the full uniform, skirt, cardigan, white shirt and school tie, gabardine coat and beret, all complete with neatly hand sewn school badges in the appropriate places.

My mother, on the other hand, had to get a special dispensation from the headmistress, to allow her time to save up for my third school uniform within three years. I was therefore permitted to wear the brown Cambridge Grammar school uniform until I outgrew it. Miss Hedley would have been able to know my exact whereabouts every morning as she stood on the stage of the assembly hall and cast her eyes over her green uniform-toting pupils, for I must have stood out like a solitary dog turd in the undulating green carpet stretching out in front of her.

Carole was a quiet, studious girl, but this allowed me to fill awkward gaps by making her laugh. I like to think I made her transition to the new school easier by warning her about the science teacher, Miss Sinclair, a skinny spinster whom the class was convinced was having an affair with the lab technician, and about the music teacher, the only male teacher on the whole staff, who was really easy to wind up. I regaled her with a description of how he had got so angry with the way the class had taunted him by deliberately singing out of tune, that he ended up storming out of the room and had slammed the door shut so hard behind him that one of the glass panes had shattered. And I told her to watch out for the Janitor if she ever needed to go to the toilet during class time, because if he saw her go in he would be sure to go outside and peek in through the gaps I had seen him scrape off the paint-daubed cubicle windows.

It must have been a couple of months after she started school when I was first invited to Carole's house after school, ostensibly to meet her dog. Blackie looked a little like Wally, but instead of the smooth pelt of a Labrador, Blackie had a ridge of raised hair on her spine, which tickled my hand as I stroked her. She was beautiful.

Carole lived in a detached house, in an Avenue. I had recently learnt that an Avenue meant the same as a Road, but that there were trees growing along the pavement. The downstairs of her house had the same number of rooms as mine, but her rooms were much larger and the furniture was much plusher. Her kitchen had pale blue cupboards along two walls, and yellow Formica worktops crowded with a bread bin, a pop up toaster, an electric kettle, and there was even a bowl of fruit. Her dining room contained not just a table and chairs, but also a dresser showing off delicately painted floral plates and dishes in shades of blue and gold. She had two sitting rooms, and the one next to the kitchen had a rose patterned three-piece suite, and a Television crowned with a v shaped aerial. But the thing that impressed me most was the red and white record player standing in the corner, winking at me. Carole could see I was smitten.

"Do you want me to put on a record? I've got the Beach Boys' "Pet Sounds" – well, it's my brother's really but he won't know because he doesn't get in for another hour."

For the first time in several months, my heart purred with contentment.

Chapter 14   The Beginning of the End

And so I am finally back to the beginning of my story: that frosty October evening in 1967 when I first found and raided the brown attaché case, which contained so many papers giving clues to the life my parents had led before they met and married each other.

After reading my father's Curriculum Vitae, I was aware for the first time that their lives must have been difficult. But, because I had experienced the kind of life led by refugees, a fragmented existence consisting of left-behind homes and border crossings, it was perfectly understandable.   What saddened me that particular evening was that the sum of their lives, with all its mistranslations, filled a mere typed page. Their story did not shock me, and, as I rarely talked about my own life experience, I did not wonder why my parents had never spoken of their memories before or during the war.

But then, I knew nothing of war.

My over-riding concern from that evening on was how to find out whether I really was illegitimate.   So my snooping that evening did not stop after reading my father's CV.   I merely methodically placed the Oath and Curriculum Vitae upside down on top of the other certificates, and checked out the next item in the bundle.

It was a certified translation of my parents' Certificate of Marriage in the "Polish Pastorate of the Roman Catholic Curatia in Nurnberg-Langenwasser", dated 1 Dec 1960. Witnesses were Pawel Steinguel and Halina Glowacka, both from the Camp.

I remembered the wedding.   It had been winter.   There hadn't been any snow – or maybe there had.   I shut my eyes and tried to call up the picture in my head.   Their wedding photo - a black Volkswagen Beetle in the background, to the right of which was a white monument which I remember stood outside the Church and commemorated all those Poles who had died in the Camp. My father stood in his good grey coat, the tallest of the wedding party, his bald head kept warm by his winter hat. Next to him on the left was Pawel, wearing a black beret and beige raincoat. To the right of my father, my mother, small hat, fur coat, or was it the blue suit? To her right Halina, in some nondescript coat, and in front of them both - me. I was holding something, but what?

Frustrated, I decided I would have to get the photo out and check. Besides, it would be a good opportunity to have another look at my father, to see if we bore a resemblance to each other. I would need to wait and ask my mother to get the photos out. I used to like looking through them, but I hadn't done so for a long time, and I wasn't sure where my mother had stored them since moving here.

By the time she came home that evening, I had tidied everything away, exactly as I had found it, and had moved from the now warm front room to do my homework at the table in the back room. I thought I would start the gas oven and get the kitchen heated up for her coming home. She saw that I was busy and merely kissed my cheek on her way past, already taking out newspaper wrapped vegetables from her string shopping bag.

"What's for dinner, Mutti?"

"Pork trotters in cabbage." Her reply wafted through to me alongside the sound of hissing fat. I much preferred my mother's creamy, slightly sour, and finely sliced cabbage to the green slush we were served at school. In fact, all her vegetables were usually served in a sauce of some type, which brought out the flavours. Unlike plain boiled carrots as taught at school - boil whole for fifteen minutes until the water is tinged pale orange, drain and serve - my mother's were sliced and boiled until they were not quite done, then in a separate pan she fried onion, added flour and then some of the juice from the carrots to make a sauce, before adding the carrots and a little cream from the top of the milk bottle.

We had just finished eating when she announced: "I was thinking of renting a television. What do you think?"

A television? I could hardly contain my excitement. A

television! I would be able to watch "The Monkees" on a Saturday, and "Top of the Pops", and "The Virginian" and be able to talk about the same things as everyone else at school, instead of sitting quietly and enviously while they discussed their favourite programmes.

"Mutti, that would be wonderful, but can we afford it?"

"I think so. I just found out from one of the women at work that you can rent a television set from Good Listening Limited on the Broadwater Road, from one month to the next! And if it is too much for me, then I can always stop renting it, nah? We shall try it and see!"

I looked at my mother with new eyes. Working with these English people at the plastics factory was having an effect on her. She had never been such a risk taker. If my mother could not pay for something up front, she didn't buy it. If she needed something she saved for it or did without.

After her announcement about the TV I thought it would be a good time to ask where the photos were and she got them for me from the little cupboard under the staircase. I unlocked my bedroom, got undressed as quickly as I could and slipped on my flannelette nightie and one of my mother's hand-knitted bed jackets for extra warmth. Then I pulled on a pair of thick woollen socks. It didn't take long for me to heat up once I slipped under the covers.

Propped up comfortably with my pillows, I upended the contents of the envelope onto my lap. Unlike the documents in the case which were neatly bundled together, and obviously in some kind of order, the photos were all jumbled up. This was because it was always me who looked through them, and I was definitely not as tidy as my mother.

My mother had her clothes neatly folded in the larger wardrobe of the two crowding my bedroom – there was no room for anything else other than my bed. My wardrobe got into such a state with clothes flung into it, half pulled out and pushed back in as I changed my mind about whether to wear this item or that, especially at the weekend, that she would feel the need to go through my wardrobe once a week and rearrange things. In her wardrobe everything was folded with the largest fold facing you when you opened the door, and each shelf was colour co-ordinated, lightest colour at the top, darkest at the bottom.

After shuffling the photos so that they were all facing one way, I dealt them into piles according to where they were taken.

There were very few photos of my mother taken once we left the Camp and emigrated, for we never possessed a camera. The majority of photos taken post 1961 were of my visits to Belgium. There were also some identity cards taken from 1947 onwards with passport size images of my mother looking very thin.

It never ceased to amaze me that even now my mother would not go out without her passport in her handbag. When I asked why she did this, she said you never knew if a policeman was going to stop you and then at least you would have some form of identification. I had never seen a policeman in Worthing other than directing the traffic once, so that didn't make much sense.

I took the opportunity to check out the one dated December 1953 and noticed that she looked much better there than in the years before: rounder faced, prettier, happier. Obviously being pregnant suited her. It made me glad to think that she had been happy that I was going to be born, even if she wasn't married at the time. I then turned my attention to sorting through the photos, putting the ones of my mother and father with obvious Camp-like backgrounds into a separate pile.

I found the wedding picture. I had been right to think that I had been holding something and now I could see that it had been a white handbag, to match my white stockings and white shoes. But I had also been wrong – I was standing in front of my father, not my mother, and my mother was wearing a chic white hat, had a white handbag over her arm, and was holding a bunch of flowers. She was wearing her beaver lamb fur coat over her suit, which made her look much more portly than she was.

Church Wedding of Brigitte and Klemens
at the Valka Camp 1960

I tried to look objectively at my father, and decided that he was a very handsome man, when he wore his hat. Compared to my diminutive mother, he must have been just under six feet, square shouldered, square jawed. I had an oval shaped face, my mother's was rounder.

He may have been blond previously, for his eyebrows were much lighter than my mother's, and she was dark haired, like me. His eyes were a greyish blue, I remembered, though not as blue as my mother's. Hers were as blue as the sky on a sunny day. Mine were hazel.

I concluded that I really didn't look like either of them.

There were five photos of the wedding in total, one of us in the process of getting out of the car, one in front of the car, a couple in front of the wooden church, and one with the old wooden refugee huts in the background. I was suddenly struck at how solemn we all were. Maybe getting married in the Catholic Church was considered a solemn occasion.

I tried to remember the party which was held in the bedroom afterwards. Somehow the bed had been moved out and they had acquired another table and enough chairs to seat all the neighbours and friends who had brought food and drink.

It was really just a meal, there was no dancing or singing

or anything resembling the high spirits I had seen in Belgium. I overheard the woman sitting next to me at the table whisper and giggle about the good-looking young priest who had helped at the marriage ceremony, and who now graced the head of our table with his presence.

When I looked at the two pictures taken at the party, I noticed that my mother was smoking, a habit which I had no recollection of her ever having.

Suddenly, my mother came into my room.

"I never knew you smoked, Mutti!"

She came over and nestled down beside me, pulling the covers over her.

"Ach, it was just occasionally. I never really liked it. It was just fashionable."

I randomly picked up the next photo in the pile, dated 10th November 1958, and inscribed by Mama Yvonne. She often wrote on the back of the photos she sent us. I was with her cousin Jeff, who was the same age as me, in the nearby city of Antwerp, visiting St Niklaas, and his helper Zwarte Piet (Black Peter) in a department store.

St Nicholas was a former Bishop who spread the Catholic faith in Turkey – or was it Greece – and brought back with him a black servant. His goodness and generous nature is traditionally celebrated on the 6th of December, his saint's day, when two men dressed up like a bishop and a black man visit children in their homes. I had a distinct memory of getting such a visit in our kitchen one evening in the Camp in Germany. The white bearded man asked my parents if I had been a good child. My mother said yes and he said he was glad he wouldn't have to leave a stick for them to beat me with. I could see his black faced helper in the background with a sack full of hazel switches.

"Mutti, if Santa Claus is based on St Nicholas, then why does the English Santa Claus visit on Christmas Eve and have elves and reindeer to help him?"

"Schaeffi, I have no idea – but I think it might be because England is not a Catholic country, and they would not want to use a Saint name, so the name got changed. They probably changed the date to Christmas Eve, when giving gifts ties in with the giving of gifts by the Three Kings. Of course on the continent they celebrate Three Kings day on 6th January. Still, we are in England now so we do as the English do, nah?"

"Yes, I suppose so." Although my wicked internal voice added that we don't really celebrate Christmas like the English do, with turkey and sausages and stuffing on Christmas Day, because there are only two of us, and there is no point in all that food, and we don't have uncles and aunties that come over and fall asleep in front of the television, or listen to the Queen's speech... do we?

I examined the other Christmas photos again. "Hmm, I wasn't in Belgium for Christmas in 1958 when this photo was taken, because here I am in the Camp in the bedroom for Christmas that year. This one is in 1959, and the colour one is 1960, our last Christmas in Germany"

As I showed her the photos, I decided that the question I was about to ask was a reasonable one. "Why are there no photos of Christmas 1957 or before?"

I wasn't prepared for her reaction at all. Flushed from the neck upwards she looked at me as though I had slapped her in the face. Abruptly she got off the bed, and in a cold voice said "It's getting late. I think you had better put the pictures away now and get some sleep." Then she turned and quickly left the room, locking the door behind her.

Chapter 15   Secrets Revealed

On returning from Carole's later than normal the following evening, I could tell by the sliver of light at the bottom of the back sitting room door that my mother was already home. But there were no welcome smells of cooking to greet me as I opened the door.

My mother was sitting straight and stiff on the worn sofa, looking as off-white as one of her hand crocheted doilies.

"What's wrong, Mutti? Aren't you feeling well?"

"That bitch!" She hissed. "That bitch upstairs, she just told me that her husband was the commandant of a labour camp!"

Shocked at hearing my mother swear, I became aware of the agitation in her face, the tenseness of her shoulders, but I still didn't know what she was so angry about.

"What do you mean?"

"Ach, nothing. Nothing you would know anything about Schaeffi, but..." she stopped and took a breath. "She was boasting!" Her exclamation burst out an octave above normal, she was almost screeching. "She had the cheek to boast that her husband was the overseer of a Polish labour camp during the war." Making an effort to control herself she hastily explained: "The Nazis rounded up Poles and other innocent people, took them away from their towns and villages, and deported them to these camps and used them as slave labour." She must have seen from my blank expression that I still didn't understand. "The Poles were very badly treated by the Nazis. The Poles and the Gypsies had it as bad as the Jews. That stupid cow needs to remember that there are a lot of Poles around here, including her neighbours on either side, and she should learn to keep her mouth shut."

I took off my coat and sat down next to her. I still didn't fully understand, but I could see she was close to hysteria. I knew that she would need me here beside her, until she had calmed down and taken time to think through whatever had caused her to feel so troubled.

I sat quietly beside her while she looked into space and picked through her thoughts. The only movement came from her hands which were incessantly folding and unfolding the material of her skirt. We must have sat like that for a while and I hoped she had recovered herself when she finally turned to look at me. Her searching gaze unnerved me. It was as though she was somehow summing me up. When she finally spoke her voice was almost back to normal.

"Ha, they all think because I am German, that they can confide in me. But I am going to tell you a secret. Yes, I am German, but I am also Jewish."

"What do you mean, Jewish? I thought we were Catholic?"

"The religion people practised had nothing to do with it, Saskia. As far as the Nazis were concerned, it was all to do with how much Aryan blood supposedly ran in your veins. In 1933, when Hitler became Chancellor, that's like a Prime Minister, one of the first things he did was to single out the Jews, and with the help of propaganda he turned them into a sub human species. There were special laws passed; you had to register if you were Jewish, you couldn't marry non Jews if you were Jewish, and so on. His aim was to purify the Germanic peoples, and become the Master race of untainted Aryan stock. He was a madman. It was just an excuse to get Jewish money into the exchequer.

"I was born in an area which belonged to Germany before the war, the Sudetenland. My father's birthright gave us German citizenship. I was raised a Catholic. But my grandmother was Jewish, and my mother was a converted Catholic, and so I was considered half Jewish. Though if they knew anything about the Jewish faith they would realise that the blood line is considered to run through the female line, not the male, and so it could have been argued that I am actually Jewish through and through!" She laughed a humourless laugh which did nothing to alleviate the growing alarm inside me.

I had learnt a little about the war, mostly from films, the odd ramblings of our French teacher who liked to talk about the French Resistance, and I had read the Diary of Anne Frank. I had also seen some war photos in an encyclopaedia once. They had been taken during the liberation of the concentration and death Camps like Treblinka and Auschwitz by the Allied Armies in 1945. I remembered the horror I had felt when I first saw the image of hundreds of Jewish dead piled up in some garish heap, some clothed in striped sackcloth, others naked, looking like nothing more than bags of bones, a jumble of legs, heads, arms and torsos.

My mother had previously told me little snippets about her childhood in what was now Communist controlled Czechoslovakia, but I had never really thought it odd that she hadn't talked about her experiences during the war, and it never occurred to me to ask.

Up until I had read the documentation in the attaché case, her history was something I had always taken for granted. Besides, the emigration application had only mentioned my father's wartime experiences, there was nothing mentioned of my mother's other than her places of work during the war years.

"Did you have a difficult time in the war, being Jewish?" I asked quietly.

She turned away from me. Her gaze returned to that point in the distance which was only visible to her. Her voice was flatter, harder than before.

"It was hard, yes, but not as hard as it was for those who were shipped to nearby Auschwitz and murdered. And we didn't really knew about Auschwitz until after the war, when we also learnt how many other death camps and labour camps there had been, and how many millions had suffered and died.

"I had to prove how much of a Jew I was, searching in church records and so on and I had to report to the Gestapo every day for work. Once, after a visit by the Police, when they beat me up, I couldn't get up for work. I was lame down one side. My friend borrowed a bicycle and pushed me to the queue to sign up for the day's work. If I had missed work they would have shipped me off straight away. It wasn't until later, when I no longer had the protection of my father, that things changed for the worse. Luckily I had a valued profession in bookkeeping, so I was not sent to any labour camp until later on in the war.

"And the local people knew me, they looked out for me. They had known and respected my father and my grandmother, who ran the inn in the next village. Besides, the anti-Jewish propaganda didn't affect older people much; they had longer memories and were wise enough to know that there wasn't any difference. But the younger ones, they got the fever more easily."

Her blue eyes looked far beyond our tiny room. I didn't dare to interrupt her thoughts. The concertina-like folding of her skirt resumed.

As I watched her face, I found myself wondering. Looking at her features, I remembered the anti Jewish propaganda I had seen in the history books at school; the pictures of the archetypal dark haired, hook nosed, brown eyed Fagin-like Jew. My mother's eyes were light blue, Aryan eyes, but her nose was slightly hooked and on the large side for her round face. Her forehead was high but sloping. I wondered what Nazis would have thought of her as they walked past her in the street.

We sat quietly together, for several minutes and I thought she might have calmed down when she continued with a more normal sounding voice. "I will tell you a secret."

She paused, clearly considering her next words carefully.

"When I lived in Jagersdorf, near the border with Poland, I was working as a bookkeeper for a big local business with lots of offices in the surrounding district, and one of my jobs was to take the weekly wages to the workers, so I travelled on the trains in the area and I got to know the train routes well. That knowledge saved me.

"Like I said, I had to report to the Gestapo throughout the war, and apart from the growing lack of food and other commodities, life was otherwise pretty normal until Father died. Then, they stopped me working for the company and moved me to work in a factory making gas masks, and we lived and slept on the premises. We knew it would only be a matter of time before they shipped us east. The girl I shared a bunk with had heard the rumours about what would happen next. I guess she feared that her life, which consisted of nothing but subsisting on our meagre diet and cleaning out the factory latrines, would only get worse. She hung herself."

I think I stopped breathing at that point. If my legs could have moved I might have run out of the room. But I was now as stuck to that seat as she was..

"I worked there for a few more weeks before we got told to get our few belongings together, and we were put on the transport. They were getting so careless, because they were losing the war and they knew the end was coming. Troops and equipment were being moved from the eastern front to the western front, and that meant the rolling stock was in great demand. Auschwitz wasn't far, so they used open topped carriages to move us. Auschwitz was on the same route I had taken so many times before. There were guards of course, but I knew where we were. I knew the layout of the land, and where the steepest dips at the side of the track would be.

"I figured out the best place and time to jump – I decided on this one embankment just before a long bend, because the guards wouldn't have a good enough view to shoot after the train started the turn. I was right. I just fell silently into a deep snow drift and not a shot was fired."

It sounded like something out of a war film. I could imagine the guards sitting on their gun turrets on top of the engine, smoking cigarettes, wrapped up against the cold, blinded by snowflakes, and my mother, a female version of Frank Sinatra in Von Ryan's Express or something similar, leading fellow fugitives over the side to freedom. I could see her coat being caught in the barbed wire; hear the rip as it was pulled free. There would have been barbed wire, of course. Perhaps someone had secreted a tool to cut the wire loose and make a hole for escapees. Suddenly I was enthralled by this horror story.

"What happened then?"

"I had the idea that if I could get a hold of a nurse's uniform, I could pretend to be a nurse. I had done some nursing training, and figured nurses wouldn't get their papers checked. So I stole a uniform. And when I found a train coming through from the eastern front, loaded with wounded soldiers, heading back to Germany, I sneaked on board, and nursed the wounded until we got to Dresden.

"I figured that if I stayed in the larger towns, there would be more confusion because of the bombings which were getting worse and worse. People were moving all the time, trying to find shelter. It would be much easier to become invisible, and people couldn't be as suspicious, because they no longer knew who should be where. It was easy to pick out Jews when they were wearing the Star of David, but otherwise we looked just the same as everyone else!

"So when I got to Dresden, I thought I would get off and take another train to Marienberg, not far from Dresden. I had a distant relative on my father's side, who owned a farm there, and I thought I might see if they could take me in. I could earn my keep, work on the farm. So I waited on the station for a connection, but it never came. And while I was sitting there I noticed this girl, she was about my age, on the same platform, sitting on her suitcase. She looked, well... furtive, I suppose. She kept spreading her coat over her suitcase, which just made me look at it all the more.

"I suddenly got this sense of foreboding, and when our eyes met, I decided to approach her. I said to her, 'It looks as though the train is delayed. Do you want me to help you carry the case and perhaps we can make a start and walk to the next station? This waiting is making me restless'. I must have said exactly the right thing because she replied, 'yes please' with such relief in her voice;. Well, we started walking, and she eventually confided in me that she had been visiting her aunt's farm, and the suitcase contained food that she had been given to take home to her family. If she had been found out she would have been arrested.

"So we continued south, along the river Elbe, for the rest of the afternoon and when it got dark, and we were a good distance from the city, we saw a deserted farm building. She pulled the suitcase open and shared some food. I can still remember the taste of that sausage. I hadn't eaten anything as good for so long. We were so exhausted, we fell asleep despite the cold. But we got woken with the whine and crash of bombs exploding and watched the rest of the night as Dresden was bombed and bombed, until it was nothing but a red fireball in the distance. How I thanked God that He had given me that gift of premonition which made me get out of Dresden that afternoon." She shuddered.

"How did you end up in Nurnberg, Mutti? Did you walk the whole way?"

She laughed again, that same desolate humourless laugh. "No, I was captured again, I was unlucky. I got stopped and of course had no identity papers. I was placed in another slave labour factory, but everyone knew the Russians were coming from the east and the Americans were coming from the west. It was just a matter of time, and the guards were becoming nervous; some were already deserting. So a group of us broke out and stole a truck, and drove south and west, until we saw the American troops. But it wasn't any easier after the surrender. They repatriated as many as they could back east, and I was returned home, where only my stepmother survived. Our house had been bombed. She didn't want me; I was just another hungry mouth for her to feed, so I ended up in the Camp that had been set up for displaced people. The Russians and the Czechs hated the Sudeten Germans. They treated us like animals in that Camp. I know it was a time of retribution for what the Nazis did, but they were cruel, so cruel. The Russians were the worst. They took women three and four times a night. I thank God I managed to escape and get back to Germany."

"How did you do that?"

She hesitated for a fraction of a second, "I paid a man to smuggle me over the border. I handed myself over to the Americans, who took me to Nurnberg, to the hospital, where I was treated for malnutrition. They had to pull out all of my upper right teeth, the gum disease was so bad. I had lots of time to reflect there. I tried to make sense of it all, of the betrayal and senseless murder, of the evil, vile things that people can do to each other. But I couldn't make sense of it, and I couldn't stay angry forever, so the only thing I could do to keep sane was to try to forget. All those that I met later, all those displaced people in the Camp, we all wanted to forget the misery of that time."

I didn't know what to say to her. She sat there beside me, hands still pleating and un-pleating in her lap, staring out in front of her, lost in her thoughts again.

I recalled the document I had found just the other day, and realised that it echoed only a fraction of what she had just described. I understood now, how the sadness I had felt even then must have radiated from the words on the paper.

Suddenly she got up. She looked stronger, more determined, like her old self.

"You were asking yesterday why there were no Christmas photos before the ones taken in Belgium... well, I'm going to tell you Saskia." She gave a deep sigh, and then said. "But first I am going to make something to eat. It's nearly six thirty and you must be hungry!"

As she moved around the kitchen, I thought about what she had told me. As the days passed I would rerun the mental pictures I had created as she described her experiences, like a film in my head. At first I couldn't get this vision of my mother nursing a wounded German on a bunk on a train, something like Julie Christie in Doctor Shivago, out of my mind. Then my inner eye jumped reels to a picture of my mother in a stone building, lying on a large mound of hay, looking out of a glassless window, towards the dark silhouettes of a distant city skyline backed by a fiery red sky. The next scene was of my mother, head covered in a floral scarf, sitting in the front of a green truck, squashed between two men, pointing ahead and shouting "At last! There they are - the Americans!"

I often had to put a stop to the frivolous projector in my head, reminding myself that what she had told me was true, had happened to her, to my mother, not to some on-screen actress. Yet it was all just too fantastical and overwhelming for me to take in properly. I could only absorb a fraction of what she had suffered - deprivation, starvation, pain, that she had witnessed death, and escaped it more than once by seeing opportunities and grasping them.

What she told me that night was seared onto my subconscious, and I was to recall what she had told me in detail, again and again, and mull it over and feel my body tremble in awe of my mother's courage and resilience. But that evening I merely waited patiently for her to tell me the one thing that was still uppermost in my troubled childish mind – the reason why we had no photographs of Christmases before my first trip to Belgium.

Chapter 16   Who Is My Father?

In the end she didn't tell me while we were eating, or even after, although I hung around in the sitting room. I realised she had upset herself too much with her memories to continue. As we sat at our meal, and I watched her pick at her food, I could see how the telling had worn her out.

Afterwards, as she tidied up, I tried to concentrate on my homework. Although I still wanted to know, I was not prepared to break the silence.

After the dishes were done, she went through to the front room to make up her bed, and when I had finished up, I went to my own room. As I lay listening to the radio, I tried hard to imagine what it might have felt like to be Jewish in terms of the war films I had seen, but of course they were about heroic battles or escape stories, from the British or American viewpoint.

I was almost ready to switch off my transistor and was therefore surprised when my mother came into my bedroom so late. I waited with bated breath as she bent over and kissed me goodnight. Suddenly, when I thought she was on the point of turning away and leaving the room, she sat on the edge of the bed and looked at me.

I knew by her hesitation that something bad was coming. I suppose that there was never going to be an easy way for her to broach the subject, but it seemed imminently cruel at the time, the matter of fact way she told it, short, and quick and to the point.

"How would you feel if I told you Klemens is not your father?"

I was as stunned as if I had been hit on the chin. I wasn't sure whether she expected an answer, but I was incapable of giving one.

"Because he isn't. I married Klemens as a matter of convenience, because I needed a father for you. I needed to get you out of the orphanage."

I couldn't breathe. Her words had delivered such a weighty punch to my unsuspecting heart that my chest felt like it was caving in.

"He needed a wife. He was a widower. We both wanted to get out of that godforsaken place and we knew that a family had a better chance of sponsorship than a single person. For me, it was a means to get you out of there."

"Orphanage?" I breathed out at last.

"Yes. You were placed in an orphanage because I couldn't look after you when you were born. It was run by the Americans, by the Methodists... I visited you every Sunday."

I was dazed. The silence dragged as I tried to absorb what she had just said. Finally I was able to ask "So who was my real father?"

Her voice softened. "His name was Karl. He was Czech... came not far from my own village. His father worked on the railways, and he seemed to think that our fathers probably knew each other. He played the violin. He had a real talent, could have been a concert violinist, if it hadn't been for the war."

"How did you meet him?"

"It was when we were applying for emigration to the United States. He took the same bus home. He lived in the DP Camp, in the wooden huts. I was living in a rented room in a guest house, on the same bus route. We planned to get married. But I failed my medical, because they found TB, and I had to go to the Sanatorium. He got his clearance papers through shortly after, and insisted he was going to stay with me in Germany, but I told him no. People waited so long for their emigration clearance, I didn't want him to lose the opportunity to get out of there. I told him he should start a new life in America, and I would follow him after the cure was complete. He left shortly after. I didn't know I was pregnant until I was in the sanatorium.... Four months gone".

"Four months? Didn't you suspect before then?"

"No. I had hardly had a proper period since the war. Malnutrition often had that effect. I only bled a little now and again. So I didn't even realise. It was a real shock to me. I wrote to tell him. He was living in Pittsburgh. He was so happy! He was the one who chose your name, Saskia. His favourite painter was Rembrandt, and you are named after his wife."

Rembrandt's wife, I let that sink in. But I still had more questions.

"Why didn't you emigrate with me after I was born?"

"I was going to join him, that had been my intention and I still wanted it that way when he wrote to me. But I couldn't look after you when you were born. I was ill, you were ill. They took you away." Her voice broke. "It just became too hard. I couldn't get a job until I was signed fit for work; I had to get a job to get you out of the orphanage they put you in. I stopped writing to him after a year."

"Why couldn't he come back?"

She shook her head slowly, sadly. "He wanted to. I didn't want him to come back. To what?" She shook her head more determinedly now. "No, he had waited for a year. There was no point in him waiting for me any longer. He had a chance for a new life; I had to let him get on with it; let him find someone else and start over." She took a deep breath and collected herself. "When I got the all clear, I got a room, and I started working again, to be able to afford to get some furniture and baby things and get you out of the orphanage. I visited you every Sunday. You know, you were such a funny baby. Not a hair on your head – completely bald! Until you were two. People used to say what a lovely boy!"

I had heard her say that before, but I hadn't known then that the people saying it were people working in and visiting an orphanage. I shivered inside, thinking of the things she had omitted to tell me, wondering which of her other anecdotes would change in the light of what I now knew.

"There was a little orphan there; she couldn't have been more than five or six years old. It was like she adopted you, Schaeffi! She looked out for you, fed you and changed you. When I came to visit I had to bring goodies for her too! You remember I told you, you never spoke until you were nearly three? She did it all for you. Got you dressed and washed. Brought you what you needed – you just needed to point! No, there was no need for you to learn to talk!"

"How old was I when you finally got me out?" I asked quietly.

"Three. It was just when they were building the new concrete blocks in the Camp. You know that memory of yours, when you saw Klemens washing and noticed he had hair everywhere but on his head? That was your first night home with us after we got married. We brought you to the first room we had been allocated.

"But you were so ill, Schaeffi, you coughed and coughed. You weren't with us long; we were so happy when we were able to send you to Switzerland to recuperate. You came back so much more healthy and fat and brown! But then Klemens was diagnosed with TB once more, and he had to go to the Sanatorium yet again, and I had the chance of a decent job and didn't want to lose it. So I applied to the Church again, and I got the application from Mama Yvonne. I knew you would be well looked after and loved by her. She wanted so much to have a baby. And…"

"Yes, I know all that," I interrupted. "But have you never seen him since? Have you never contacted this Karl again?"

"No." She sighed.

"Is there any way we can contact him now?"

"No… I don't think so," she said slowly. "I don't have his address anymore, and he could be married and have children of his own, and ..." she lowered her head. "I never thought we would end up like this. I thought I was doing the right thing."

"Do you have a photo?"

"No," She shook her head firmly. "I lost all that with moving…it didn't seem to matter so much once I married Klemens and we were going to be able to emigrate and start a new life as a family."

She looked at me and, as if seeing for the first time my desperate need for more details, she added: "You have his hazel eyes, almond shaped, one eye slightly more pointed than the other. And his hands. You have his hands. Look."

She picked up my hand and traced her finger along the outer edge of the palm. Under the little finger it sloped quite markedly outwards and then back in. She held up her own and pointed to the same area but there was no sharp outward curve on her palm.

"You see? It's quite unusual to have the palm shaped like this. His hands were like that. And lovely, long fingers. Now you know why I wanted you to learn the violin. You were gifted, you know, but, ah, well." She let out a long sigh.

"Is that why he called you Curva? Klemens, I mean. Because you had a child by a different man and you weren't married?" It must have hurt her to be asked the question, but I couldn't help myself.

She shrugged. "He knew what had happened. Things were difficult after the war. We got introduced by some mutual friends, and he wanted to be married again. Both his previous wives had died of cancer. It was a Marriage of Convenience. He took you on as though he was your father, gave you a name, and he got the wife that he needed to look after him.

"And we *were* happy in Germany. We both had the same goal – to get out of that Camp. It was only once he came here that he turned nasty. Thought he was a big shot drinking with all the other Poles. Suddenly I didn't fit in, I wasn't Polish. I wasn't prepared to carry on the way we had. I wanted more out of life. If he had been prepared to work hard, we could have invested the money we had saved. I had thought that we could buy a house and turn it into a bed and breakfast, and then he wouldn't have needed to work outside in the cold. But no, he preferred drinking our savings away. Then he went sniffing after that Polish woman..."

I turned to the wall as I felt the tears start to fall. I didn't need to hear another diatribe on Klemens and all his shortcomings.

I wasn't aware of her leaving the room.

Chapter 17   Labels and Guilt

I cursed my life again and again that night and the other sleepless ones that followed. I was an outsider not just to those I had come into contact with during my thirteen nomadic years of existence, but now I was also a foreigner to myself.

One particular night, as I lay tossing and turning, my skin itchy from harbouring this unlovable stranger, I contemplated turning on the gas tap situated on the hearth. The thought of having to endure this life any longer felt like a burden impossible to bear. Every bump and drone from upstairs simply reinforced the fact that I was living within the same walls that housed a lunatic, a one eyed man and the wife of a commander of a Nazi labour camp.

No wonder my mother was eaten up with bitterness. Life had dealt her a similarly awful hand. What was the point of carrying on faced with this bleak future? What made her even *want* to go on?

The answer came to me the next instant. It was ME. She had invested her future in me. I had provided the reason for her to carry on hoping.

Somehow I got through the next day, and the following ones. Soon I thought less of what I had discovered about myself and more about what I had discovered about her.

Suddenly I wanted to learn about the war and what had happened to those victims who had shared the same fate as my mother. All those neighbours in the Camp, had they endured the same as my mother? Had they also told lies to cover the reasons they continued to live, while so many others had died? What made them carry on? Did hope never die despite the loss of everything else?

I immersed myself in reading about the holocaust. Although I was far too young and naïve to be able to fully comprehend what it must have been like to be Jewish trying to survive in Nazi occupied territory, I became driven by a need to try to understand.

For the first time I became truly aware of all that humankind was capable of - intolerance, prejudice, cruelty and, in the worst instance, total sadistic inhumanity. And the reasons for such base immorality were totally perverse. There was no valid excuse. A person's colour, creed, birth right or imagined threat was all the justification required. The behaviour I had seen in the playground didn't seem to necessarily disappear with the onset of adulthood and supposed wisdom.

And yet as I reread Anne Frank and other stories of courage and survival my feelings of self pity morphed into pride. I realised that for every bad human trait there was a good one.

I seemed to grow up very quickly over the next few months. Suddenly I was fiercely proud of my mother's bravery and ability to survive. I began to look at her with new eyes.

Aware that the subject was painful for her I asked my mother questions from time to time over the following few years, about my real father and the war. I never found out any more details about my father from her, I sensed this was a closed topic and did not want to hurt her by bringing it up too often. The incidents she had described that particular evening in 1967 were alluded to occasionally but never more fully explained. I suppose they were the most traumatic for her. I asked no questions – a mistake that was to haunt me later in life.

But I did find out one new fact. When I read about the anti-Semitic Nurnberg Laws that were passed in 1935 to restrict any Jewish influence in daily German life, for example stopping Jews marrying non-Jews, I asked her about how these laws had affected her. She said anti-Semitism had grown prior to the annexation of the Sudetenland, but that she was a practising Catholic and although she knew that her grandmother was a non-practising Jewess, they all considered themselves Sudeten German first and foremost. They therefore thought themselves excluded from any threat. It wasn't until the annexation in 1938 and the same laws were adopted in her homeland that Jewish heritage suddenly took on a new meaning.

Almost overnight the atmosphere changed. Suddenly she was tainted with an identity that she had never had or believed in. For the first time in her life she was labelled "Mischling" – mixed race – a mongrel - and shunned for something that was not of her own doing. Suddenly she was an outsider whose original birth right and ensuing human rights no longer belonged to her. She could not marry the man to whom she had become engaged. She asked her Catholic priest what she had done to deserve this change in her fate. He could give her no answer other than that God acts in mysterious ways.

A few friends and colleagues turned away from her, others remained constant. Although they could not marry, her fiancé stood by her, but his mother refused to have her in her house. This particular recollection seemed to cause my mother considerable pain. After a suitable pause, I asked her what happened to her fiancé. She said that he was condemned because he would not give her up. He was forcibly sent to the western front and his mother blamed her for his fate.

She never saw him again. Even worse, she never even told me his name, and I never was able to bring myself to ask.

I can see now, with hindsight, that all those times my mother recollected bits of her background she was incapable of describing her feelings. It was a trait that was passed on to me in the way that such subconscious characteristics insidiously pass themselves on from parents to their children. I always drew my own conclusions from her dry descriptions of events.

I realise now that this is a form of self-preservation. Memories that are too painful can only be recounted in feeling-less monotones, if they have to be recounted at all. It is much easier for the human race to try to forget trauma, ignore feeling, and struggle with the humdrum of living until the pain passes and numbness grows over the wound.

In the months that followed the revelations of her survival of the holocaust, and the circumstances of my birth, as I came to understand how my mother must have suffered, I was able to change my attitude to my own identity. So I was illegitimate. It was just another label. My mother had been mentally scarred by more life-changing labels than I had ever experienced. I eventually understood that the bitterness she sometimes showed was because she could never attain the label she felt she deserved.

I also decided that humankind's insistence on labelling people is the world's curse. It classifies, divides and derides, causing untold pain and misery.

I recalled the Bible story of the Tower of Babel, where the forefathers were so puffed up with pride they decided they would build a tower so tall it would reach heaven. God cursed them for their lack of humility and decided to teach them a lesson, by making them unable to communicate with each other. In my budding teenage opinion, you only had to label someone according to the colour of their skin, or their accent, or their looks, or the prejudices passed on by your peers, family, or the media, to see the curse of miscommunication in action. I concluded that the people who translated the Tower of Babel story from the original manuscripts into English should have taken the liberty of renaming it the Tower of Labels.

Sometimes, though, as I continued my isolated adolescence, I simply lay in bed, music blaring, and daydreamed about what my life might have been like, if my mother had not had TB, and she and Karl had managed to emigrate together, and I had been born in the United States.

Sometimes I stood in front of the mirror and examined my almond shaped hazel eyes and held up my hands and pretended to play the violin.

Occasionally I was plagued with doubts about the story my mother had told me. And as soon as these thoughts rose from the sludge of my mind I was swamped with guilt for even letting them surface.

When the song Son of Hickory Holler's Tramp by O.C. Smith was released the following year, I worked out from the lyrics that this was the story of a boy whose mother had turned to prostitution to make ends meet to feed her large family. The thought crossed my mind that my mother might have done something similar - after all how did she bribe her way across the border into Germany?

Once it occurred to me that I had simply been an orphan and that Klemens and my mother had adopted me so they could improve their chances of emigration. I chose to bury that particular thought deep.

I also wondered at the timing of her disclosure.

Maybe she had realised that I had been looking in the attaché case and rationalised that I would find out about being illegitimate by myself. Maybe she thought a love story might be what I wanted to hear. Maybe she wanted me to forgive her for the abnormal life I had with her as a mother.

I was too scared to ever ask.

PART 2

Chapter 18   Surviving Brigitte June 1992

I knew my mother was dying. I had prepared myself for a quick heart attack, some morphine controllable pain, a gentle falling asleep and a never awakening. A dignified end.

My naive optimism had not prepared me for the maelstrom of her last days; manifestations of rage alternating with confusion, dark incoherent memories suddenly clarified by sparks of lucidity, her wasted body shrinking into the whiteness of the hospital bed, her normally vivid blue eyes dulling with fear.

My heart cried out in anguish for the three weeks I watched the mainstay of my life slipping away from me, a ship slowly hauling anchor to drift from my world towards another.

What made it more heart breaking was that I was just really starting to get to know her again.

She had suffered a slight heart attack some seven months earlier in November 1991. I drove the 600 miles from Scotland, where I now lived with my husband and two sons, having been alerted by a phone call from the hospital. The consultant told me that the symptoms caused by her failing heart could be controlled with water pills in the short term, but that she was frail and that I should start making arrangements for her care. This had given me enough warning that there was not much time left.

In January, once she had made a relatively quick recovery, I took the opportunity to move her from her flat in Worthing, to a flat in the same village where I now lived in the west of Scotland. She was not bed-ridden, and still wanted her independence, but the security of being a phone call and five minutes away, as opposed to a twelve hour drive, was a comfort we both needed.

I am thankful that we shared those final months together.

It brought us closer than we had managed to be since I had left Worthing 19 years earlier in 1973. My twice-yearly visits home to her had once been a necessary duty. However, when my first son was due and the challenges of motherhood loomed, I realised the advice I had run away from for most of my adulthood was something I now desperately craved.

Her bi-annual visits to my marital home had always been a little fraught. She had not had a very good opinion of men in general after Klemens, and, during the early years of my marriage, my husband did nothing to encourage her to change her views. I ended up being piggy-in-the-middle, smoothing over the slights that flew backwards and forwards, some deliberate, some accidental, and I often felt guiltily relieved to see her depart after her two or three week stay. As the years passed, however, her toleration of her son-in-law grew to something bordering on respect, and by the time she came to live nearby, they got on reasonably well.

I realised that it was not going to be easy for her to move so late in life. At 76, with a record 26 years of living in the same home, and a solid circle of friends and church colleagues, the prospect of starting over cannot have been easy. Her mobility was not great, but the new flat was within short, and, more importantly, level walking distance of the village shops. It was not as well appointed as the flat she had rented in Worthing, but it was on the ground floor which meant no worrisome stairs to struggle up, and had the added bonus of central heating, a luxury which she had never had before. I felt extremely lucky to have been able to find this rental property so quickly. I hoped she would be able to enjoy the bright and warm living areas during the remainder of the colder Scottish winter which she was going to have to endure.

As winter turned to spring she regained her strength, and I was relieved as she ventured out more often and began to make herself some acquaintances. Naturally sociable, she would stop to talk to her new neighbours working in their gardens. She often popped in to the local craft shop to pass the time of day and talk about her needlework to the shop owner and any unsuspecting customer who ventured in while she was there.

For the first time since their birth, she was able to enjoy having her eleven and six year old grandsons come to visit her after school each day, helping them with their homework and then lavishing them with her home-baked treats. And when my husband worked evening shifts I had the pleasure of savouring her cooking as the four of us ate our evening meal together. We would sit round her gleaming drop-leaf table, and relish the family favourites that she had eventually taught me, although my efforts were never quite as good. I was too impatient to expend the same effort that she put into her preparation. My mother's cooking was always the best I ever tasted.

One warm Friday evening in May, during my final visit of the day to check all was well, she told me that the doctor had visited her that morning. She had a soft spot for him, a neighbour of mine she had met socially while visiting me over the years. I sat down on the bed, ready to have a concluding chat with her now that she was sitting comfortably propped up by her mass of pillows, her bed-jacket to hand should she need it later, and "The Lady" magazine lying open beside her.

"Do you know what he asked me? He asked me if I was prepared to die! Well, I couldn't believe it! I was so shocked at his question."

Not as shocked as me, I thought, my heart suddenly beating as fast as if I had been running a marathon.

I took a deep breath. "Och, mum, you know he's a committed Christian. It's not surprising really that he would try to give you some comfort if you needed it. And anyway, that's good doctoring, isn't it? Not just treating your flesh but also your spirit."

"Hmmm, well, I just told him I hadn't considered it at all. But then I did get to thinking about it and I want you to know that I want to make a will. I bought one of those do-it-yourself ones in the book shop. Oh, by the way, you know that nice lady I told you about? The one I started talking to in the craft shop, well she's invited me for tea next Saturday."

"That's great mum, I'm really glad you're starting to

make friends. You know, you should go to the community centre – there are lots of groups and activities on in there. In fact, I'll take you up there tomorrow and we'll have a look at what's on."

"Don't change the subject, Saskia. I wanted to tell you about the will. I want you to help me fill it in tomorrow. I've saved some money, and I want you to put some aside for the boys' education. There's enough in my bank account to cover funeral expenses. I want to be buried, not cremated. And I've decided I'm going to go to church on Sunday."

"Oh, ok, I'll drive you."

"No, no, I'll walk. You've got enough to do with the boys. I want to go to the church round the corner. The one the doctor goes to. He was telling me all about the wonderful fellowship and I want to see for myself."

"OK, mum. I…I think that's a great idea." I said, unsure how to handle her sudden revelation. Although she had been a regular church-goer in Worthing she had not yet shown any interest in attending the only church of her denomination in a town ten miles down the coast.

"Right, well, off you go now. You'll need to get ready for that party you're going to… John did you say?"

"No Jim. It's Jim's fortieth party."

"Can you quickly make me some tea before you go, and put it in the flask?"

I wandered off into the kitchen, dazed. Nothing had changed in regard to the way we handled life-changing discussions, but then we had a history of my mother springing surprises on me. I decided I would have to think about how to broach the subject again when I helped her with the will. Hard as it would be for me, it was definitely something we needed to talk about.

"What do you want me to do with this bread?" I shouted through to her, looking at a pile of neatly cut bread cubes heaped on the breadboard. I switched on the kettle, and tidied away the few dishes she had washed and left to drain.

"Bread?"

"You know, this bread you've chopped up. What are you

going to make with it?" I asked as I walked back into her bedroom. She looked at me blankly.

"Bread? I didn't chop bread."

"You must have..." I stopped. "Could it have been the home help?"

"Why would she cut bread?"

I was concerned by her increasing forgetfulness, but further questioning stopped as I noticed a slight gurgle emanating from her chest as she was breathing. "Have you taken your water pills yet?"

"Yes."

I picked up her pillbox, compartmentalised into days of the week, and checked whether she had taken her day's allocation. I made her tea, and decided to leave the bread where it was. If it was indeed for breadcrumbs, it would benefit from drying out. I placed the flask on her bedside table, and bent over to give her a kiss goodnight.

"I'll pop up tomorrow, and we'll go shopping."

"Yes, but don't come too early, you know how long it takes those pills to work. I seem to spend my whole morning on the toilet. If I had a pound for every pint I pass, I'd be a rich woman. Good night, Schaefi, enjoy yourself."

The party was in full swing when the phone call came. The duty doctor told me he had been called out by her, her breathing had become laboured, and she needed to go into hospital. I drove like a maniac. By the time I got to her flat, the ambulance was waiting. I ditched the car and sat with her in the ambulance, shaken by the sudden change I saw in her since our conversation a few hours earlier. The matter of fact practicality she normally displayed had totally deserted her. She looked pale and frightened, gagged by an oxygen mask, her white hair loose and tousled. Her imploring eyes made me kneel on the floor of the rocking vehicle, so I could hold her hand and try to calm her. I had never seen her so needy before.

They took her away to a cubicle in the emergency department, and I sat silent and stunned for an hour until I was approached by a nurse who told me she had been moved to a ward, and that I could see her for a while. She was sedated, her mask still in place, but I sat beside her and held her hand, and tried hard to think of the right thing to say. Thoughts whirled in my head, and I became convinced that our earlier conversation had been prompted by a premonition on her part.

During the next two weeks there occurred a change in her personality which traumatised me. She became increasingly confused; berating the nurses, refusing to eat, pulling out her catheter, and even swearing at the doctors. I found it extremely distressing to visit her and try to talk normally to her, for her mind was increasingly wandering, and she often spoke nonsense, saying that there was a man in the locker behind her bed, lying quietly one minute then suddenly catapulting herself upright to sit rigid, arms at her side, blue eyes wide and staring out in front of her at some unseen phantom, mouth moving with silent words, then just as suddenly falling back on to her pillows.

Once she had suffered the final heart attack, her body became weaker and the manifestations of violent confusion decreased. She lay on her back and occasionally rambled in German about fire and bombs and hiding and I think she may have been reliving those traumatic war experiences she had first divulged to me when I was thirteen. She spoke less and less over the following days as her body shut down physically, and I was not sure if she was lucid enough to hear and understand when I told her that I loved her.

I was unashamedly glad when she could finally lie at peace, her expression benign rather than panicked or irate, more like the mother I preferred.

I phoned the minister of the church that she had intended to visit. I asked if he would perform the funeral service, even though she had never been a member of his congregation and he had never met her. He kindly agreed and we fixed a mutual time for him to visit to discuss the arrangements, and for me to provide a synopsis of her life story.

On putting the phone down I was hit with a feeling of complete desolation. I spent another sleepless night, but instead of being haunted with visions of my mother's wrestling match with death, on this particular night I had to mull over what I would tell the minister. Would I repeat the glib whitewash story she occasionally painted to new acquaintances, which glossed over a life of displacement and suffering, or the truth as I knew it? I still had no answer to this question when I got up to face the second day of my life as a motherless being.

I drove up to her flat to look for her bible and flicked through it for any passages having special meaning for her which she might have highlighted. She often read her bible, although it struck me as I leafed through the black covers that I had never really been sure of how strong her faith was. Her religion seemed to be more about fellowship and belonging to something, than strongly professed beliefs. I found a single little piece of paper stuck between the pages, with a notation on it: Romans 8:35, 38-39.

On looking up the verses I read the following:

35 Who shall separate us from the love of Christ? Shall tribulation, or distress, or persecution, or famine, or nakedness, or peril, or sword?

38 For I am persuaded, that neither death, nor life, nor angels, nor principalities, nor powers, nor things present, nor things to come,
39 Nor height, nor depth, nor any other creature, shall be able to separate us from the love of God, which is in Christ Jesus our Lord.

Later I reflected that nights of sleeplessness can affect the brain and perhaps I was deluded, but as I read these words they seemed to me to be a sign straight from my mother. They confirmed for me that she had publicly questioned why she had been allotted a life filled with every one of those trials, had even asked someone for some words of comfort. How else had she got the reference? I hoped that they had given her solace. I decided that her funeral should be a tribute to her courage, resourcefulness and survival, and that I would tell the minister the little that I knew about her past life.

As I opened the curtains on the morning of her funeral, and gazed at the clear azure sky, I thought my heart would break. There would be no one attending who had known her as I knew her, no relatives, no friends from Worthing, as I had no means of contacting them. Once again, it would just be the two of us sharing our own private existence.

The minister's eulogy was wonderful. It seemed to me that his voice was filled with awe as he described what life had meted out to her, and he concluded by saying he wished he had had the opportunity of knowing her. I was able to hold back my tears until her coffin was gently lowered into the grave, knowing that she was gone forever.

My husband's and friends' tender words of support couldn't diminish the raw feeling of isolation that overwhelmed me during that bleak day, or the lonely ones that followed. I went through the normal motions, getting my sons off to school, household chores, preparing meals, but once again I felt remote, an outsider observing the everyday activities I was performing from some great distance, like watching myself act in a play from the back row of the theatre. It was reminiscent of the feelings I had experienced as a child. The details of my fragmented childhood had not been shared with anyone. Since moving to Scotland, I had become an English ex-pat with a strange name and I only cared to enlighten the very few whom I thought might be genuinely interested with the bare bones of that life. Strangely enough, the description I gave was almost a replica of the simple sentences which had summed up my mother's life on the application for emigration I had discovered in the attaché case. Life, love, marriage and children had diluted my teenage angst and the magnitude of my mother's revelations in Pavilion Road all those years ago.

I knew that the weeks ahead would be difficult. Grief would come looking for me when I was not busy with my normal household activities. It crept up on me most when I lay in bed trying to sleep, and surprised me with a gift of sweet memories, which turned to bitter feelings of loss as I was reminded that where there had once been two of us sharing our private bond of history, now there was only one.

My first trial would be clearing the flat that she had just started to get looking as though she belonged to it, and trying to decide which pieces of her past life to keep and which to throw out. Walking from room to room, not knowing where to start, trying to decide which pieces meant the least, which ones I could squeeze into my own home, which ones I could sell or donate to charity, I looked at the furniture that was the sum total of her life; each item with a memory attached, tributes to her survival. I finally sat down on the sofa in the living room to try to let my head clear. But the mahogany glass cabinet filled with her trophies - pieces of china and crockery which she had hunted for in the antique shops of Worthing, made me recall how determined she had been that she would one day find that elusive piece that would be worth a fortune. And she had indeed stumbled across a rare piece: a 1909 edition of Grimm's Fairy Tales with pen and ink drawings by Arthur Rackham. The sunlight, vainly reaching its warming fingers into the room where I sat shivering, sparkled on the glass panes of the oak bookcase (bought with savings from that first factory job while we still lived in Pavilion Road), which proudly exhibited her hard hunted treasure on its middle shelf.

The sandalwood carved chest given to her by Mr Moss, the old man for whom she had been housekeeper and carer, sat despondent in the middle of the room, still bearing the half full teacup and saucer she had abandoned to its care. Inside it still harboured the linen sheets, embroidered tablecloths and her own hand crocheted doilies, once intended as my "Bottom Drawer" or dowry, a tradition that my mother had clung to despite the changing times.

My eyes filled with tears and I got up abruptly and moved into the bedroom. I ran my hand over the burred walnut chest of drawers that had been a legacy from the Brighton Road flat where we finally ended up in Worthing, and where she had felt that at last, she had something to show for all her years of hope, hard work, patience and struggle.

Gathering my thoughts I tried to focus on the challenge ahead, and finally decided that I would try to make a start by sorting through her clothes. In the second drawer down, tucked under the neatly layered pullovers, I found a large envelope. The first items I withdrew were her bank book, and two smaller envelopes with my sons' names on, each containing the promised £1000 cash carefully counted out and bound with elastic bands. I marvelled how my mother had had the means to stockpile all this cash, for she had been living on a meagre German pension topped up with a UK State Pension for the last fifteen years. I speculated how much she would have had to save a week, to accumulate this much, but never finished the calculation as I pulled out a further bulky envelope addressed to me, opened it and discovered £1500 in used notes.

The envelope was still not empty however. Tucked away in a corner I found the key to her brown attaché case.

She had carried it around with her over the years, from one flat to the next and on all visits to Scotland, like a child carrying its security blanket. In reality, the lock was so flimsy the case could easily have been opened with a sturdy knife, but she had carefully hidden the key anyway.

I wiped my brimming eyes, put everything back in the envelope and concentrated on emptying the drawers of her clothes, sorting them into bags for donating to the local charity shop. When I finally located the case down at the bottom of the wardrobe I sat on the bed and looked at it. I was in no hurry to open it. I needed to prepare myself mentally to look through it again. I recalled how I had first raided this same case, and like Pandora's Box, how it led to dreadful discoveries just as I had been on the brink of adolescence; becoming more self-aware and humiliated by my strange family circumstances.

Hanging my head in shame, I remembered how my

consequent snooping and questioning had finally forced my mother into revealing those secrets about her origins and mine, and how the innocence of childhood seemed to have disappeared in one evening. No longer able to control the grief, I drew comfort from the sudden huge sobs of loss and regret that burst out of me like a thunderstorm.

Chapter 19   More Secrets

I finally summoned up the courage to open up my mother's case several months after she had passed away. I had made myself visit the grave for the first time since the funeral so that I could inspect the stone and place a flowerbox of miniature roses on the plinth I had requested for that purpose.

My friends had advised that visiting the grave was a therapeutic experience, but I have to admit that it was rather the opposite. Standing on the unevenly patched grass in front of the marble headstone, and reading the gold lettered inscription, all I could see were words that were incapable of conveying even an iota of what I felt.

The graveyard was on top of a hill and as I lifted my head and took in the magnificent view over the village towards the Clyde Estuary and the violet peaks of Arran in the distance, it occurred to me that she would enjoy the view if she could see it.

Suddenly I had visions of the graveyard coming alive at night with ghostly apparitions sitting along the boundary wall, chatting to each other about this or that, looking over towards Arran, reminiscing to each other about their annual visits to this popular holiday destination. I could hear my mother telling her companions about her visit to the island the summer her first grandchild had been born and how well he and his brother were doing at the primary school that was just visible between the rooftops. Then I thought of the graveyard in winter, the bleak stone wall battered by icy northerly winds, and I shuddered.

It was my only visit until several years later.

I found it easier to talk to my mother in my head. Imaginary conversations with her were much more comforting than visiting a piece of grass. I would ask her what I should make for dinner, or what colour of curtains I should chose for the spare bedroom, or where she would want her furniture to sit in my living room. I talked to her as I weeded the garden, remembering how she had vigilantly tended to her indoor and outdoor potted plants. I talked to her as I washed and ironed, as I did dishes, as I vacuumed. I probably talked more to her in the year after she died than I had during the six months when she had lived nearby.

My dreams were filled with her. They always took place in our former home in Worthing. In one dream her face was covered in blood and she told me, in that matter of fact way that she had, that all her teeth had been pulled out. In another she was sitting crocheting on the old sofa bed in the front room, sun streaming in through the south facing bay window, as she told me dispassionately that I was naïve to think that people were good.

I repeatedly told her she could rest in peace now.

Every night, getting ready for bed, I would look at the attaché case sitting under the bay window in my bedroom, feeling it staring back at me, daring me to liberate its secrets once again. I did not speak to my dead mother about it. As in the past, I was too scared.

Finally, on one exceptionally warm Sunday for September, when my sons had gone down to the beach with their friends, armed with football and soft drinks, I brought the case downstairs into the living room, knelt down on the rug in front of the fireplace, and with shaking hands, unlocked it.

There were more envelopes than I remembered, but they were all neatly stacked. My hand hovered momentarily as I wondered if I should start at one end or the other, but then, once again, I chose at random.

It contained a mix of papers of varying hues of white, cream and yellow. My German was rusty, but a cursory look informed me that these were official letters from the local benefits offices in Nurnberg asking my mother to confirm her work history from 1947 to 1951 in order to establish what benefits were owed to her. There were also some medical papers, from different medical institutions, indicating that she had been unable to work at certain times and the reasons why.

I did not have the patience to study them at length. I put them back in the envelope and pulled out another.

This one contained applications for UK citizenship dated 1982. There was also an application to the US Embassy for a work visa dated 1966, the year my mother had been studying to be a nurse.

There was a bulky envelope containing various hand written letters, mostly still in their envelopes, and there were five addressed to Kings Walden, which intrigued me. Two were written in a middle European language, probably not Czech because there were few accents on the letters, so most likely Polish. The hand writing looked the same on both. The third was typed in English and dated 8th June 1964, signed by someone I had never heard of, who offered himself as an intermediary in attempting reconciliation with Klemens. Suspecting that the other two letters might be from him, I put them aside and decided I would have them translated.

There was a letter from Jeff in Belgium, and the final letter was a double sided typed sheet, with no signature, possibly indicating there was a missing page. It was mailed from Luneberg in Germany, dated 20th July 1964. I read it briefly and reckoned from the contents that it was probably written by the girl whose housekeeper role my mother had taken at The Bury.

I picked another envelope, and noticed that the words Divorce were written on the outside. It contained some correspondence between my mother and her lawyer. The earliest letter was dated 17 July 1968. I had known none of the details of this communication other than being told at some point when we were in Pavilion Road that Klemens was suing for divorce on grounds of Desertion. She was going to fight it, because she had not deserted him - he had changed the locks - and she had witnesses. But I guess the witnesses either had not been willing to testify or possibly were not traceable, for the Decree of Divorce that I picked up next stated that the divorce, on grounds of three years' desertion, could be made absolute within three months of the 1st December 1969 if no defence was forthcoming.

When I unfolded the Decree Nisi Absolut I saw that it was issued on 4th March 1970. I did not remember her telling me that the divorce was finally concluded. Maybe it didn't mean that much to her in the end. Or maybe she was ashamed of it. After all, for her generation, divorce still carried with it a social stigma, as did illegitimacy. My generation had seen those attitudes die out as the Pill and the ensuing sexual liberation begun during the swinging sixties changed British society's prudish attitudes forever.

The next envelope contained a Deed Poll document changing her surname from Pietkiewicz to Langley.

I remembered the discussions we had on the subject of changing our surname, and how we considered at length what new name to adopt. She had decided on Langley because there was a place called King's Langley not far from King's Walden, and her maiden name had been Langer, so to her it was a good English sounding alternative. I had a similar Deed Poll document which I kept with my birth certificate to show proof of identity once I had left home. Mine was dated 1970, so I was astonished to see that hers was dated October 1967, before she was even divorced! I was even more surprised when it occurred to me that she must have already changed her name around the time that she told me about her war time experiences.

Memories flooded back as I recognised the wedding certificate of her parents, and her wedding certificate to Klemens, the same ones I had found when I was thirteen, and the same ones which my mother had shown me herself three years earlier in 1989, during her visit to me that July to take part in my eldest son's eight birthday celebration.

In hindsight I think it may have been the location that inspired the heart to heart we shared that afternoon. There was something about that kitchen that invited conversation. We had not long moved to this house, my third and last during the course of my marriage. It was a four bed roomed semi, built of yellow sandstone a century earlier, a time when the train had finally arrived in the local village, and brought with it merchant middle classes from Glasgow wishing to build family holiday homes by the sea.

It had a solidness and character that our previous bland modern homes had never had, and its spaciousness and high corniced ceilings reminded me of the flat in Brighton Road. My mother was as impressed by our new home as I was. I loved to run my hands down the Scot's pine banister, and look through the glass panel above the solid oak front door at the sea glinting some quarter of a mile away. Whenever I opened the heavy velvet curtains of my bedroom every morning, I never failed to be astonished by the vista that greeted me, and I thanked my lucky stars that life had been so good to me to grant me my two sons, a comfortable marriage, and this house. I felt that my mother was also finally happy at the way my life had turned out.

There was still a lot to be done to the house. My husband and I had already put a new carpet in the second sitting room downstairs, and turned this into her bedroom for the duration of her visit. We planned to make it a cosy den for the winter, when heating the much larger front room would prove difficult.

The kitchen needed the most work. We replaced the old yellow Formica covered kitchen cupboards with modern beech ones, and extended the work surfaces with matching worktops. I had stripped off the old brown wallpaper and finished decorating just before my mother's visit.

Lastly I had also bought an old pine dresser and enormous kitchen table, which reminded me of the one in old Mr Moss's kitchen, and simply beckoned anyone to sit and talk around it, as soon as it was installed in pride of place in the centre of the room.

"Schaefi, I want to show you something."

I was in the kitchen, just finishing the dishes after lunch, when she appeared with the attaché case in her hand. She made me sit at the table and placed it carefully onto my pine dresser displaying the blue and gold hand painted porcelain dinner plates which she had helped me find a few days earlier in an antique shop, pointing out that they would look just right against the bright blue flowered walls.

I looked at that brown faux leather case in trepidation, uncertain whether to tell her I had already made my acquaintance with some of its contents. As my mother carefully picked out various papers she told me about the genealogical research she had been forced to do during the war, in order to prove her bloodline.

The anti-Jewish legislation which was passed by Hitler's government originally in 1935 in Germany, and extended to Sudetenland in 1938, was known as the Nurnberg Laws. They stipulated that the purity of the Aryan nation would be established through the classification of an individual's bloodline using the religious affiliation of their parents and grandparents. In practice it meant that all members of the population had to prove from church records which religion their family members had belonged to. Their aim was to identify and label anyone who had converted from Judaism to Catholicism or Protestantism during the previous half century.

If anyone had four German grandparents, they were classified "of German blood". If a person had three or more Jewish grandparents, they were classified Jewish. If there was either one Jewish parent or two Jewish grandparents, they were called a Mischling (person of mixed race) of the first degree, and anyone with only one Jewish grandparent was labelled Mischling of the second degree.

"Look, Schaefi, this is your great grandmother's death certificate." She gently unfolded a transparently thin piece of paper and I stared in awe at the spidery script in both Czech and German, the words 'Israelit' standing out in stark relief. Cezilie Lamm had died of bronchitis in the hospital of Jagerndorf, in 1932, aged 76.

"And you know what, I had to do research to find out who my mother's father was. My grandmother never married, as you know..." she said offhandedly.

I hadn't known at all. This was yet another revelation, thrown at me out of the blue. As the irony of this newly discovered illegitimacy hit me, I almost blurted out that history has a way of repeating itself.

"There was no birth certificate" she continued, "but I remembered my grandmother talking about a guardian, so I went to the town hall to see if there were any records pertaining to guardianship."   She handed me an official-looking letter with a stamp which looked like a Third Reich Eagle with a swastika beneath it dated 1942. It was in very convoluted German, but stated that her mother Paula's guardian had been one Markus Pollack. Court case records named the father as Adolf Berger, who had been born Jewish but had converted to Catholicism in 1881. They couldn't locate the actual court records, but that didn't matter.

"As far as they were concerned I had a Jewish grandmother and a Jewish grandfather, which made me a Mischling of the first degree. Finally it was official. They even gave me a certificate. But I was safe for a while. The Nazis were unsure of the reaction of the general populace and couldn't make a decision about transporting Mischlings because their disappearance directly affected their German, or should I say Aryan, relations. The "Final Solution" worked fine when Jews were rounded up into ghettos, walled up and removed from visibility, to be transported as and when their schedules dictated, at the crack of dawn when the good Germans were sleeping ignorantly in their beds." Bitterness tinged her voice. "But in the end, it came down to who you knew.   My father was a respected German, with some influence."

"So you were safe while he was alive."

"Yes, it was after he died in 1943 that my former life came to an end." She turned away and went back to the box. When she turned back she had in her hand some white tissue paper, which she unwrapped carefully to reveal a small brooch, no larger than three centimetres or so, shaped like a beech leaf, and made up of numerous tiny garnets, all roughly the same size except for five larger ones, set in silver, with the silver forming the veins of the leaf.

"This is an heirloom from my father's side of the family. Look."   She turned it over and pointed to some engraved initials, Rudolf's mother's and his grandmother's.

The Garnet Brooch

"It's beautiful." I said, running my finger over the black-red knobbly gems.

"It's yours now."

"Was your father's family wealthy?"

"Oh yes, well, at least until the breakup of the Habsburg Empire after the end of the Great War. Suddenly their money was worthless, just pieces of paper that had to be loaded into wheelbarrows to go and buy a loaf of bread."

"So you lost everything?"

"No, things settled down after the first few years of political upheaval. Financially we were not as well off as we had been. But we were a respected family in the area and that counted for a lot. People looked out for each other." She was back at the file, pulling out another envelope. "Ah, here it is, your grandparents' wedding certificate."

I studied it with care. "Mum, Rudolf married Paula at the age of 36, that's rather late in life isn't it? And she was only nineteen, that's, let me think… seventeen years younger than him. That's a bit unusual isn't it?"

"No, it was normal for men to wait until they had a career and could support a wife. It was a love match, pure and simple, but of course my mother had to convert so they could get married. It was normal for women to convert to the religion practised by their husbands."

The Langer Family - Rudolf Langer c 1940, Paula Lamm c1912, Brigitte Langer 1947

We gathered all the documentation together and I drew out our family tree back to the mid-eighteen hundreds onto a sheet of A4 paper. It occurred to me that we might have been re-enacting what some Gestapo official had done whenever she had supplied these same certificates and papers. My blood ran cold at the thought of the lengths thousands of people like my mother had had to go to, people with no interest in or claim to the Jewish faith or race, in order to provide official documented proof of their bloodline, knowing that whatever was discovered would eventually decide their fate.

I wondered how present day Scots, who had likewise emigrated all over the world, would feel if there was suddenly a call by the government of their adopted country ordering them to go to the town hall and present birth certificates and evidence of the religion of their forebears, knowing that their future residency and security was at stake. How would they react when they were forcibly put on trains to be dispatched to an unknown destination and made to work for the government of the day? And before the thought was even fully formed, I berated myself for being so naïve. How could I have forgotten the sadistic way humans regularly treated their own kind - the Highland Clearances, the mass removal of Greeks from

Turkey, the Moslems in the partition of India and Pakistan, the racial laws in South Africa and the USA, ethnic cleansing in Bosnia and Rwanda – all bore witness to man's inhumanity. And time and the repetition of history made no difference – humans never seemed to learn from their mistakes.

"How did it feel when you were suddenly labelled Jewish, or had you been labelled that already?" I asked.

Her face fell. I waited anxiously, aware that I had overstepped the mark by asking such a direct question. Feelings were still not something the two of us normally discussed, even in our more modern society, where openness and discussion of emotional turmoil were increasingly the order of the day on television and in films.

"Ashamed." Her voice was matter of fact. "My mother's heritage brought shame onto the Langer name. Not that my father cared, but my stepmother loved to rub it in. It wasn't too bad before I left home to start working in Hungary, but by the time I returned anti-Semitism had grown along with Sudeten support of Hitler, and I felt like an outcast, an outsider in my own homeland."

"Would you like a cup of tea, mum?" I asked, hoping to take the edge off her pain. But I also realised this was a good opportunity to quiz her about her childhood.

I put on the kettle, and asked nonchalantly "Do you have any memories of Paula at all?"

Chapter 20   Brigitte Langer   1915 - 1939

"No" she sighed sadly. "I don't have any memories of my mother. My only memory is of a scent which I have always associated with her: the faint trace of eau de cologne that clung to my mother's bed-jacket. My grandmother gave it to me, as a comforter I suppose. Perhaps it was grandmother's perfume I smelled, but I always made the association. I dragged that thing around with me until it fell apart. I was only three years old when she was incarcerated in the local mental institution, suffering from Melancholy.

"My grandmother told me many years later that my mother had in fact given birth to a still born baby girl just months before, and the "Melancholy" stemmed from grief. I suppose nowadays it would be called post-natal depression, and we know that people can get over it, but in those days we were ignorant of such things, and once you were locked up in that kind of institution you were lucky to get out. Anyway, we were never to know if she might have improved in time, because she contracted Spanish 'Flu, and died."

I had heard of this particularly virulent strain of influenza that reached pandemic proportions, rampaging across the world in 1918 and 1919, causing an estimated 32 million deaths.

"My father was inconsolable," she continued. "Not only had he lost his wife, but the family fortune was slowly being eaten into as post war inflation ran ever higher. He was working as a customs official at the border crossing with Poland, which lay a mile or so from where my grandmother lived. So I suppose my first real memory was of being bundled up in blankets and sitting beside my father in our pony-and-trap, jolting down the long road from my house to be delivered to the warm kitchen and care of my grandmother. And the best part of the trip was being able to feed the horse a lump of sugar. Vati held me up and I stretched out my hand

and its whiskers tickled my palm as the cube disappeared into the enormous soft lipped mouth. And then Vati would put me down, climb into the trap and drive off".

I poured the tea, and brought it over to the table. She took a sip and continued.

"My grandmother Cezilie ran a small inn in Dobischwald, on the main road between Olomouc and Jagersdorf, in the district of Silesia. I don't think that district exists anymore, but then it was part of the Austrian Empire. Her father, my great grandfather, had been a successful businessman and merchant whose family had moved from the area known as Monrovia within the same Empire, and settled in Dobischwald in the middle of the nineteenth century. After his relatively early death in 1882 Cezilie had invested her inheritance in the inn. She had never married and needed to find a means of making a reasonable living for herself, her widowed mother and eventually her daughter.

"How I loved my grandmother. She sang all the time, folksongs from the region, and gossiped about the guests. I can still picture her preserving cherries and pears grown in the orchard behind the inn, helping her to label the jars and line them in rows on the shelves in the pantry which was the size of this kitchen. How hard we worked preparing food for the winter, pushing great metal hooks through the stiff tendons of enormous smoked hams; filling and winding tubes of handmade sausages, so that they could be hung from the beams in the cellar. My favourite chore was picking herbs from my grandmother's garden. I loved the pungent smell of the bay leaves and marjoram which we used in abundance when preparing the evening meals intended for paying customers."

She took another sip of her tea, and no doubt prompted by her train of thought, asked me what we were going to have for dinner that evening.

I suggested that she might like to make an apple streusel cake, since all her talk of her grandmother's cooking had reminded me of that particular favourite of mine.

"Do you have any yeast?" she asked, knowing that it was

not something I kept normally, not being a keen baker myself. I did not have the patience to wait for the dough to prove.

"Of course, mum, I bought it especially for you coming!"

"Alright then. I'll make some streusel. Or what about that cheesecake you love? Do you have lemons?"

"No, and I don't have curd cheese either, but we could get some tomorrow if you want."

Years later I learned that after the Great War the Habsburg Monarchy broke apart and with it the Austro-Hungarian Empire. As a result of the growing feelings of Nationalism sweeping across post war Europe, the three and a half million native German-speakers who had settled in the areas formerly known as Silesia, Bohemia and Moravia over the previous centuries, wanted their own independence. In 1918, the German "Deputies" who ran these regions refused to adhere to the newly created Czechoslovak State, and proclaimed their intention to create four new states, one of which was called Sudetenland, hoping that they would eventually be integrated into Austria. Czech troops quickly extinguished the insurrection and in 1919 The Treaty of St Germain confirmed once and for all that the areas covered by the four proposed states were destined to become incorporated into the new State of Czechoslovakia.

The insurrection was not forgotten however, and the seeds of aggravation sown between the Czechs and the now self-termed Sudeten Germans took root. Those seeds were fertilised by anger at the mistreatment of one by the other. The Czechs tried to subjugate the German majority. German was no longer to be spoken in public. Czech soldiers patrolled the borders and Czechs policed the streets. High ranking posts in the civil services and factories established centuries previously were systematically taken over by them, or moved to the predominantly Czech populated regions. It was not surprising that, as unemployment and poverty levels rose during the depression, so did a burning desire for self rule. Eventually those seeds bore fruits of discontent and grievance so great, that they were taken to Adolf Hitler by Konrad

Henlein, self styled leader of the Sudeten Germans, and a Nazi sympathiser. Hitler was happy to use the Sudeten grievance as a reason to press for annexation.

My mother did not mention these political matters and how they affected her as she was growing up. The most important place in her world was simply her grandmother's kitchen.

I let her talk while I started getting the ingredients together.

"I spent more and more time with my grandmother because, although I dearly loved my father and understood his loneliness, I could never comprehend his choice of replacement wife and mother. I just couldn't stand Hedwig. The way she would cry "Rudi" in her whiny voice, whenever a battle of wills needed settling. I know I was an obstinate child, but we were fighting for my father's attention I suppose. And of course she was barren, and couldn't give him a son, so that twisted her view of me too."

"Did your stepmother hit you?"

"Oh, yes, all the time - with the carpet beater!" She looked at me and I caught the twinkle in her eye, and we laughed together, remembering how the carpet beater had always been her chosen implement for my chastisement. I only ever got threatened with it, however.

"And if my father ever tried to stand up for me Hedwig would give him such a tongue lashing it was almost as if she was hitting him too. I could see he couldn't stand up to her, and he soon gave up trying. The best times were in the evenings when Vati got out his banjo, and I accompanied him on the piano. And we both harmonised along to Hedwig's beautiful voice. I'll give her that – she did have a beautiful voice. And a different kind of harmony reigned for the hour or so we sang and played together."

"So you avoided confrontation with Hedwig by spending most of your time helping out your grandmother at the inn?" I prompted ten minutes later, as I took a turn at kneading the heavy dough.

"Yes. I was of invaluable help to her, and she taught me

book keeping, which came in useful later. And of course I had a group of friends I hung around with in and out of school. We skied and tobogganed, skated on the lake when it froze in the winter and walked and picnicked in the summer. Yes, and don't look so startled Saskia! I can ski – although I preferred the toboggan."

"I didn't realise there was skiing where you lived."

"Oh yes, we had hard winters, and there was a ski resort nearby. And of course it wasn't the expensive sport you indulge in now, all those fancy ski boots and waterproof jackets at £80 a time."

I remembered when we had taken her with us to Aviemore one January, and she had browsed through the ski shops, overawed by the range of skiwear and tutting at the prices. She did concede the jacket we bought her was extremely warm. She had never let on that she could ski.

She concentrated on placing the dough into a plastic bowl, covering it with a clean dishcloth, and finally set it on the work surface below the window to prove in the warm sunlight. I was peeling and coring apples when she continued.

"Of course my grandmother realised that she would not always be able to give me her protection, so she encouraged me to train as a governess when my schooling was finished. I suppose she knew it would be better for me to find employment away from Hedwig. So I trained for six months and on completion of the course in June 1932, I left home having just turned seventeen to work as aide to a governess in the household of a lawyer in Losanc, about fifty kilometres over the border of present day Poland."

I knew from the death certificate that her grandmother died at the end of that same year, a few months before Hitler came to power in Germany.

"Three years later, I successfully applied for a position as governess with the von Hermann family and joined their very affluent household to look after the two children. After a while, the whole family moved from Budapest in Hungary to Vienna in Austria, and the happiest period of my life began. I spent my days off visiting the city's museums, eating pastries in its opulent cafes, going to concerts, feeling part of its vibrant culture. It was wonderful. If you ever want to see something worthwhile, Schaefi, you should see Vienna. I know I haven't seen Paris like you, but aah... not like that, Saskia, do it like this, see?"

She instructed me in the proper way to prepare the streusel breadcrumbs.

"Did you meet anyone in Vienna, you know, go out with anyone there? I mean, did no one ever chat you up while you were at a concert, or something like that?"

"No, not really..." she said dismissively, although I thought she turned a shade pinker. "I was there too short a time to get know anyone, really. Just a few months later I received word from Hedwig that my father had suffered a stroke, and I gave up my position to return home and help her care for my father. He ended up in a wheel chair, and Hedwig had to nurse him constantly, something she never stopped complaining about.

"Using the bookkeeping skills I had learned helping out at the inn, I started working in an office in Jagersdorf. My income boosted the meagre pension on which the household had survived since my father's retirement, and life became more bearable as I rekindled old friendships. I finally came to understand the changing political scene and the growing influence of the Nazi ideology. Of course I had no idea what the end result would be. But I remember most of the social events I went to - parties and meetings for coffee - were dominated with political discussion, inspired as we were with Hitler's rhetoric and propaganda. My friends were hopeful that his economic policies, promising a brighter future for the Germanic race, would indeed improve living conditions in the area, and I believed it too, was taken in, just as they all were. Hitler was a fascinating man, don't let anyone tell you otherwise. His speeches could whip a crowd to a frenzy. He was the new hope."

"You believed it? " I was dumfounded that she could have been taken in by the rhetoric. "How could that have been, when you were to suffer for being the wrong race?"

"Well, I suppose it was because I thought of myself as a German Catholic, first and foremost. I know Hitler's hatred of the Jews gave Hedwig the opportunity to shame my mother and grandmother's Jewish roots whenever she could, but really it was just another name I was belittled with on a daily basis, and I didn't really listen to anything she said anymore. The only blight was when my fiancé's mother started putting increasing pressure on him to finish with me. Racial intermarriage was forbidden, and she thought any open romantic attachment to a known mixed race Jewess would be sure to bring him trouble in the future. We were so naïve. He insisted we would marry, although we had no idea when or where any future wedding might take place. But I suppose it was my first real experience of being shunned by someone who knew me and my family personally."

That final comment obviously hit a raw nerve, for she suddenly redirected the conversation to the streusel cake, and the preparations for her grandson's birthday party. If I had known what was to come, I might have been brave enough to seize the moment and ask the name of her fiancé.

I had learnt over the years that Hitler's hopes for a better Germany were outlined in his book, Mein Kampf. His vision was to unite the German speaking people by consolidating all former Germanic territory into a newly envisaged Third Reich. Inspired by popular 19th Century race theories, he believed that purifying the Germanic people of lesser races would create a new Aryan master race. This would require the elimination of all so called "Non-Aryans" (Jews and other "undesirables") from the social and economic fabric of Germany.

The Nurnberg Laws passed in Germany in 1935 were intended to begin the purification process. By providing a pseudo scientific means of determining the difference between the two "races" they were used to put a stop to further interracial breeding. The stripping of all rights of citizenship from Jews followed in 1936: Jews were banned from all professional jobs, effectively preventing them from having any influence in education, politics, and industry.

Increasing numbers of laws were passed to remove all means of livelihood for Jews in Germany and Austria after it was annexed to Germany. For example, in January 1938 the "Law Regarding Changes of Family Names and Given Names" was issued to make it more difficult for Jews to escape persecution by changing their names.

Laws were also passed to ensure the general public knew they too had a responsibility to the state in enforcing the policy of Aryanisation. They faced persecution for not upholding the anti-Semitic laws, and, in April 1938 it became a crime for a German to disguise the fact that a business was owned by a Jew. By July 1938 all Jews in Germany were required to carry identification cards. Open anti-Semitism became increasingly acceptable. In October 1938, when Germany annexed the Sudetenland, Konrad Henlein welcomed Hitler with open arms, as did the majority of the Sudeten Germans. Nazi sympathisers, including some Sudeten Germans, took part in the violent demonstrations of "Kristallnacht" (Night of Broken Glass), a phrase that was coined later to describe the night of 9th November 1938, a night of blatant anti-Semitic brutality when 1000 synagogues were set on fire, more than 7000 Jewish businesses and homes were looted, some one hundred Jews were murdered and as many as 30,000 were rounded up and arrested in Germany.

Six months later the Czechoslovakian state ceased to exist as Hitler marched into Prague, encountering no resistance. Konstantin von Neurath was appointed Reich Protector. On June 21, 1939, von Neurath issued a long list of anti-Jewish decrees, essentially identical to those in effect in Germany, designed to destroy the economic viability of the Jewish population and confiscate all Jewish property.

In October 1939, the first Czech Jews were rounded up and deported to concentration Camps in Poland. By October 1942, seventy-five percent of Czechoslovakian Jews had been deported, transported initially to a holding Camp, Theresienstadt, which was situated to the north of Prague, and then on to various other death Camps. Most of them were killed at Auschwitz, in Poland, less than a hundred kilometres from where my mother lived. Jews who were married to Germans and mixed race Mischling Jews were spared the early transports. Afraid of the backlash, the Nazis could not openly attack spouses or children of law abiding Aryan citizens. In Germany the rounding up and transportation of Mischlings only began in early 1944.

It always amazed me how accepting people seemed to be of the mass movement of a designated population, but I was initially unaware of how common a political practice this was during the 19th and early 20th centuries. However, what was not common knowledge at the time was the end result of these deportations. Nazi Propaganda advertised the transports were intended to take the Jews east, to give the Germans "Lebensraum" – room to live. Relatives could correspond and send food parcels to those incarcerated in transitory holding camps like Theresienstadt. Censorship of outgoing letters kept the general population in ignorance of the real circumstances in which its detainees lived. It was only when escapees finally whispered the truth about conditions in the holding, labour and death camps, and their stories slowly filtered through to the community in which my mother lived, that her friends might have been shocked to realise that the ultimate destination of the transports that regularly passed through the area on their way to Poland were not what they had originally thought. It was not until the liberation of the death Camps by the allies that their true nature was finally made public.

Chapter 21   Brigitte's Box of Secrets

During that same visit to celebrate my son's birthday in 1989, my mother also told me she had a claim to fame, on her mother's side. Her grandmother's uncle had been Leo Fall, a famous composer of operas and operettas at the turn of the century in Vienna.

I duly added his name to the family tree I had drawn up under her guidance, and after my mother left that summer, I mentioned the name to an acquaintance of mine, who was somewhat of a music buff.   She did some research and eventually gave me a photocopy of page 216 of the Oxford Dictionary Companion of Music, where it showed that Leo Fall had indeed been a popular Austrian composer of operas and operettas, which were performed in Berlin, Hamburg and Cologne, as well as London.   Most notable of his works was "The Dollar Princess" which had run for 486 performances. My friend also told me that Hitler's identification and repression of all Jewish talent led to once popular tunes penned by Jews being banned from performance, and consequently they were lost to future generations.

As a result of my mother's revelations during that holiday, I felt a sudden surge of pride in my heritage. After I mailed the photocopied excerpt about Leo Fall to my mother, I went to our local jewellery shop and bought a gold pendant of the Star of David, the pentangle that is emblazoned on the Israeli flag, symbol of the Jewish Race, and worn as an identifying badge by Jews from 1941 until the end of World War II.

Of course it was easy to show it off in the 1980's. The Israeli cause was still looked on favourably by the west, when the Holocaust and the Second World War were reasonably fresh in the collective nation's memory. I naively wore it as a symbol of belonging to something. I could not really imagine what it might have felt like to wear that same five pointed star on my coat, to be identified as a member of a specific caste, an outsider, a worthless sub-human being. To have former friends and neighbours turn their backs on you, ignore you, make you step off the pavement in deference, look at you blankly as if you no longer had any place in what were once the streets that had been walked by, had belonged to, you and your family for decades.

Now, three years later, and just a few months after her funeral, sitting in my front room, having finally found the courage to look through my mother's attaché case, I held that photocopied sheet showing Leo Fall's acclaimed works in my hand once more. It had been shoved between two envelopes in the next handful I was looking through. I reached for the gold pendant at my throat and was overcome with a feeling of gladness that I still wore it. My mother had noticed it once, and I had answered her questioning look with a hasty "I don't want people to forget, Mum." She had merely nodded and said nothing more on the subject.

Focusing back onto the present, I noticed one of the envelopes in my hand had *Saskia* written on it in my mother's writing. I opened it tentatively, to find the original copy of my birth certificate.

I say original because it was dated 3rd February 1954, in the name of Saskia Langer, with details of the date of birth, the full address in Furth, and my mother's name, occupation, religion and place of residence. There were no details regarding the father.

I could see quite clearly that it was not the same as the copy of the birth certificate I always showed along with my Deed Poll papers whenever having to supply proof of identity. The one I used was dated 4th May 1960, and simply stated my name as Saskia Pietkiewicz, and that I was born in Furth on 31st January 1954. I had always wondered why it was dated six years after I was born, and had assumed that it was a copy of the original, which had possibly been lost, and reissued prior to our emigration with my mother's married name on it instead of her maiden name. I could only conclude that my later dated certificate had been obtained prior to our emigration, in order to make it look like Klemens had been my father.

I went and found the copy I had and compared them. The one dated 1954, in the name of Langer, was called a Geburtsurkunde, and the later one was called a Geburtschein. Geburt means birth in German, but I duly went and got my German dictionary, to double check the difference in meaning of the two suffixes. I discovered that Urkunde meant document and Schein meant certificate, so I was still none the wiser.

My frustration led me to pick up all the certificates, put them back into their envelopes and place them into the dark innards of the attaché case, and then I banished it back to the bedroom. I had had enough for that day.

A few days later, it was back in favour, released and open, ready to share its contents with me once more. I was determined to get this box sorted out once and for all. I was fed up with being teased by it, like a dog being slapped on the nose every time it was given a biscuit. I figured that I needed to persevere and get to the bottom of the pile of documents. I waited until I was once again alone, settled down in Mr Moss' old red armchair and pulled the case closer.

Having noticed some paperwork at the bottom on previous forays: booklets, loose cards and odds and ends, which I supposed my mother hadn't got round to cataloguing, I thought I would concentrate on these first.

I discovered her notebooks from when she was training to be a nurse in Papworth, with a photograph of her in uniform taking a patient's pulse. There was an inventory of all the furniture she had kept in and moved from storage in Hitchin to the flat in Pavilion Road, Worthing. It made me very sad, to see the meagre number of worldly goods she had managed to acquire by the age of fifty. I was grateful that she had been able to settle down in one place after 1970, and that her careful budgeting had allowed her to acquire the treasures now accommodated in my own home.

I found a little Flemish prayer book which I had been given at the time of my christening in Belgium, a rent book for Lavender Croft, a cheque book for the Bayerische Vereinsbank, with some signed cheques dated 1954 which had never been cashed, and a booklet in German entitled Bestallung des Vormundes, "Appointment of Guardianship". Inside the booklet was an appointment card dated 12th May 1960, addressed to Brigitte Pietkiewicz, asking her to attend the County Court in Nurnberg regarding the matter of her daughter Saskia's guardianship. Highly intrigued, I looked in the booklet and discovered that my mother had become the guardian of Saskia Pietkiewicz on 16th May 1960.

Why would my mother need to make herself my guardian?

It occurred to me that the second birth certificate, the one which only stated my name and gave no details of my parentage was dated 4th May 1960, eight days before the date on the appointment card. Was the second birth certificate issued with only my name so that all semblance of my illegitimacy was removed? Did she make herself my guardian, because this new certificate did not link me to her as my mother? Was the whole purpose of the second certificate in fact a means to cover up my illegitimacy, in order to give the semblance that we were one family all surnamed Pietkiewicz, for emigration purposes? And did my mother take out legal guardianship to ensure that I was legally tied to her, and not to Klemens?

Anger erupted in me like a volcano. This damned box was still hurling out more secrets, secrets I had no means of making sense of now that she was gone. I threw the leaflets I had gathered in my lap across the room in a rage, stormed out of the room and got the vacuum out. I had always found vacuuming very therapeutic. By the time I had vacuumed the four upstairs bedrooms, the landing and stairs I had calmed down. I was even able to laugh at myself. Where had my resolve gone? What was I getting into such a state about? My life was one big unanswered question anyway, this was nothing new. I went back into the front room and started to gather the papers.

Suddenly I noticed that there was a card lying on the floor next to the Flemish prayer book. I discovered, to my amazement, that it was my baptismal certificate. I had been christened on 8th September 1959, in the name of Saskia Langer, my god parents were identified as Frans Meersman and Maria van Steen, the nurse who had looked after me when Yvonne had been sick. There was my mother's name and address in Nurnberg, and, to my absolute astonishment, on the next line, my father's details. Not Klemens; a different name.

It felt as though someone had hit the pause button. I stared at the name while the card seemed to grow in my hands. Slowly I mouthed the two words, and then repeated them out loud. Oldrich Kaluba. They sounded strange and stilted to my ears, but they tasted like honey.

His address was given as "currently residing in the USA".

I knelt down beside the case and hugged it.

It wasn't until I had the two Polish letters addressed to Kings Walden translated that I next went back to the attaché case. I discovered that the letters were indeed from Klemens, as I had suspected, not because they were signed by him, but because of their content. My translator actually had great difficulty in comprehending the letters, for each one consisted of a long string of words that made up one whole sentence. Obviously the author had never learnt the art of letter writing. We had to work together to determine the meaning. I eventually figured out that the first letter, dated May 1964, was basically asking my mother to return to him, stating that he had given me a name and fulfilled his part of the bargain, but that she had broken hers by leaving him to fend for himself.

This letter, badly written as it was, provided proof to me that their union had indeed been a marriage of convenience, just as my mother had stated.

The second letter, dated two months later, indicated that he was desperate for her to return; that he had lost everything; that his condition was now worse than in Germany for he had no one to look after him, that he lived, ate and slept in one room, and that if she had decided not to return to him for the sole reason that I did not want to go back to him, then she would have problems with me in future, being such a spoilt, wilful child.

I smiled when I heard that, for I suddenly recalled that occasion in Kings Walden when my mother had asked me if I wanted to go back to my father, and I had said no. I had not realised my wishes had been given as a reason for not returning to him.

I wondered briefly what might have happened if I had said yes.

What I had discovered in Klemens' letters galvanised me into looking for more revelations. This time I went back to the attaché case with some enthusiasm. I decided to concentrate on the older German documents to which I had only paid scant attention the first time I had looked through them. I resolved that I would sort them by date and try to figure out where my mother had lived and when, and if there was any mention of me in the ones dated 1954. Most of all I hoped I would find something which would give me more information about my father.

My diligence was soon rewarded. I figured out from her correspondence with local government offices in Nurnberg that my mother was making a claim for back payment of sickness benefit for those times when she had been unable to work. There were references from employers, proving when and where she had worked, and letters from various doctors with dates and reasons for inability to work.

I therefore discovered that she had been in the Heilstatte Oberfuhrberg, Waldsanatorium, 28th December 1953 to 17th May 1954, because of Tuberculosis of the lung. It didn't take much to figure out that this did not tie in with her story of not discovering she was pregnant until she was in the Sanatorium. She would have been at least seven or eight months pregnant with me in December. Unless she had been in a different Sanatorium prior to this one, it suddenly left a big question mark regarding the truth of what she had told me.

In a letter dated 24th March 1954 from the Town Hall asking my mother for a copy of my birth certificate, and from another letter dated June 1954 I ascertained that I was in a home called the Martha Maria Heim, Stadenstrasse, Nurnberg, and that my mother was asking for confirmation of whether the costs for my upkeep would be paid for by the state.

Finally I held in my hand documents proving beyond all doubt, that she was indeed my birth mother. Tears of relief started to fall down my cheeks.

In my heart of hearts I had not doubted it since the birth of my younger son, when I was stunned by the resemblance he bore to her. My tears however, were more for the fact that at least some of the fears that had haunted me since her revelations in 1967 had at long last been dispelled.

But Brigitte's box of secrets was not done with me yet. I should have known from its previous pattern of behaviour – the way it alternated between giving succour in one instant and throwing me into a further crisis of identity the next – that worse was still to come.

I continued collating the documents. In a five page transcript of a medical examination dated October 1955, which I gathered had been performed on my mother to ascertain whether she was fit for employment, I discovered the following. In 1944 she had suffered Neuritis in her left hand and left leg, and was left wondering if this explained the incident when she had been unable to get to work and her friend had taken her to sign up with the Gestapo on his bicycle.

From May to December 1948 she had been in a Sanatorium for TB, and again in September 1949 until April 1950. I marvelled how on earth she could ever have thought that she would get into the United States with a medical history like that.

And, finally, in the middle of a page of cold clinical terminology describing my mother's physiological history, I read a few simple words that rocked my already unstable world all over again.

Two normal births, 1945 and 1954. The first child died.

My heart swelled ready to burst, I could feel the blood pumping in my ears. My body shrank into the armchair, becoming as inanimate as the rest of the objects in the room. All I was aware of was my aching heart, my coursing blood, and my thoughts, screaming at me that she had had a baby and she had never told me.

I don't know how long I sat in that catatonic state, but while my body was frozen in inactivity, my mind was hyper active.

Who was the father? Her fiancé? Her school sweetheart - who had stood by his intention to marry her at some point in the future, refused to "renounce" her, and had been forcibly sent to the Western Front? Was it possible that the baby had been his and the reason for her seemingly voluntary repatriation at the end of the war, back to the Sudetenland, was in order to wait for his return?

I knew that on her return to the Sudetenland she had been held in a Camp at Freiwaldau before her illegal crossing back into Germany in 1947, and I had gathered from her comments that she had hated the Russians more than the Nazis. My heart felt as though it was being squeezed in a vice as it dawned on me for the first time that she might have been raped by a Russian.

But the timing was all wrong – if the baby was born in 1945, even at the end of the year, she would have had to have conceived it in the early part of the same year, which would have been when she was on the run, escaping from Auschwitz, witnessing the bombing of Dresden. Had she been raped when she was still in forced labour before she was put on the train to Auschwitz?

Why couldn't she tell me? Was shame - the shame attached to the act of being raped - the reason she could never find the words to tell me that I had once had a sister or a brother?

The document didn't state when or why the baby had died. Had it died as a result of the poor conditions and malnourishment my mother had experienced at the hands of the Russians? Had she to watch it suffer slowly as her milk dried up, its eyes sunken and large, its belly distended, too weak to cry. I could understand her hate now. The Nazis had never done this to her. How long had it lived? Why had she waited two years before she made her escape? Was she too distraught at first, too hopeless to summon up the energy required? I could not help but wonder to what lengths she had gone in order to secure her freedom. How had she paid for the crossing? My mind was in overdrive.

I was inconsolable. I could not sleep for several days with these thoughts see-sawing through my head. Seeds of doubt took root. I questioned the strength of the relationship that I thought we had shared. I could not understand why she had kept that box of secrets for me to find, to provide me with little pieces of an enormous jigsaw puzzle, to be left with so many unanswered questions. It seemed incredibly cruel. Had she wanted to punish me? Had I somehow let her down or done something to cause her not to trust me enough to divulge her secrets, and provide explanations, while she was still alive?

I put the case away. I couldn't bear to look at it anymore. It sat in a corner at the bottom of the wardrobe in the spare bedroom, dark and unseen, denied, gathering dust... just like my mother's secrets now sat in a little wounded corner at the bottom of my heart, dark and unseen, denied, but gathering toxin like an abscess.

Chapter 22   Breakdown June 1994

My back garden was being transformed. I had pulled out
weeds and trimmed bushes, painted the garden shed a rust
brown, and was now scrutinising the strawberry patch, which I
had just finished covering with netting to keep off marauding
birds. I wiped the sweat from my forehead and stretched my
aching back. It was time for the boys to come home from
school, and I was listening out for their chatter. Suddenly I
felt a tightening in my throat, as though an unseen hand was
clenching my jaw and squeezing down into my neck. The
constriction lasted for half a minute or so, and then
disappeared. When the episode was over, I went into the
house and starting thinking about what to make for that
evening's meal.

Obviously I wondered at the strange affliction I had just
suffered, but I wasn't the sort of person who normally
panicked at strange twinges. It was an under-reaction I had
subconsciously cultivated as a direct result of my mother's
overreaction to the slightest indication of ill health. When I
was about eight years old, in Ickleford Road, I had complained
to her of intermittent pains in my knees – she diagnosed
rheumatic fever. In Pavilion Road, I had a heavy cold and
complained of a stitch in my side - she diagnosed pleurisy.
Both times she was irate at the doctor for not taking her
seriously. It was the same for her own ailments, of which she
had many, but most, it seemed to me, were insignificant. She
spent a lot of time lying in bed, keeping warm – her cure-all
for every physical complaint – while berating the general
incompetence of doctors.

Two days later I woke up with a tingling sensation in my
right arm. I put the cause down to having lain awkwardly on it
in my sleep. But when I was preparing breakfast and picked
up the kettle to make a cup of tea I felt less sensation in the
fingers of my right hand than normal. Intrigued, I searched for

a pin in my sewing box and pricked the fingers of my left hand and then the fingers of my right. There was definitely less sensation in those of my right, especially the little finger.

The only medication I took on a reasonably regular basis was Imigran, a drug newly released to the market for the migraine-like headaches I had increasingly suffered for the last decade. These were concentrated around my right eye, often making it water, and made me feel nauseous. Although not true migraines they were acutely debilitating, often lasting more than 24 hours. I had tried Migralieve, the most common migraine combatant on the market, but it knocked me out and did not always clear the headache. I was overjoyed when I was prescribed the new drug as it gave me relief within a half hour. However, on taking the tablet, I often felt a tingling sensation down the right side of my face, neck, right arm and hand, which lasted for twenty minutes or so, and the similarity in sensation made me wonder if I was suffering some kind of side effect from the drug. I made a mental note to call the doctor for an appointment but forgot as the responsibilities of my day took over.

Having suffered a further bout of the strange constriction of the throat a few days later, and the tingling in my right arm refusing to go away, I did go to see the doctor. He arranged for me to go into hospital for some tests. After two weeks I was released without the consultant having reached any satisfactory diagnosis. Although aggrieved that so much time had been wasted inconclusively, I came home feeling a bit of a fraud. My symptoms were negligent in comparison to the sufferings of the other patients I had encountered. But my doctor was not happy at the outcome. He asked me if I would be prepared to pay for a private consultation with a neurologist, specialising in the nervous system, who might be interested in taking me on as a test case if I was indeed suffering an unusual drug induced side effect.

My appointment came through a few days later.

I felt tense as my husband and I took the elevator to the third floor of Ross Hall private hospital, hidden away in a suburb of Glasgow. Rejecting the ministrations of the overburdened National Health Service and paying to "jump the queue" was largely frowned upon by the majority of staunch socialist Scots, which may have been the reason why the location of the only private hospital in the region was so badly signposted.

"You know I hate being late for appointments." I said sullenly, "We should have set off much earlier." I had inherited my mother's obsessive need to arrive in good time; my husband's genes were altogether more laid back. It was a constant gripe of mine, the way he always had to find something to do at the last minute, as I paced the driveway, looking at my watch, itching to set off. We invariably arrived at our destination in time, but that did not stop me fretting for the duration of each rushed journey.

Perhaps my tension helped bring on another of the throat-constriction episodes, but at least the consultant got an opportunity to witness it. After it had passed she tested my reflexes, made me stand on one leg with my eyes closed, sounded my chest, all very similar checks I had undergone in hospital, although she did prick me with a needle on various parts of all my limbs, asking on a scale of ten, how sensitive the pricks were. She asked me various questions about my headaches, when and how often they occurred, what thoughts I had on what might cause their weekly onset, and finally she told me that she wanted me to have an MRI scan and some other tests. I left quite satisfied, knowing that at least the investigation was ongoing.

I was advised by mail that the scan would take place some three weeks later, however I never made it for the appointed day, because my symptoms suddenly grew worse.

My children were in bed, my husband was out for the evening, and I was in bed reading, when I had another throat-constriction occurrence, but this time the tightening developed into involuntary movement of the muscles in the lower half of my face. It was now contorting as though I was in a slow motion "gurning" competition, trying to reproduce the twisted facial mask from the Scream movie. The episode lasted for about five minutes.

Surely, I asked myself, this is not the normal side effect of a drug?

By the time my husband got home, I had calmed down, having rationalised that it would not be long until the tests were due. Perhaps my reaction was an indication of the common sense attitude I generally adopted, but more probably I was simply determined not to let my imagination run riot.

We settled down for the night. I had difficulty getting to sleep, but must have dozed off. I woke around three in the morning to feel the muscles in my face twisting as before, but now my legs and arms were also in on the action. I must have looked like a marionette whose strings were being pulled by puppeteers kneeling on all sides of the bed. Waking my husband, I asked him to call the doctor. As he switched on the light and stared at my writhing body in horror, threads of fear began tightening around my heart.

The first rays of pink dawn streaked the purple sky, as I was strapped to a gurney, taken down the stairs and loaded into an ambulance. My last plea before I left my home was that my husband would not bring my sons to visit me until these symptoms abated. I could not bear to have my boys see me like this, could not face a repeat of the involuntary recoil I had observed in my husband. The doctor suspected lockjaw, and I was being taken to a hospital in Glasgow specialising in infectious diseases. I was quarantined in a room, and observed. The symptoms reoccurred every few hours, but over the following three days, changed in nature. Sometimes only my face contorted, or my throat constricted, at times I rocked slowly from side to side, (bars were put up on the bed to stop me falling out), and in between I was perfectly normal for hours at a time. I could no longer sleep for my mind was in overdrive, aghast that the side effects of a drug could have transformed me into this thrashing being, scared of what my body was going to do next.

The staff concluded I did not have lockjaw, and after three days, on instruction from my consultant, I was moved to the hospital in which she was based. I was sitting in the reception area of the ward, waiting for my bed to be prepared, when I took a kind of seizure – my whole body went rigid for about 30 seconds and I slipped off the chair; I could still see and hear, but I could not move.

The following morning I had the MRI scan. I lay petrified in the humming metal casing. Later that afternoon I had another test. As I was being subjected to the taping of electrodes to my head and lying with my eyes shut looking at multicoloured kaleidoscopic patterns passing in front of my eyelids, I self diagnosed a brain tumour. All my rationalisation and reasoning disappeared like a breath of warm air in a sauna. I instinctively felt that I was going to die. Strangely I felt a rush of relief, for the thought that I would be leaving this unbearable state of living, to see my mother once more, was incredibly appealing. The next instant a tsunami of guilt washed over me. How could I say that I loved my children, if I could not bring myself to worry about their future without me?

I waited for the test results with grim fortitude for three interminable days until I was finally called into the Consultant's office to hear the news. I was dumbstruck when I was told that the results proved beyond doubt that there was nothing physically wrong with me. I was suffering from stress.

If I had not had the utmost respect for this consultant and admiration for the manner with which she had treated me every time I had seen her, I would not have taken the prognosis seriously. It was incredulous that nervous tension could have caused the physical symptoms I had experienced, but the consultant assured me that it did happen on occasion, that she had encountered it before.

She asked me if there was anything in my life that would cause me stress. I told her my mother had died two years previously. She asked about my mother, and I revealed that she had been a holocaust survivor. When she asked some more questions about my childhood, and I had given her a brief synopsis, she commented most astutely that there seemed to be a lot of loose ends in my life. She excused herself and left the office.

I sat in the chair facing her cluttered desk, put my hands on my belly, bent double and rocked backwards and forwards, desolate and afraid, until the tears finally flowed and I heard myself wailing "Oh mum, mum, what am I going to do now?"

I will never forget how lost and alone I felt as I sat there trying to make sense of what my body had done to me. And I still wonder why I instinctively said those particular words. Was I disappointed that I would not be joining her after all?

The Consultant's assistant came into the office and sat down beside me. I suspected that she had been listening at the door, and felt somehow guilty at my outburst. She put her arm around me and suddenly I found myself holding onto her as though she could give me the comfort I so longed for from my mother.

When my sobbing subsided I asked what would happen now. I was told that they would arrange for me to attend bereavement counselling sessions with a psychologist. I was discharged that same day, and the symptoms inexplicably disappeared as quickly as they had started.

The questions on the form were so obviously intended to flush out whether the subject was suffering from depression, it was almost laughable.

I had no problem getting up in the morning, I ate normally, I slept normally, I worked, I cooked, I cleaned. I did not cry, I did not mope around, I had a healthy appetite, I slept like a log,

Admittedly, death had certainly seemed a welcoming option three weeks earlier when I was undergoing an MRI scan, convinced that the strange symptoms I was displaying were caused by a brain tumour. But suicidal I was absolutely not.

I looked at the other attendees dotted about the hospital waiting room. In one corner sat a young bedraggled looking man whose clothing and nails had seen better days; over the other side an even younger looking emaciated girl with greasy hair was struggling to interest her restless runny-nosed two year old daughter in the toys littering the table in the middle of the room.

An attractive, slightly-built dark haired woman of about thirty five appeared at the door and called my name. As we walked quickly along a warren of corridors, I noticed the form I had been asked to complete was attached to the front of her clipboard. She guided me into a small white-walled room, blandly furnished with a scratched pine coffee table on which sat a notepad, pen and a box of paper tissues, a jar of water and a solitary glass. I wondered at that. The table was flanked by three reclining chairs that had seen better days. After asking me to sit down, she introduced herself.

"My name is Jacqui. I'm a clinical psychologist. I'll be taking notes as we talk but you shouldn't concern yourself with my writing; my notes are simply reminders of our topics of discussion, which I will use after our meetings to consider our progress. Everything we talk about will be confidential." She paused and smiled at me. "I think we should meet every fortnight or so, but you're welcome to call me anytime if you want to bring forward an appointment. Here's my card." She suggested we could meet in various clinics that might be a little closer to where I lived than this hospital.

This same hospital where my mother had died.

I nodded in agreement with everything Jacqui said until she stopped for breath, when I finally blurted out the question that had been haunting me since my diagnosis. "Am I mentally ill? Did I have a nervous breakdown?"

It struck me Jacqui must have heard the same questions a myriad times; her answer was just too slick.

"We don't use labels like those nowadays. There are lots of reasons why we have people referred to us. The physical signs you experienced were a means for your body to express its state of anxiety. Talking about your feelings relieves some of that pressure. Have you been able to talk about how much you miss your mum?"

"No, not really. Initially my husband was very supportive. But his father died in 1990, and then his mother the following year. Three deaths in three years. It was a lot to deal with."

Her reaction was noncommittal. She didn't nod assent at my comment. She didn't look sympathetically at me. I felt I had to continue, if only to fill the cavern of silence.

"I didn't want to go on about my mum after the first few months. He wasn't very talkative about his own parents' deaths and I could sense it was all still rather raw for him. I spoke to a couple of my friends about her, but how often can you talk about someone no one knew?"

Another pause. Still no comment from her. I continued. "People are not really good listeners, you know. They feel the need to interrupt with a similar experience. Most of my friends are talkers. I don't mind, I'm more of a listener than a talker." Ironically she took that as her cue.

"You don't have any brothers or sisters or other relatives you can talk to?"

"No, I'm an only child. I don't have any other relatives. There was only ever my mother and me."

"Ok, let's go back to the beginning then. Tell me about yourself."

This was more familiar territory. I sat back and gave her my normal spiel.

"I was born in Germany, and lived in a Refugee Camp in Nurnberg until I was seven. My parents were Refugees from the Second World War. I was fostered in Switzerland and Belgium until I began school. We emigrated to the UK in 1961, as a result of the United Nations' "World Refugee Year", and our family was sponsored by a Teacher's Association whose fundraising helped set up our family in a home in Hitchin, Hertfordshire."

Stopping for a breath, I continued. "My parents separated when I was nine, and my mother moved from job to job until we ended up back in Worthing, the first place we had arrived in when we emigrated, under the auspices of the British Council for Refugees. When I was thirteen my mother told me that my father was not really my father, and that she had made a marriage of convenience in order to get me out of the orphanage where I had spent my first three years..."

I finally realised why there was only one glass. I filled it with water and took a couple of gulps. Then I smiled at her. "You know, I usually never get as far as this before getting interrupted with comments like, "Oh my goodness, what an interesting life you've led!", or "I didn't know they still had Refugee Camps in 1961". I waited for a response, but as usual she was not forthcoming.

Taking another deep breath (or perhaps it was a sigh), I continued with a brief outline of my mother's story or at least the one she had told me that dreadful night a few months before my fourteenth birthday. About half way through, I knew why the hankies were on the table.

"Did you feel different?"

The silliness of her question took me aback. "Yes, of course I felt different. It was not a normal childhood in comparison to that of the people I know. I still feel different."

I stopped, unsure of how far I was willing to go. It was one thing to tell a story that most people found interesting, quite another to take that extra step and begin baring my soul. Yet, I had ended up here because of my body's manifestations, which were obviously some kind of cry for help. I made the decision there and then that I would be totally honest, and hope that I didn't sound too much like a lunatic.

"The rocking that I did as a child, that I still sometimes do, is abnormal. I know that. It's obviously something I do for comfort. Probably something I began doing in the orphanage. I don't know. Do abandoned children often do that?"

Jacqui didn't reply. It was unnerving. I had no option but to try to explain further.

"Sometimes I feel as though I'm standing outside of myself and watching what goes on around me rather dispassionately. I sometimes feel - I don't know how to describe it exactly - removed, I suppose. Removed from the action around me. Like I am there but not part of it at all. Not emotionally part of it. Does that make sense?"

Was that a slight nod? Probably not.

"Well, sometimes I think I don't respond the same way emotionally as other people do. I don't seem to feel as strongly about certain things as others do. For example when someone gets angry because they think life has treated them unfairly, I don't understand. What has fair got to do with life? I seem to be more matter of fact, and practical, and I think it has to do with my life experience. When I worked with autistic children one summer, and studied up a bit on the condition, I wondered if I was slightly autistic. But I know I'm not. I can look back now and I understand that I probably grew emotionally detached because of moving from one "mother" to another in my early years.

"Does that make you angry?"

"Angry?" I was surprised at the question. "No, my unusual childhood was nothing compared to the life my mother led. I was loved - by my foster families, by my mother. How can I be angry?" Suddenly I felt more tears in my eyes. "Not angry. I don't have any words to describe my feelings. I just seem to start crying."

She handed me another tissue, and let me compose myself.

"We've made a good start. Can you please continue talking about your life, not your mother's, in more detail on your next visit? You might want to write it down, in preparation and feel free to think about how you felt at the time. You could write your thoughts and memories down in the form of letters to your mum. It might help to focus your feelings, put them down in concrete form. Let's meet again in a week. But if you need to talk before then, give me a call."

My first hour was up.

In the coming months, as I detailed the minutiae of my life and my relationship with my mother, I was to find the accuracy with which Jacqui knew that the hour allocated to me was over quite disconcerting.

During the following days I gave more consideration as to how and why I felt "different". Unlike my mother whose accent remained obvious throughout her whole life, I was able to speak English with no German accent at all. Physically I did not look any different. To anyone I talked to, I would have seemed a normal, traditionally raised Scottish person, although sometimes an oddly pronounced word meant that the listener had difficulty in placing my Scottish accent. And perhaps I was a little difficult to place into a particular social class.

However, the fact that I had grown up between cultures meant that I had no constancy in the terms of reference that are subconsciously transmitted through interaction with family and relations. My mother's social norms were not the same as the average Joe Bloggs'. I often felt hindered because seemingly normal behaviours and customs had simply not been in my mother's experience for her to hand on to me. I had also totally missed out on absorbing the accepted rules of conduct subconsciously learnt from family and community because I had been moving constantly from one culture and country to another. My mother and I had lived on the periphery of British culture, and were therefore socially reclusive.

For example, when my son was born I learnt from my mother-in- law that I was supposed to visit my husband's extended family and show off the baby. I had not had an extended family myself from which to pick up such customs. As my baby grew and I watched my mother-in-law make him giggle whenever she played "round and round the garden" on his little palm, I realised I was totally unaware of the sayings, finger games and nursery rhymes that British children grow up with. I could only remember one German word game that my mother and I played in the Camp.

I had to buy books and learn British rhymes along with my firstborn. I learnt from an old Janet and John Reading book which I had bought in a jumble sale to read to my son, that after attending a party or getting a present it was normal to write a thank you note. I recall blushing at the thought of how the breaches of etiquette I constantly performed in ignorance must have seemed extremely rude to people who had shown me kindness. I often felt gauche when I realised I had made a social "mistake" – and what made it worse was being unable to explain this social ineptitude because if I did I would divulge just how different I was.

On the other hand, I also realised the life I had led had given me attributes and attitudes which set me apart in a different, more positive, way. I had subconsciously learnt by my mother's example that a single parent could be resilient and could survive all kinds of set backs. These life lessons often stood me in good stead. I had learnt life was tough and my expectations were therefore grounded in reality. I was not materialistic. I was practical. I was empathetic to people's problems and able to offer wise advice. I was also not afraid of change or the spectre of the unknown, a characteristic that keeps many people from moving on.

My only regret was that I had not allowed myself to dream or aspire enough.

Over the next few visits I told Jacqui all that I could remember about my mother, interspersed with stories from our life together. Between visits I sifted through my memories for all the little details my mother had told me. I told Jacqui how distressed I felt that there was so little that I knew, so many opportunities I had missed, because I had learnt about Brigitte's life too young to ask for the finer details and then later was too wrapped up in myself as a teenager. Once I had moved away to Scotland, I became even more distracted by my husband and children.

Jacqui tried to reassure me this was not unusual. Children could not really become interested in their parents as adults until they had become adults themselves, complete with some life skills of their own against which to gauge other people's lives and experiences.

I continued to recall the life we had led in Germany and in England, before and after we had left Klemens, and I tried to skew my memories and look at my mother through the eyes of an adult. As I described my life to Jacqui I finally managed to put things into perspective. I had always looked at these memories as instances of what was happening to me, living as I did in my child's world. Reflecting for the first time through grown up eyes on what my mother had been trying to achieve, I finally tried to interpret how her mind might have worked.

Alone and unsupported by the normal network of family and friends that most of us take for granted, she had started her working career doing what every woman was trained to do in the decades prior to the sixties. Her house making skills gave her career a kick start at The Bury. Her caring skills were brought into play working for Mr Moss, and she started to build on these skills by working as a care assistant in the NHS. She must have seen that the only way to forge ahead and make a decent living would be to train as a nurse.

She had struggled to learn English and while training at Papworth she was struggling to learn a new medical language. I had found her notebook, and in it a spelling sheet – where she had tested herself over and over writing out complicated terminology.

In order to attain her career goals she had to sacrifice living with her daughter and saw her only once a week. Luckily she still could rely on the foster families in Belgium to help with childcare during the long summer school holidays.

Her plan was good but it was not foolproof. Unfortunately, her health failed her. I never did find out what was diagnosed - another one of those questions I failed to ask her - but she was unable to continue her training. I can only imagine how frustrated, angry and impotent she must have felt.

In November, 1966 when we moved back to Worthing, she was able to convalesce with the assistance of the British Council for Aid to Refugees. I do not know what my mother would have done without the constant lifeline the BCAR gave her, and I will always be grateful that their charitable support was there for us.

Chapter 23   Betrayal, Guilt and Anger

When I told Jacqui in detail about the night my mother revealed her escape from the train to Auschwitz, her marriage of convenience, and her description of my real father, I cried. The emotion of this particular telling was strangely at odds with all the other times I had told people that my mother had been a holocaust survivor. My normal down-to-earth manner deserted me. On this occasion the tears streamed down my cheeks from the moment I began recounting opening the door to our sitting room that fateful evening.

I had enough knowledge about the art of counselling to know that the counsellor's or, in this case psychologist's, expertise is the ability to listen and reflect the interviewee's feelings back to them. It feels less of a challenge than being asked a direct question, it is non judgemental, and it removes the possibility of leading the discussion anywhere other than where the interviewee wishes to go. Of course, not every interviewee is willing to explore their inner feelings and motivations. I, however, was desperate to find out what my body had been trying to tell me.

At the beginning of our meetings I often felt aware of Jacqui's prompts to get me to talk.

Her prompt when I had finished telling my mother's war experience was "You find it very distressing to talk about this."

When I had recovered myself I explained that I was obviously upset that she had had such a difficult life, a near death experience, and yet the most intense feeling was anger at myself because I had not asked more questions at the time. I did not even know the name of my mother's fiancé.

"I know that normally when people talk they jump from one scene in their head to another and the order of events is often overlooked, but when I look back and try to put her recollections into some logical chronological order, there are all kinds of holes in the story that I just ache to fill with details".

"Why is it important for you to put the incidents she described in order?" she asked.

I was surprised by the question.

"I suppose I am logical, I like things to be in order, for them to make sense. When I read through the documents she left behind there were so many gaps. If I had asked simple questions like where was she incarcerated before they put her on the train – what happened after the night she witnessed the bombing of Dresden, when, where and how was she recaptured? Where was she taken to then? Which labour camp did the husband of the woman from upstairs run? Where and when? It would all have made more sense. I would not have had so many doubts about what she had told me."

"Did you think she had made it up?"

I hung my head in shame. "Yes, there were times I thought she made it up to get me to feel sorry for her. I still haven't figured out why she told me when she did."

"Couldn't it have been just a momentary lapse? Perhaps it was brought on by the mixed feelings she would have felt after speaking to the woman from upstairs?"

"I suppose I hadn't looked at it like that. You think it was purely impetuous? But no, that wouldn't have led her to tell me that I was illegitimate. She came back into my room and told me that. She could have kept that a secret. It had nothing to do with the war."

"Perhaps she got herself into the state of mind where, once she was finally recounting what she had kept silent about for so long, she had to tell everything. Or perhaps she felt you were simply old enough to know about your birthright. To be finally able to get it off her chest must have been a great release for her."

I let this new concept sink in. I had learnt from my own experience about the effect that holding in painful memories can have on your body. I would not have wished that on her. I understood the relief that can be felt when a problem is told to another person, that unburdening feeling like a weighty rucksack being lifted from your shoulders. I could comprehend how she would have relished that feeling of release.

And the next thought that struck me as suddenly as a thunderbolt, as I sat there and mulled over what Jacqui had pointed out to me, was that my mother had *trusted* me enough to tell me. Who else would she have told her secret to without fear of being judged, than her own daughter?

And with that insight there followed the horrible realisation that I had in fact judged her; completely and utterly belied her trust in me. I started to cry.

"I betrayed her, you know."

I looked everywhere but at Jacqui as the words finally slipped out. Some of the guilt I had imprisoned in that particular compartment of my heart for so long was about to be liberated. Mentally I hefted my backpack of guilt so that it started to slide down my arms.

Jacqui waited silently.

"I let her down." I said slowly. "I betrayed her worse than that time with Frau Muller, at school in Germany. I could have lied and I didn't." I stopped as the tears fell in big splotches onto my hands. Jacqui pulled another tissue out of the box on the table and handed it to me.

"It happened the following summer." I finally managed to control myself enough to continue. "I was woken up by voices. It was too early for school, my alarm had not yet gone off. I wanted the noise to go away, but the persistent tones of anger stopped me from falling back asleep. Suddenly I heard my mother yelling my name, and there was such a note of alarm in it, that I sat up with a jolt. I ran to the window because the voices had come from outside. She called my name again, insistent, needy, scared. I opened the window, jumped out and ran along the path to the paved area behind our kitchen. To one side there was a lean-to from which I could hear scuffling and as I peered in I could see my mother, a broom stick in her hands like a ninja fighter, backing away from Franz, the lunatic man who lived on the first floor. "Run, get the police!" she shouted to me. I didn't stop to think, simply jumped on my bike which was leaning against the garden wall, and pedalled as though the devil was trying to catch me. I didn't even think to be embarrassed that I was in my nightie; I was far too scared for my mother. The Police station was a good mile away from the house and by the time I got there my lungs felt as though they were on fire. There was a policeman sitting behind the counter, but I couldn't get the words out to tell him my mother was in danger, I was panting so much, and my inability to communicate was compounded when I burst into tears. Finally I managed to blurt out my address and said my mother was being attacked.

He said he would get someone out there right away, left the room and a little while later appeared with some tea and a blanket. After an interminable length of time, while I was left wondering what had happened back home, I was taken to Pavilion Road in the back of a police van, along with my bike. I quickly got dressed, and then joined my mother and two policemen in the front room.

My pale faced mother was sitting on the sofa, next to one of the policemen who was reading her statement back to her. The other man sat watchfully in Grandfather Moss's chair.

'I was emptying the rubbish into the bin at the backdoor at 6.30 or thereabouts when I heard a strange snuffling noise coming from the garden.

'I walked round the back and traced it to the old rolled up carpet that lay in the lean to, and thought that there was some kind of animal inside the carpet. So I got my broom from the kitchen and poked the pole into the carpet to scare off whatever animal might be in there. I got a shock to discover that it was Franz from upstairs who had rolled himself up in the carpet and the noise had been him snoring. I have no idea why he was there.

'He started shouting at me, saying I was a nosy old cow and that there was only one thing women were good for. Then he hit me and started pulling me into the lean to, and that was when I started fending him off with the broom. I shouted for my daughter Saskia, and when she appeared I told her to go and fetch the police, and he ran off.'

When he finished he asked her if that was correct and she nodded. She signed the document, and then the policeman asked if I had seen the man my mother had described. I replied yes. But when the policeman asked me to look at my mother's face and confirm that her face was swollen where he had allegedly hit her, I could not honestly tell whether it was swollen or not. I stood in front of her, and her eyes locked with mine. I knew she was willing me to say yes. I slowly said I didn't think it looked swollen because I could not bring myself to wilfully lie. I saw the blue of her eyes darken in disappointment before she looked away from me. She must have felt that I had made her appear to be a liar."

Jacqui cut in "You're being too hard on yourself. You weren't a witness to what happened."

"No, but I let her down. I know I did. I knew I should have lied. I made the decision not to, simply to spite her. To pay her back."

"To pay her back for what?"

"To pay her back for doing what she did to put me in this world and giving me such a shitty life!" I exclaimed with an anger that had surfaced and burst out as suddenly as a geyser. I put my hand to my mouth as soon as the words had spouted forth, and started to cry great sobs of release and guilt.

At our next meeting Jacqui said that she felt my show of anger had been a milestone for me.

"Being angry is nothing to be ashamed of. It's perfectly normal that you should be capable of feeling anger and love. One doesn't preclude the other. You can be angry with someone and that doesn't mean that you love them any less. But it seems to me you have a problem with people being angry, am I right?"

"Yes, I know I needed to be good to keep in with all the people who looked after me. I didn't want them to reject me. I needed approval, that measure of love. I know that now, though I didn't then. But really I never experienced much anger from anyone other than her. I couldn't cope when she got angry. The smallest frustration would set her off. Like one day when she couldn't open a tin of sardines. Suddenly she wrestled the can opener off the rim of the tin, and then she was hitting the tin against the table, screaming that her life had been nothing but struggle and shit, and that she always got kicked back down as soon as she got ahead, and that people were bitches, and what had she done to deserve this."

"How did it make you feel when she lost her temper like that?"

I had to search for the right word. "Helpless. I cowered in the corner until she had got it out of her system and the tirade of foul mouthing everyone, but mostly my stepfather, stopped. Then she picked up the can and got a cloth and cleaned the bits of sardine off the walls and the table and the plates. She picked out the remainder of the fish through the hole she had managed to make, and five minutes later we were sitting eating. And you would never have known that Vesuvius had just blown."

"Did you feel that she blamed you for her hard life?"

I had to consider that one carefully. "I suppose I might. Did I? I don't know. No, I didn't – she was so proud of me. I was the apple of her eye. I was what gave her a reason for going on. She wanted so much for me. In her eyes I could have been anything. She thought I could have been a great violinist. She thought I could have been a great actress. She thought I was so gifted and I knew that wasn't true. It was a burden actually, because I knew that I would always end up disappointing her."

"It's quite a common feeling for teenagers to be overawed by their parents' hopes for them. Did it make you feel guilty when you thought you could not live up to her expectations?"

"Yes." The words got caught in my throat and I had to clear it. "Sometimes I hated her when she went on about how wonderful I was."

"A very normal feeling for a teenager, Saskia. But let's take things back to your mother's anger. I want you to think about how you coped with these displays of anger for the next time we meet."

I was often given a task to consider over the weeks between meetings. It helped me to focus on one particular aspect of our relationship, and of course brought back all kinds of memories, and raised all kinds of questions. I wondered whether I had been frightened of my mother. Had I evaded asking questions because I was scared that she would throw a tantrum? Or had the insecure existence that I had led up to that point in my thirteen year old life, taught me that I should not rock the boat because I had no control over what happened anyway? It seemed to me I had grown up accepting and unchallenging of the world around me. As an adult I had often been accused of being too easy-going and accepting of the status quo, of not standing up to bullies.

I mentioned this to Jacqui at our next meeting.

"Some people may choose not to challenge because they feel more in control accepting change than trying to change things."

"Is that what happens?" I asked. "I know I rarely get angry. I know I don't like getting angry. It always seems such a waste of energy because nothing really changes as a result of that loss of control. Is that because I saw my mother railing against the unfairness in her life, and to no avail? Did I learn from her frightening violent bursts of anger, that it was a futile emotion?"

Jacqui chose not to answer. I suppose I had already worked it out for myself. Instead she asked me another question. "Thinking back to the incident you described, when your mother threw the can of sardines, do you think she felt better after her outburst?"

I could see where she was going with this. "Are you saying it helped her to vent her anger?"

Her answer seemed too diplomatic. "It can be for some people. Letting out your frustrations some way can give feelings of release and allow acceptance. I'm not saying that everyone should throw cans of sardines. Anger is a healthy emotion. Just like laughter shows that you feel good or happy, anger is a way of showing that you feel bad or frustrated. And it is emotionally healthy to feel both."

It seemed to me she stressed the "emotionally healthy" part very slightly.

"But some people can't handle their anger – they get violent, surely that's not healthy?" I asked, astonished. "Look at the physical abuse that occurred when my mother got angry with my stepfather! And now I'm not even sure whether he was the instigator, or she was!"

"Obviously violent anger can hurt people. People with too much anger have to learn to control the emotion. Anger Management teaches people to let out their frustrations in a positive way. But I don't want to get sidetracked here. I'm not saying that your mother had anger problems. I am simply saying that your mother felt angry at times and quite healthily let that anger out. I don't think it was her intention to scare you. The anger was not aimed at you was it?"

"No, she was not angry at me. She was angry at life." I paused as I thought about what I had just said. "And I suppose she had every right to be."

"Yes, she did. Unfortunately she didn't know that her angry outbursts frightened you. So don't be so hard on yourself now because you were too scared to ask the right questions, or because you reacted like a normal teenager who was put on the spot and felt angry because of it. You didn't do anything wrong by telling the truth or by being angry. I am sure your mother forgave you for it. It's time for you to forgive yourself a little."

Chapter 24   On Deviousness and Lying

On 20th July 1969 I watched man's first step on the moon taken by Astronaut Neil Armstrong on a television set that was located in the lounge of a small old people's nursing home in Worthing, where my mother was working day and evening shifts as a nursing auxiliary. I was aware that it was a momentous occasion for humankind, just as I was increasingly aware of the momentous struggle my mother was facing in earning a living for the two of us.

She had lost her job in the plastics factory, once again due to illness, the nature of which I was not made party to. We had also moved out of Pavilion Road to one large single room in a boarding house renting rooms to British people, who kept themselves to themselves. This move away from BCAR owned housing suited me after our encounters with the neighbours in Pavilion Road.

The house was not far from the breezy seafront and at the west end of the busy town centre. In the winter the wind whistled up and down the streets and caught my umbrella as I tried unsuccessfully to steer it in the right direction and stop it from turning inside-out as I walked the mile and half long route to school. In the summer the smell of dried seaweed wafted into our windows from the busy promenade at the end of our street, where the old people who came in droves to Worthing to retire would walk, sit, and breathe in the pungent sea air.

Our room was on the first floor, with a shared bathroom half way up the landing. It was a large bright room, with a high ceiling and two windows facing south east. There was a cupboard topped with a sink unit under the other window, and beside it another cupboard, on which stood a small grill/oven topped by two hot plates. Cooking drove my mother to distraction because there was no work surface to speak of, and she cursed the hotplates, they took so long to heat up. There was a tiny table and two chairs nestling in the bay window and to the right of the door was the sofa bed from Pavilion Road. When the back of the sofa was up you didn't notice the single bed behind it in which I slept, and beyond that there were crammed the two wardrobes from my former bedroom. They loomed on either side of the chimney breast which housed a gas fire. My only concern was that our cat Tootsie be allowed to move in with us, and it was my job to carry her down the stairs to the front door whenever she needed to go out.

I started working on a Saturday in the local Woolworths, in the hardware department, petrified at first that I would not be able to add up without pen and paper on which to do my calculations. Multiples of twelve are so much more difficult than counting in tens. The tills in those days did not add up the prices of goods, nor calculate how much change to give. But I enjoyed selling yards of curtain tape, which had to be measured off a roll and cut to the required length, curtain rods, nails, hooks, screwdrivers, cup hooks, bradawls, hand held drills with bits, tin openers and other assorted hardware, whose purpose I managed to gradually work out from the packaging and talking to the customers. It was useful to know how to change a fuse or plug for my mother, or be able to advise customers on how many curtain hooks were best to create a natural looking drape when hanging curtains.

Although we had moved home once again, I had been in Worthing High School for Girls for two years now, and had finally acquired that sense of belonging that I had yearned for. I had a small group of friends, and no enemies. My school reports were improving, and I even won a school prize, much to my mother's delight.

My confidence grew further when I auditioned for a part in the school's Senior Dramatic Society's production of Much Ado about Nothing by William Shakespeare. I played Don Pedro, Duke of Aragon, a fairly large role, though not a lead one. The play was performed in front of two full houses in the school hall in March, and my name was mentioned in the local paper. Our English teacher, Mrs Brooks, who was the co-producer, wrote me a lovely thank you note after the show, praising my acting ability. I certainly enjoyed acting, and was not at all nervous about standing up in front of people and being looked at. I think it was because I felt that the audience were looking at the character I was playing, not me specifically.

I am sure everyone else with larger roles got a similar note, but for my mother it was an indication that I was destined to have a career on the stage.

I had already mentioned to Jacqui how I found my mother's hopes for me difficult to deal with. On one of our meetings we discussed it further. I told her how, if I was praised in any way for something I did at school or by someone we knew, my mother considered whether that praise indicated a gift that should be encouraged in order to make me famous. In fact, the merest hint of any ability was taken up as a personal crusade by my mother. It was often embarrassing for me. She insisted on telling all and sundry that I could have been a ballerina if I hadn't been so large boned, or that I could have been a great violinist, but she couldn't afford to keep up the lessons.

Like all girls of my era, I had dreams of becoming a renowned ballerina, and later a movie star, just like the boys I had known had dreams of being a legendary footballer like George Best; but I was never so star-struck that I ached to fulfil those dreams.

As I continued to do well in school her ambitions suddenly turned towards enabling my educational future. She even started paying for me to take Latin lessons so that I did not miss out on future academic opportunities. After all, you needed Latin to get into Oxford or Cambridge, or to become a doctor.

So it transpired that twice a week, on my way back from school, I stopped off for an hour at a retired Latin teacher's house, and sat at his living room table, going over an old Latin text book that looked very like the French school book I had in my school bag. Each chapter started with a passage requiring translation, and was followed by some verbs to learn off by heart, some exercises covering that particular chapter's grammatical lesson, and ended with a list of vocabulary, also to learn off by heart. The content of the passages differed very little - the French Resistance preparing for skirmishes were replaced by stories of Roman Legates preparing for battle.

I did not enjoy Latin lessons. I was not able to grasp the rules of grammar at all. Because I was a native speaker and could converse without trouble I did well in German, but I could not conjugate a verb or write an essay without amassing an array of grammatical mistakes. I had the same problems with French.

Besides, I did not care for the Latin teacher. He had false teeth which he continually loosened and moved around his mouth, making strange sucking noises and looking rather like a cow chewing the cud. Occasionally, as I worked at the exercises on the living room table, he would disappear into his kitchen and come back, jowls moving, smacking lips, teeth, and tongue, having drunk a couple of swigs of the yellow liquid in the tumbler that he was now carrying. I did not want to continue with the lessons, but I knew I could not simply tell my mother that I hated Latin.

I admitted to Jacqui that, with hindsight, I could see that I was scared of my mother's reaction if I stood up to any of her decisions. The result was that I became devious in the way I handled her. Knowing that she held men who drank in poor regard, for it reminded her of Klemens, I told her that the Latin teacher smelled of alcohol. After she went to see him to get a report on my progress and sniffed the fumes off his breath for herself, the lessons were stopped.

My deviousness had reverberations. In the course of one of my mother's fits of rage when she yet again poured out her diatribe at life in general, I discovered that she had taken this failure to secure Latin as one of my school subjects as a personal set back. Once again, her attempts to improve our situation by safeguarding my future were confounded.

The result was that I became less devious, and more overtly a liar.

For example, that summer of '69, I became friendly with a girl called Karen who worked at the next counter to mine in Woolworths. She was very pretty, with a short blond twiggy style haircut, big blue eyes and long eyelashes which she caked with mascara to make them even more alluring. She was sixteen, and much more worldly wise. Boys used to come up to her counter and chat to her and she would giggle and flutter her clumpy eyelashes. She told me that she and her friend had been invited to a party and did I want to go? I didn't think my mother would let me, so I was surprised when she raised no objection, other than that I would have to leave at 10.30pm. She didn't want me to walk home in the dark, even though the party was only a couple of blocks from where we lived.

I'm not sure what my mother expected this party to be like, but she put some cash towards the money I had saved from my job and helped me buy a red trouser suit especially for the occasion. Did she think it was a coming out occasion for me?

Saskia (15) with Brigitte in Worthing 1969 - check out that trouser suit

I look at that suit now and it looks horrendous, but then it was the latest fashion – a red tunic top with a navy stripe down the sides, which matched the stripe in the slightly flared trousers.

I also bought my first pair of high heels to complete the outfit. I had toyed with the idea of buying a pair of Levi Jeans, but they were more expensive than the trouser suit and shoes put together.

My mother insisted on walking me to the flat where the party was. Strangely I was not mortified at this, although I was concerned about the way my trousers flapped around my ankles. I suppose I understood she would want to know where I was going. It did not occur to me that my mother might be checking out the people that were going in and out. If she was she would have been disappointed for the party was already in full swing and the entrance to the place was deserted.

One of Karen's friends was turning sixteen, and her parents had allowed her the run of their flat for the party. Karen had told me her friend was intending to have sex with her boyfriend that night to mark her coming of age. As I looked at the small front room crammed with adolescents, I wondered which room they were going to have sex in. The curtains had been drawn to shut out the daylight and give the place some atmosphere but the music was not that loud. I realised I was by far the most conservatively dressed, most of the girls being in Levi jeans and smocks, and I felt instantly out of place. I felt as though everyone was staring at me as I went over to say hello to Karen, who was in the far corner, sitting on a boy's lap. He was rather good looking but I flinched at the mocking look in his eyes. Karen told me to go into the kitchen and get a drink. As I poured some coke into a greasy looking glass, I considered leaving. The door opened and a tall, slim, swarthy looking boy, with long wavy dark hair that curled at the ends where they swept over the collar of his blue shirt, asked me to dance. I suspected I heard a foreign accent.

Flattered that he had followed me into the kitchen just to ask me to dance, I agreed. Besides, I loved dancing; I had developed my own moves and the girls at school had even asked me to teach them so I knew I was good. It was one thing to have people look at your outlandish outfit, it was quite another to know that they were admiring the way you moved to music. Sly and the Family Stone's "Dance to the Music" was playing, and we followed their instructions.

Pierre was French. I told him I was Saskia, and I was Czech. The next record was Marvin Gaye's "I Heard it Through the Grapevine". I was in my element, but I must either have extremely embarrassed Pierre, whose dancing merely consisted of stepping from one foot onto the other, or totally impressed him with my sinuous movements. Whatever the reason, he was suddenly filled with the urge to stop me mid-step, grab a hold of my shoulders, and press his lips to mine, forcing my lips open with his tongue and plunging it into my mouth. As first kisses go, it wasn't an unpleasant sensation.

We spent the next two hours snogging on the sofa, coming up for air only once when he got us both a glass of coke, and a couple of other times when I asked him what time it was. There was no other conversation. At 10.30 I told him that I had to go. I wiped my face with the back of my hand, sorted my tunic, which had managed to twist itself to one side, and without a backward glance, left the room and walked down the stairs and out on to the street, where I found my mother waiting.

She eyed me suspiciously and asked if I had enjoyed the party. I wasn't sure if my lower face was red from the two hour snogging session, but I replied nonchalantly that the music was quite good, but that other than that, it hadn't been up to much.

As I lay in my bed that night, my mother snoring gently on the sofa bed at my side, I pressed the back of my hand against my lips and pretended it was Pierre. Licking the back of my hand proved a poor alternative. I also wondered briefly if Karen's friend had lost her virginity.

Chapter 25   Lying A Little Is Better Than Lying Too Much

At some point during 1969 my mother left the nursing home to wash dishes in a little café near Worthing Pier. The only perk of that particular job was that the owner would bring me a mashed banana and marmalade toastie, as I waited for my mother to finish up at 5.30pm. After a few months she started working at a dry cleaning shop. She complained about the ether fumes, claiming they gave her headaches. During that summer my mother also earned a little extra by helping to clean some of the holiday flats owned and rented out on a weekly basis by our landlady. Mrs Schiffenstein thought that my mother would be happier if we moved into the first floor flat of one of her other houses - a terraced house in Milton Street, with a single mum, Sharon, and her two young children living on the ground floor.

My mother was initially pleased with the flat. She was able to reclaim the rest of our furniture out of storage, and turned the bare front room into a homely looking sitting room. There was a kitchen with a small table and chairs, a bathroom, and at the back of the house, at the mid landing, there was a small bedroom, which contained the hot water tank and consequently stayed quite warm. My mother slept on the sofa bed in the living room.

The only drawback was that there was no dividing wall or door to separate the two flats. Sharon's bedroom was the downstairs front room. The second room belonged to the children and could be accessed from her sitting room, which lay directly under my bedroom at the back of the house. Consequently the only use Sharon made of the downstairs corridor was to reach her bedroom, or to access the front door if she was not using the other exit from her flat – the back door of her kitchen.

This arrangement was not a problem for us until spring

1970 when Sharon acquired a boyfriend. He often strutted back and forth between rooms dressed in only a towel, which riled my mother terribly.

She complained to Mrs Schiffenstein, and as a result I was moved out of the back bedroom and into the attic room on the second floor, which had been locked until now, and used as a storage facility. Ever a business woman, Mrs Schiffenstein duly increased the rent to include the extra room, which further annoyed my mother.

Once again circumstances beyond my mother's control had disturbed her peace of mind. Furthermore, she started working shifts in a home for the blind situated on the seafront, a five minute walk away from the flat. Every few weeks she had to work night shift and she slept fitfully as the weather got warmer, and the windows had to be kept shut to keep the noise level down.

However, I liked my stuffy little attic room. It gave me the freedom to listen to my music without disturbing my mother too much, which had always been a necessary consideration when we had shared the single room the previous year.

I often lay on my bed and rocked to the music, when I should really have been studying. In fact, apart from an afternoon's cramming for each of the nine 'O' Level subjects I was taking, I studied very little prior to the examinations I sat that June. I was therefore extremely surprised to be woken one morning in August by my mother, opened results-envelope in hand, face beaming, excitedly telling me that I had passed all nine subjects. To show how proud she was of me she bought me a watch worth nine pounds, a pound for each subject passed. I suppose I should have been more excited, but I would rather have spent the money on a pair of Levi jeans.

Her pride was even more suffocating when I went back to school in September to find out that I, Carole and Gillian, another of my friends, were the only three pupils in my school year who had passed in all nine subjects. The only reason I was happy was that I could use the opportunity to persuade her

I deserved to go to a party along the street with Gillian. I was not averse to occasionally going out without telling her when she was working nightshift, but Gillian had to stay overnight, so I needed her agreement.

My social life earlier that year, when I had reached the age of sixteen, had consisted of the occasional disco or visits to the bowling alley whenever my mother was working late shifts, accompanied by those of my friends who were allowed out.

I knew that boys were put off girls wearing spectacles, so on these occasions I removed my glasses. Needless to say I did not bowl; it was just a place for teenagers to hang out, eyeing each other up while sipping a coke at the snack bar. Not that I did much eyeing up, I would only have been able to do that if a boy actually came up close to talk to me.

Once I asked my mother whether I was ugly. She told me that I was not classically attractive in the English tradition that appealed to young boys. She could see that my continental style appealed to older men, because she had seen them look at me as I walked along the street. This was not what I wanted to hear. However, her truthfulness saved me a fortune, for when I realised that I was not the type to get chatted up, I stopped wasting my money hanging out at the bowling alley.

Consequently, my hopes were therefore rather high for the party Gillian was taking me to. She had only heard about it though her older brother, and had not been invited, but said not to worry, it was quite easy to gate-crash parties as long as you mentioned the name of a friend of the person who was holding the party.

Unfortunately there was no French boy to recognise and appreciate my continental good looks at this party, but there were plenty of well spoken long haired boys who seemed greatly impressed by Gillian's long blond hair and long shapely legs.

I spent most of the evening alone, trying to make out the lyrics of the progressive underground rock music being played, straining to listen to conversations either side of me and remember the names of groups being bandied about: Deep

Purple, The Moody Blues, Yes, Pink Floyd, Emerson Lake and Palmer, Led Zeppelin – groups seldom played on daytime Radio 1.

At one point there was a track playing that consisted only of birds singing and cows lowing; I felt terribly naïve somehow, how could I have missed all this variety of sound, listening to the radio as much as I did? I resolved to browse the channels in future. I had already calculated that if I had saved hard, I could buy a record player within a year, if I didn't buy any clothes at all. But I had also concluded that there was no point, as LPs were so expensive to buy, that I would only be able to afford one every three months. Besides, I would have had to live like a hermit because I could not possibly be seen in public in the hand-me-down clothing my mother increasingly wanted to kit me out in. She rarely sewed these days, not having the time or will to spend hours slaving away at her sewing machine after work. In fact these days she was acquiring clothing more cost effectively from the charity shop she had recently discovered, than it cost her to buy yardage of material from the haberdashers or Remnant Kings. And anyway, I still had to save up for a pair of Levi jeans.

In September, I started Lower Sixth Year. My mother began talking about career choices, as did the form teacher at school, and it was agreed by all concerned that languages were my forte. For my three "A" Levels I chose to do French, German and History. This was because the new French teacher who had taught me during the last year was a big improvement on the previous Resistance-reminiscing teacher and had managed to get me interested; I was naturally able to speak German; and, finally, because the History teacher was my favourite. I had no idea what I wanted to do as a career, although teaching was recommended by my career guidance teacher.

This was not an unusual state of affairs for a girl in the late sixties. The single parent family was still a rare phenomenon, as was the idea of woman's liberation. Other than the burning of the bra, which got much attention in the press, the idea of woman as single and independent, unmarried with children, or, most horrific concept of all, main breadwinner, was not typical of school or career guidance talk when it came to discussing one's future. The underlying assumption was that careers were still very much what men had, and women started and then gave up, devoting the rest of their lives to rearing children and making life comfortable for their hard-working husbands.

In October 1970 we moved again. It was to be the last one for my mother until her final relocation to Scotland 22 years later.

The new flat was on Brighton Road, the former highway hugging the seafront as it linked Brighton to Bognor Regis through the West Sussex coastal towns of Hove, Shoreham, Lancing, Worthing, and Littlehampton. It was a busy road, whose volume of commuter traffic continued to increase over the following two decades, despite the development of the inland dual carriage way linking these same towns. In 1970 we were woken by the rush hour traffic between eight and nine of a morning, and ate our dinner to the accompaniment of droning engines between five and six of an evening. By 1992, that same road carried nose-to-tail traffic for the best part of the night and day. Whenever my mother visited Scotland she was astonished at the peace and quiet of the world away from Brighton Road.

However, at the time we moved there, the traffic noise emanating from the road was not a problem. The tastefully white washed end-terraced building was of regency style proportions, and our first floor flat was distinguished by a black balcony embracing the enormous bay window of our front room. Access to the flat was either from the main front door, followed by a second door set in a glass fronted partition, or from the back of the building. There was no rear garden. The land behind the house had been sold to a garage, and been covered with tarmac for use as customer parking. As I described the flat to Jacqui, I suddenly understood why this flat had appealed to my mother. Access was private and secure. She had the use of a south west facing balcony to the front and a south east facing balcony at the rear of the flat on which she could cultivate nasturtiums, busy lizzy, geraniums and even hibiscus. The enormous living room was bright and welcoming, as was the double windowed bedroom. The kitchen was contemporarily functional when we first moved in. The previous tenants, who were emigrating to Australia, sold us some of their furniture, including the gas powered fridge in the kitchen - the first fridge my mother had ever owned. They also asked us if we would look after their cat, Olive.

Tootsie was not enamoured with Olive. It was obviously one thing to put up with frequent moves of territory, which she had done with good grace, but to be expected to take on a sitting tenant was quite a different story. After several encounters of the fur flying kind, we had to keep Olive in the kitchen, and Tootsie in the front room and make sure that neither was outside at the same time. Eventually my mother realised this lifestyle was not good for either cat, and she phoned the RSPCA to pick up Olive and take her to an animal shelter where, she explained to me, someone would find her and give her a new home in due course.

I cried when I found out that the RSPCA only held animals for a couple of months before they destroyed them. I felt that we had not kept up our end of the bargain, but my mother said we had done what we could, given the circumstances.

I took my mother's hard heartedness very badly. With hindsight I can see that it was the right thing to do, but at the time it seemed to be another characteristic of my mother's that I added to the list of annoying habits she had, and I spent more and more of my time in my bedroom, in order to keep my irritation with her under control.

As I told Jacqui these things, it gradually dawned on me that I had harboured a great amount of resentment against my mother, and I was surprised at myself for not having recognised or admitted it to myself sooner.

I reflected that after she had died, my mother had seemed almost saintly. All I could remember at that point in time was the pain she had suffered, and how awful her life must have been. I had forgotten how I had shied away from her company for the last few years of my life at home with her, and how I had grown to resent the burden of her expectations of me and her bitterness at life.

I finally sensed that I was coming to terms with Brigitte, not just as my mother, not as a holocaust survivor, but as a human being.

Chapter 26   Going with the Flow or Not

One spring morning in 1971 my mother had a slight stroke shortly after opening up the sofa bed on her return from working a nightshift. Recognising the symptoms she stumbled down the stairs and asked the neighbour on the ground floor to call the doctor. The stroke left her partially paralysed. Her mouth hung loose on the left side, her speech was slightly slurred, and she had restricted movement in her left hand and arm. She exercised her arm and face muscles every day as she lay convalescing on the sofa bed, and all movement returned back to normal within a few months. She counted herself lucky.

She applied to the BCAR to get a phone line installed and line rental paid for out of the trust that had been established by the Teachers' Association for my family, and she felt safer knowing that if she needed to call a doctor at short notice, she would now be able to do so. We therefore had a phone that we only used for emergencies or very special occasions, but we still could not afford a television.

I started working as a waitress in a local hotel, over the weekends. My mother encouraged me to look for a job in France over the summer holidays so that I could improve my spoken French. I applied to an agency and was a little surprised when I landed myself a job as an au pair with a family in Paris within a few weeks. My astonishment grew into amazement when I learned the family I was to join lived in the 8th Arrondissement, the most well-to-do part of Paris, and their apartment was two streets along from the Champs Elysees, on the same street as the entrance to the President of France's Residence. Moreover, I would be spending a month in Paris and two months in the family's country house in Normandy.

When I arrived I was picked up by Mr Swoboda and his five year old daughter, Anne, at the Gare du Nord, and taken to their apartment. Mr Swoboda was in his early fifties, of Polish origin, whose family had emigrated to France before the Second World War. His wife, Suzanne, was away ensuring the holiday home was ready, and I looked after Anne for a few days before Suzanne returned and I finally met her. When she found out I was born in Germany she nearly phoned the agency to get me dismissed and replaced with another au pair. In my broken French I tried to explain to her my mother's background, but she insisted she could hear a German accent in my spoken French and it reminded her of when the Nazis were occupying Paris. She said she would never forgive those Germans who had terrorised her neighbourhood, and arbitrarily shot her cousin, as a means of retribution for someone else's misdeeds.

Suzanne did eventually calm down as she learnt about my mother's experiences, but I was taken aback at her vehemence – I had never encountered such hatred before. Perhaps the feelings had not been as intense in an unoccupied country like Britain, where only those sent to fight had first-hand experience of the brutality of war. I realised for the first time that those immediately suffering a disaster would forever feel more passionately, and more fearfully, than those that had only read about it or watched it in a film. It was an important lesson to learn.

When I got home I asked my mother why she didn't hate the Germans for what they had done. She said that a nationality is not evil, it is individuals that are. For every person who had meant her harm during the war, she had encountered many more who had tried to help. I still wondered at the difference in her forgiving attitude and Suzanne's continued bitterness.

My duties were to spend time with Anne, to try to teach her English, and take their Afghan hound called Tzarevitch for daily walks. This was not as easy as it sounded. Anne was not interested in learning English, and the dog was petrified of cars. He trembled for the duration of our quick walks around the block, the only route we could take, as crossing a street with him proved impossible. I had to be wary of the street inspectors who roamed the streets of Paris trying to catch dog owners illegally allowing their dogs to foul the pavements. I was stopped twice by babbling men holding up shields, both times telling them in broken French that I did not understand what they were saying to me and hurrying off. I got away with it on those occasions and once we left the noisy, hot streets of Paris for the lush green Normandy countryside, there were no such problems.

I experienced my first taste of the good life. The summer passed in a pleasant routine of playing with Anne and the dog, sunbathing, listening to radio quizzes with Suzanne, and playing poker for matchsticks in the evenings, all performed in pleasant surroundings, eating wonderful food and tasting a variety of French wines.

When I returned to England in September I had gained a confidence that everyone remarked upon. I had even acquired a little French style – and started sewing and embroidering my own clothes. I also felt a restlessness I had never encountered before, probably due to experiencing a lifestyle that was so alien to the one to which I was returning.

A few weeks after my return home, my mother and I decided to take a day trip to London ostensibly for me to look for some new clothes patterns and material, and for her to get a valuation on some coins she had accumulated.

My mother had recently discovered a passion for antiques and coin collecting. She thought she would make a fortune one day, certain that the little pieces of chipped pottery she occasionally brought home with a self satisfied look on her face would sooner or later be revealed as rare pieces of great value. She had been collecting and storing old shillings and pennies, sure that, with the change to decimal coins that had just occurred, this 1921 half penny or that 1901 penny would eventually be highly sought after.

My mother was a great window shopper, but personally I found wandering around Kensington rather depressing, knowing that the cost of any one item in any of these upmarket shops was way beyond anything we could ever afford.

She was looking in the window of a shop that sold carpets from the Middle East in Bond Street, and decided to go in to ask about a small rug we had which she insisted was from Iran, and therefore of value. I wandered around the shop and wasn't really paying much attention to the conversation struck up between my mother and the woman behind the counter.

Suddenly I was called over and introduced as having just come back from France, and hadn't the style rubbed off on me – look at the lovely outfit I was wearing. Admittedly I was actually looking pretty good in the burgundy flowery dirndl skirt and pink cheesecloth top I had treated myself to in France which went perfectly with the wine coloured ankle strap shoes my mother had bought in a charity shop.

I half listened as the conversation topic turned to the shop owner's son, who was due home next week, and how much she was looking forward to seeing him again. I wandered off once more. My mother must have spent another twenty minutes chatting before we left the shop, by which time I was thoroughly bored and desperate to go home.

It wasn't until the green fields of the South Downs were zipping past the train window that my mother told me we were going back to London the following weekend.

"Whatever for?" I asked, knowing full well that the train fare itself wasn't cheap and mentally counting the cost of eating out twice in one week.

"We've been invited to afternoon tea!" she said in her best posh accent, a smug look on her face.

"Oh!" I exclaimed, thinking that they must have got on really well.

"She's Jewish you know. And her family comes from near where I was born! They emigrated to London before the war, but afterwards moved to Israel to help build up the country. She and her husband moved back to London to open the shop, but her son is still living there, working on a Kibbutz."

We duly made the trip the following weekend, and ended up having to take a taxi to find their relatively modern apartment block in Golders Green.

The flat was immaculately furnished with antiques. Monsieur Swoboda, who was an antique dealer, had told me that he only needed to sell one of the pieces of furniture in his shop to pay all his staff for a month. I guessed this family was pretty well off.

When I was introduced to the son, I was rather surprised to see a stout serious looking man with a little round cap on the back of his head, dressed in a dark suit. I had been told he was 23, but he looked about 40. I had heard of hippies going to work on kibbutzes in Isreal to experience life in communes, but I could not imagine him hanging out and smoking pot around a Campfire. Still, I assumed he had another persona when he was not with his parents, like I had when I was not with my mother.

I was, however, disappointed to discover he could speak no English. I could make out a little of the Yiddish he spoke occasionally, because the language has German roots, but conversation was out of the question. We had a traditional afternoon tea with scones and jam, and then we all went for a walk in the unusually balmy October air, our mothers walking ahead as we walked alongside each other in companionable silence. I was far too surprised when he gently took hold of my hand to pull it away from him.

Suddenly the penny dropped. They had been matchmaking! I could see my mother jumping at the chance of a match with a boy from such a prosperous family. Forget waiting for her pennies to grow in value, why not take the opportunity to marry into a fortune! I felt extremely uncomfortable and indignant.

When we arrived back at the apartment I felt even more compromised, for his mother asked me straight out what I thought of her son. I was glad that my mother was in the bathroom and unable to interfere, for it allowed me to be honest. I replied that he seemed a nice boy but not my type. Her face actually fell. I suppose that was a compliment to me, but it didn't feel like it.

We left shortly after. My mother couldn't wait to ask me what had happened. I guess she had sensed the change in the atmosphere. When I told her she looked at me as though I had stabbed her in the heart. I told her I was far too young to be getting involved with a 23 year old anyway. She just said "aach" as though my opinion on such matters was stupid beyond reason, and what did I know about these things.

Yet again I had managed to thwart her dreams.

Despite my much improved spoken French, studying was onerous, and I did rather less well than anticipated in my 'A' Level Prelims. But the push was on at school for applications to University, and I received an invitation to interview at Warwick University for a place on a BA course in French and Theatre Studies, which I was keen to be offered.

The pressure was on. The trip was planned for weeks; I even borrowed a pair of tan boots to go with the rust brown dress with Cossack sleeves my mother had splashed out on for me for the occasion. The train journey was long and arduous; I had to cross London; the interview was at two in the afternoon, and when I got back it was late in the evening. Before I could go to bed, I had to go over the interview word for word with my mother. Unfortunately she took umbrage at one of the responses I had provided, stating that it would ruin my chances of being accepted, and stormed out of the room. She didn't talk to me for three days.

In the end I was made a conditional offer, but my results were not good enough, and my mother had to suffer the shame of telling all that I had failed to get into university.

I don't remember being terribly upset about it. I had basically adopted an attitude of letting life happen to me. I felt somewhat disassociated with my surroundings. Everything my mother wanted for me felt too much of a burden, a cross that I either felt incapable of or didn't want to carry, knowing I would only end up hurting her if I openly rebelled.

I let my mother push me into applying for a Bilingual Secretarial Course, at the local College of Further Education. I couldn't see myself being a secretary, but I went with the flow. I also let her organise a job for the school holidays, through a contact she had in the BCAR. I therefore spent the summer of 1972 working as a waitress at Birer's Court, an exclusive Four Star Hotel near Littlehampton.

At least this move of my mother's led to my meeting some celebrities: David Jacobs, compere of the television programme Juke Box Jury, and Cliff Richard. But it was most memorable for me because it allowed me to meet Paul, who worked as a commis-chef in the kitchen. He was nineteen; extremely good looking; dark haired and olive skinned; shunned by his mother who lived in Brighton; a chess genius - during his free time he challenged guests to games which he invariably won; and he wrote poetry, most of which I did not understand.

He also took LSD. Sometimes I didn't know what he was talking about – was he tripping or reciting poetry? But he made me feel special. He picked me out of the three other girls who worked there as chambermaids. Once, when we were working well past the normal lunch hour, cleaning glasses in preparation for a wedding reception later that afternoon, I was desperate to get some painkillers to soothe the agonising period pains I was suffering. I asked him to pick them up for me from reception, but when he saw me bending over in agony, he swept me off my feet and carried me, rather unsteadily, out of the scullery area. I was redder faced than him when I asked him to put me down once we were outside, but the gesture was the sweetest thing I had ever experienced, and I was overwhelmed.

We spent all our free time together, and I didn't get much sleep during the six weeks I worked there that summer. Not that we did anything other than kiss, but we became inseparable during that time. I had never really talked intimately at length to a boy before; it was a revelation to me when he described his interests, feelings and desires, and I discovered he was really quite similar to me. He also had a mother with whom he could not get on.

When college started he surprised me by writing letters to me addressed care of the college, for I never would have given him my home address. I just knew that my mother would not have approved of him. He had nothing, and was nobody. I had already experienced the kind of relationship she considered desirable, and I knew he would fall well short of her criteria.

We saw each other a few times over the following six months or so, on his days off, during the Christmas break, or whenever there was a special function on at the hotel, and I would get a phone call to work the weekend. I was therefore shocked to discover, when I arrived at the hotel one Friday evening, that he had left the hotel and had joined the French Foreign Legion.

The woman who ran the hotel was as astonished as me. She handed me a photograph, taken on the prom in Worthing, on one of the days we had arranged to meet that summer. We stood arm in arm, me smiling, as happy as an eighteen year old with her first boyfriend could be. I was already stunned because he had given me no indication he was leaving, but what hurt most whenever I thought about him during the following months, was that he hadn't even cared enough to take the photo with him.

In hindsight, maybe he left it for me as a reminder of him.

One day in May 1973 I was called out of class at college and told to go home. I found my mother lying on the sofa, a little puddle of sick on the carpet beside her. Her face was grey, and she looked worried. With laboured breaths she told me the doctor had called an ambulance because he thought she might have had a heart attack. She asked me to clean up the sick on the carpet, and to phone her friend to ask if I could stay with her for a while.

She was in hospital for three weeks and in a convalescent home for a month. I stayed with her friend, sat my exams at college, and went with the flow. It never occurred to me that she might have died.

Chapter 27   Breakthrough

Whenever I told Jacqui a story I told it in a fairly laid back manner. It was as though I could stand back and look at the scene, like a film editor splicing the action. I think Jacqui felt she was getting somewhere if I displayed a spark of feeling or even anger.

Jacqui by now had probed enough to understand the ambivalent relationship between my mother and me. She knew that I did not lightly offer up information that disparaged Brigitte. But as the weeks and months passed by and I told Jacqui my recollections, I had the opportunity to examine the nature of my relationship with my mother. Meeting by meeting, as I reflected and described little incidences echoing subconscious feelings of guilt, I was able to offload the burden I had carried on my shoulders.

When I first attended our "meetings" I thought my mother and I had a very strong loving relationship, and that the reason I was there was because I was missing her and needed to come to terms with her death. I knew she had suffered and that I could never make it up to her, and somehow I felt responsible for not being able to give her the life she had deserved or wanted in her later years.

As a result of my meetings with Jacqui, and being able to tell my story in depth, through adult eyes, I finally made the leap of understanding I required. I could actually identify with the course of my mother's life. Her early years had been controlled by an uncaring stepmother, anti-Semitic laws, and circumstances enforced on her by the war and its aftermath – it was a life very much destined by the influence of others. On leaving my stepfather, she finally had the opportunity to take control of her own destiny. And she did so to ensure things would finally go *her* way, as opposed to any one else's.

It was this need to control that had caused our relationship to founder. As the weeks of consultation turned to months, I slowly realised that the anger I had harboured towards my mother was born out of my impotence in the face of her need to control her own fate.

Perhaps my reaction to her controlling behaviour and deep need to get away from her was normal for someone of that age, like all offspring leaving the nest. But as I grew older, married and had children of my own - in short, as I became aware of a woman's lot in the world - I realised that she had suffered more than the average. I began to recognise the enormous guilt I had nurtured over the years since moving away and leaving her to fend for herself. And I came to acknowledge that these same feelings of guilt, anger and impotence had always lurked in the background whenever I spent any length of time in her company in later years.

I ultimately understood how good I had become at compartmentalising my feelings, and how securely I had locked the lid of the safety deposit box marked 'guilt' in the vault of my mind.

Jacqui was pretty upbeat when we started our next meeting. During the previous consultation I had told her about my reaction to my mother's matchmaking attempt and had displayed some anger. We had also started talking at some length about my mother's death.

She told me she wanted to do an exercise with me.

"You have unfinished business with your mother, unanswered questions that arose after her death. It may help if we do this particular role play."

I listened with interest.

"I want you to imagine that your mother is in the room with us. I want you to ask her anything that comes into your head."

My first reaction was that it was a strange request. But as I recalled the conversations I had had with my mother in my head after she died, I realised that not once had I asked her any questions about our relationship. I had never been able to ask her about things that I knew would hurt her, for fear of her reaction. Suddenly I was willing to play this game.

"Your mother has just walked into the room and is sitting

on that chair beside you. She is waiting for your questions," prompted Jacqui.

"Why did you not tell me about the baby?" I faltered with my first, but burning question. There was a silence. I looked at Jacqui. I looked at the empty chair. I tried to visualise my mother and I could see her now, calm, at peace, her head bent over her hands, busy crocheting a fine lace tablecloth, not looking at me.

I wanted her to look at me.

"Were you raped? Who raped you? Was it the Russians you hated so much? Were you ashamed to tell me?"

Her silence became a solid thing, like the wall that had always stood between us, that I had to tear apart. I felt the anger rising in my throat like a rumbling geyser.

"Did you not trust me enough to tell me? Was our relationship a sham? Was it me? Did I push you away? Did I let you down?"

My rage boiled over. I knew she would never answer me. I could have screamed. Tears poured from my eyes, but I continued – if she wouldn't answer me, then at least I would have my say.

"Did you hate me that much for frustrating your ambitions? You could never understand that I couldn't give you what you needed, could you? Couldn't you see, your shitty life was NOT MY FAULT!"

For the first time in my life I had shouted at her, finally unfettered by fear, free to express how I felt. I slumped back, exhausted with the effort of freeing myself from the shackles of my guilt. I finally understood.

Jacqui looked at me calmly. "How do you feel?"

"I'm okay." I swallowed. I tried to pull myself together but the relief left me worn out.

"I'm sure it feels good to get it off your chest." I could see now she had planned it this way. Well, perhaps not planned, is counselling that predictable? But certainly she must have hoped that the role play would provide the outlet for my anger.

"Saskia, you have every right to be angry. Your mother's

unrealistic expectations for you were based on her lost opportunities. But we both understand her need, don't we?

"Yes"

"Can you forgive her?"

"Yes"

"I don't think she 'let' you find out about the baby because she wanted to punish you. I would be surprised if she even remembered that the facts about the other baby were in the paperwork she left. It is a well known fact that holocaust survivors wanted to forget. They felt guilty too, for surviving when so many others had died. It wasn't their fault they had done whatever needed to be done in order to survive. Survival is a primeval force of nature. I think maybe she simply didn't know how to tell you. Maybe it was just too painful for her to talk about losing her baby. But in the end, it was her right, and her decision not to tell you. Can you accept that?"

"Yes"

The release I felt after I was finally able to admit the anger I had harboured for so many years towards my mother, was as tangible as a steel band of pressure being lifted from the crown of my head. When I left the meeting that day I felt as though I walked taller than normal.

I met Jacqui once more after this pivotal meeting, and we mutually decided that I did not need to see her again. I figured I had come to terms with my past.

Gradually I realised that the year I had spent talking to Jacqui had given me a fresh outlook on life. When I visited the consultant at the end of the treatment period, she told me she was amazed at the change in my demeanour, and that she could sense a new confidence and calmness about me.

I thanked her for seeing my diagnosis through, for getting to the root of those awful symptoms. As the interview drew to an end, I took the opportunity to ask her a question.

"I was wondering, do you think my mother's many strange illnesses were also symptomatic of the emotional trauma she had encountered in her life?"

"It's highly likely. Post traumatic stress disorder is a relatively new diagnosis which has finally recognised and rationalised a whole series of symptoms that the sufferer can experience. For women it can be headaches, "women's" problems or depression. Unfortunately there was no counselling available for people like your mother. There was no "closure". They just had to get on with things and come to terms with their loss and guilt by themselves."

As I walked out of the room, I was filled with a sense of gratitude for being able to live in an era where I had been provided, free of charge, with the means to understand myself and come to terms with my past.

As I drove home I resolved it was time to shift from living in the past, to concentrate on living my life to the full, and begin making it up to my boys for the time spent on my introspection.

I was ready to move on.

Chapter 28   The Search Begins 1994

Since the day my mother's box of secrets had revealed his identity, printed on my Baptismal certificate, I had wondered about searching for my father.

My mother's view had been that his life was his own after their intimate relationship and single year of correspondence had ended. I did ask her once again before she died whether she had ever wanted to know what had become of him, but she was very quick to say that it would not be fair to try to contact him now, that he would have made his own life, had possibly married and had children, and anyway, what was passed was the past.

Her sentiments echoed in my mind now and again, and I wondered if it would indeed be fair of me to try to contact him. Yet a deep need to feel part of a real family, a desire to know if there were indeed half brothers and sisters, to be reassured that I might have someone in the world that was blood kin, kept gnawing away at my heart.

I knew that I would have to take my chances if I ever found him or any extended family. I would have to be prepared for his decision at that time; that he might not wish to see me, or allow me to visit his family, because of the pain and disruption it might cause to lives ignorant of his history. But a more selfish part of me wondered if a new family should be spared the truth, denied the fact that there had been a child fathered during a different existence prior to his arrival in the United States. Why deny them their roots? And while I acknowledged that "what was passed was the past", why deny myself a future?

Yet again I was torn between emotion and practicality. I calculated that, if he had been around the same age as my mother, he would now be between 75 and 80 years old. The figures were not encouraging. Finally I decided I was putting the egg before the chicken. I made up my mind that I could defer the decision whether to make physical contact with him if and when I ever found him, alive or dead. And so I began my search.

I had very little to go on. I knew my father was Czech, that he had emigrated to the US in 1953, the name of the Camp he had left in Germany, and I knew his name.

The only problem was that the name on the Baptismal Certificate - Oldrich Kaluba - was nothing like Karl, the name my mother had used to refer to him. It occurred to me that Karl might be a pet name for Kaluba, and that the name had been inverted to show the surname first, as sometimes occurred on old official papers.

Knowing it was a long shot, at the end of 1995, I wrote a letter to the Red Cross Head Office in London, asking if they provided the service of tracking those who had lived in their post war DP Camps. Their reply provided me with a contact name and department, to which I duly wrote, asking if it was possible for them to search their records for any details on an inmate of the Valka Camp in Nurnberg during the years 1952 and 1953, named Karl or Kaluba Oldrich. I had read about immigrants to the US changing their names to sound more English, so for good measure I added the name Charles, the English equivalent of Karl.

About three weeks after mailing my letter of enquiry, the Red Cross replied and asked for more details. I phoned the signatory and explained my situation, and was told that, without a place or date of birth, it would be very difficult to trace my father and to ascertain a date of departure from Germany, but they would certainly do their best.

I went to the library for help. I learned that there were plenty of means available to aid the tracing of relatives if they originated in the UK, from church records, or birth or death certificates at local registry offices. No doubt the same help might be available from the Czech authorities, but I had no means of finding that out. I didn't even know where he had been born or lived, although I did remember my mother saying that it wasn't far from where she had originated. This led me to try to find out where Jagersdorf was located, but I could not find the town on any map of modern Czechoslovakia.

I learned that the world leaders in genealogical research at that time were the Mormons, based in Salt Lake City, Utah. Unfortunately, apart from knowing that Karl had written to my mother from Pittsburgh in Pennsylvania from his arrival in 1953 until I was a year old, (so up until around 1955), I had no other information to provide to enable a search of their records. The search, of course, would need to be paid for. I figured that unless he had joined the Mormon Church or had married someone who had, the chances of there being any details on him were very slim.

It dawned on me that I was looking for the needle in the proverbial haystack. I had absolutely no idea what else to do. I consoled myself with the thought that finding him was not to be, and anyway it was probably better like that. Who could tell what can of worms might have been opened?

Putting my yearnings behind me, I concentrated on living.

I decided the time was right to try to tell my mother's story to my sons, aged thirteen and eight. Like sex education, the more complex details were inevitably toned down in the telling, but I did not spare them the graphics as we settled down to watch Steven Spielberg's "Schindler's List" when it first appeared on video release. My sons watched me with trepidation as the tears streamed down my face. I tried to explain to them that, for me, it was as real an image as possible of the type of living conditions my mother had endured, and this was what had made me so upset. I was not sure whether they understood. Did they view my mother's life in terms of this film, just as I, at the age of thirteen, had compared it to the films I had seen? I think it was a more realistic portrayal of the era, and much more explicit than the Hollywood depictions I had access to when I was their age.

Watching the film left me very unsettled. I realised that I was still raw where my mother was concerned, but recognised that counselling had allowed me to face my emotions rather than ignoring them. Moreover, on this occasion I worked my way through the emotional trauma without having to call on Jacqui for help, as I might have done the previous year. I was proud of this new ability to put the past and the present into perspective.

My husband was less able to understand the change in me. Deep mental and emotional fissures had seemed to crack open between my husband and I during the years that I grieved for and finally came to terms with my mother's life and death, and ultimately my own identity.

After a year of agonising over the life changing events that had slowly chipped away at the foundations of our marriage, I realised that the crevice between us was simply too deep to bridge, and in 1997 I made the decision to leave my husband. He taunted me that I was following in my mother's footsteps in giving up on my marriage, and I battled with feelings of guilt as I moved into rented accommodation with my sons.

And so I too experienced single parenthood, though my struggle was by no means comparable to the experience of my mother. I was a professionally trained languages teacher and therefore employable, if there had been any permanent posts available. I therefore changed career, and though the motherhood gap years and my inexperience in my newly chosen career in the field of whisky exports put me well behind in the salary stakes, at least I was still using my languages to some extent. Furthermore I had a network of friends who supported me emotionally as I built a new life for my small family.

Unfortunately the split became acrimonious and charged with emotional blackmail. I had to fight for access to my share of the marital home, including my mother's box of secrets and the pieces of furniture and memorabilia that had been her legacy to me. It took three years for me to overcome the emotional scarring of our separation and eventual divorce.

In 2000 I started working for a large company which allowed its employees the right to use the internet during the lunch hour. Suddenly I was able to surf a whole new wave of opportunity. Swept along with enthusiasm I splurged out on a home pc, found my way into instant chat rooms, and within a few months began an online romance. Richard was working and living in Germany, and the relationship grew through email, followed by monthly visits which were enabled by the sudden onset of cheaper flights from a local provincial airport to the continent.

During the first year Richard and I got to know each other, I discovered a wonderfully kind man with whom I could be myself, a man who had seen more of the world than most, and had experienced his own troubles. As we shared our pasts, I was astonished by Richard's ability to empathise with and articulate perfectly the feelings and emotions I had experienced. I finally felt understood and it encouraged me to talk as I had never talked before. As I opened my heart to him, and told him of my grief and counselling, he made me feel it was not a shameful episode, rather an ordeal I should be proud of for coming through.

My life was changing. A year after we started our online relationship, Richard moved from Germany and we started living together. Nine years after my mother died, I visited her grave for the second time, taking Richard with me. I wanted to introduce him.

The world was changing. Changes in politics, the information explosion on the World Wide Web and cheaper air travel were opening up forgotten European capitals as tourist destinations. In early 2002 I was planning a trip to Prague with Richard and some work colleagues, and wondering if it would be possible to visit the area from which my mother originated. I had discovered web sites displaying the old Sudeten German maps and town names, and stumbled into a community of knowledge sharers who were able to provide me with the equivalent new Czech town names.

Of course, I had to haul out the old attaché case and go through the documents again, to get place names for translation. I wanted to try to locate where my mother had worked during the war and where she had lived as a child, as listed in the Curriculum Vitae I had first discovered all those years ago. I was relieved to find this time that my reaction to looking through the documentation was much calmer than on the previous occasions. Ten years had passed since her death. Working with Jacqui and time had definitely helped me. I felt extreme sadness as I handled each envelope, but no tears came and I reflected on the great strides I had made in accepting my lot in life, and my mother's past. Jacqui's word "closure" rang in my ears, and I knew that this sudden urge to seek out my mother's birthplace was most probably the final part of this process.

I discovered that Freiwaldau, the Camp in which my mother had been incarcerated after the war, was actually the name of a town, now called Jesenik, and that her home town Jagersdorf, also known as Jagerndorf, had had its name changed to Krnov. Both lay in the far north east of the Czech Republic near the Polish border, as she had described to me.

This was a good distance away from Prague and would require a substantial detour away from the friends with whom we were spending the holiday. I was advised via the websites I now regularly visited, that older people would still be able to speak German, so I knew I would be able to communicate with the locals. I was told that visiting the Town Halls in each town would be the best start to my research. I also intended to visit the local cemeteries in the hope of finding the gravestones of my grandmother and grandfather, and perhaps even the resting place of an infant with the surname of Langer.

In June, Richard and I finally embarked on our seven day trip to the Czech Republic. After what I had heard from my mother about how badly Iron Curtain countries had suffered under the Soviets I was surprised at how relatively prosperous and unscathed the country seemed. As we drove from the airport into the city centre, I saw the infamous communist era concrete blocks, but beside them nestled well maintained red roofed one and two storey houses, similar in style to those in Germany.

Because of the annexation in 1938, Czechoslovakia had never suffered bombing during the onset of World War II in the same way as those countries affected by the advancing

Nazi Blitzkrieg. The countryside only suffered destruction during allied bombing as the Eastern Allies and Russians proceeded westwards to rout the Nazis during the last months of the war. As a result Prague could boast many relatively unscathed historical buildings, and it was these which drew increasing numbers of tourists now that the country had become more accessible to westerners.

We spent the weekend in Prague with friends, sightseeing and enjoying the hot weather and general good humour of the people around us. The city's beautifully restored medieval buildings and monuments were truly astonishing to view. My favourite was the Baroque Church of St Nicholas, gleaming in the sunlight, stucco decorations and frescoes taking my breath away. We laughed at the somewhat unprepossessing marching performed by the guards at the Castle, and marvelled at the view of the city from the St Vitus' Cathedral Tower. We tasted a variety of beers in a beer hall we stumbled across frequented more by locals than tourists, and I finally tucked into the knodel I had been anticipating with relish, only to be disappointed that they did not taste as good as those my mother used to cook.

As we walked through the busy streets of both the old and the new town I was amazed at the number of jewellers with window displays dripping with garnets - rings, earrings, lockets, brooches - set in both gold and silver. This gem was obviously highly prized by the locals, much more than the handful of diamond rings cowering dejectedly in a corner. I remembered my mother's brooch, the one she had given to me during that visit when we had both delved into her attaché case. My interest piqued, I looked more closely at the displays, searching for something similar in style. I noted that the prices were not cheap, £120 sterling for a gold ring with four garnets of roughly the same size as those larger ones in the brooch. It came as a revelation to me that the brooch I had worn occasionally in her honour over the years must have been worth a fair amount and I decided to get it valued on my return.

My friends, who knew of my history, were as keen as me

to visit the Jewish quarter and were greatly moved by the higgledy piggledy headstones in the Jewish Cemetery and the memorial to the Jews of Bohemia and Moravia in the Pinkas Synagogue. With tears in our eyes we read the hundreds of names printed on the walls, a list of those exterminated during the holocaust, and viewed the original artefacts left behind in the holding Camp of Theresienstadt, where Jews were isolated in the first instance after being rounded up within their local towns and villages. I watched my friends experience that same sense of outrage and incredulousness at man's inhumanity which I had experienced so many years previously.

On Sunday Richard and I said farewell to our friends. We rose at daybreak on Monday to make our way to the bus station and board the first bus to Jesenik. As we wound our way east through the fertile plain in which Prague was situated, through decreasing numbers of industrial towns and then past increasing numbers of fields of vegetables and grain crops, I understood why this country and its inhabitants gave off an aura of prosperity. It must have been totally self sufficient, and must have been greatly envied by the Soviets for its resources.

Gradually the landscape became more undulating. We passed signs for spas and eventually, as the hills became more pronounced, ski resorts. I remembered my mother telling me how she had bobsleighed as an adolescent, and I laughed at my naivety in thinking that her hometown would have been some medieval village. To my shame I realised that I had harboured the concept that modernisation since the 1950's was something that had only happened in Britain. I blamed black and white films and photographs for colouring my images of pre-war Europe with an aura of austerity.

Consequently Jesenik was not what I had expected. It was a relatively large town that was strung out on either side of the main road. We got off at the bus station, situated not far from a fairly modern shopping precinct through which we walked in search of the town square. It basked sleepily under the midday sun and hardly anyone was walking its scorching pavements. We located the Town Hall, but discovered it was closed for lunch.

Stopping a solitary passer-by, we managed to get directions to the cemetery. It was a long slow walk, a mile back along the road in the direction the bus had come.

The cemetery was rather unkempt. Its whitewashed perimeter wall looked well enough maintained from the outside, but the ankle-high grass was badly in need of cutting. Strangely enough, it was as though our appearance spurred the cemetery's caretaker into action, for while we were wandering between rows of gravestones searching for anything resembling the name Langer, an old man suddenly appeared with a lawn mower, and began his mowing meanderings with such gusto, it seemed as though he was determined to cut the grass before we had finished viewing each aisle.

As I realised there were many graves that had no stones at all, I started retracing my steps over the newly cut areas in case I had missed any small stone indicating a child's grave. But I never found anything resembling Langer. I realised I had no proof whatsoever that the baby who had "died in infancy" would in fact have had the surname Langer, or had even died in this town. I had simply made the assumption that my mother would not have left a living child while she was incarcerated in some Camp in this town in order to make her "illegal crossing" back into Germany. If anything the infant's death would have given her the means, motive and freedom to escape. And then it occurred to me that I might have had it all wrong, that she might actually have made a dangerous journey in order to save an ailing, starving child.

The temperature seemed to have gone up a few degrees as we sat down in the shade of a solitary tree and ate the sandwiches we had brought with us for our trip. I contemplated what we must have looked like: obviously tourists, with our backpack and small trolley suitcase left at the entrance gate, wandering back and forth. It was not surprising that the lawn was being cut in our honour. I wandered over to the grass cutter and asked in my regrettably broken German if he knew where I could find the church holding the records for those lying at peace in the cemetery. He told me it had burnt down and that we should ask at the Town Hall. We finally gave up our search and started heading back into town, figuring the return from lunch break would surely have breathed some life back into Jesenik.

The town centre was in fact as quiet as before, but I did manage to get into the Town Hall, and ask regarding the possibility of tracing a child who might have died between the years 1945 to 1947. I was taken into an office where a pretty young woman in her twenties received me and we discussed what I was looking for in German. She said that a search with only a surname and no specific date of birth or death would take a long time to perform, and how long would we be staying? When she understood I wanted to do some more research in the town of Krnov and that we only had a few days, she gave me her card and asked me to email her on my return to Scotland. I came out of the room feeling a slight sense of unease at the subtle way my request had been deferred.

We found our way back to the bus station and caught the next bus to Krnov. As we left Jesenik behind us, I reflected there had been no sign of barracks or any memorial to the Camp, and, even more unusual, not a single Germanic name on any of the gravestones.

Chapter 29   My Mother's Hometown

Krnov turned out to be much larger than Jesenik. A busy industrial conglomeration, it was split into old and new town. It took us a while to get our bearings and once we found the Town Hall it was close to 5.00pm. I did get admittance to an office but was kindly and firmly asked to come back in the morning to discuss my request further.

We wandered around the town square and were impressed by the old ornate buildings which had remained intact on two thirds of the square. We booked into a hotel and discovered the receptionist could speak English. When he enquired politely the reason for our visit, and I told him I was searching for anything related to my mother who had come from this area, he became very chatty and we talked at some length about my somewhat romantic plans to retrace my mother's footsteps. He said he could give me a street plan showing the old town with its original German street names. From this I concluded we were not the first who had come to Krnov on a similar errand.

We spent an enjoyable evening in one of the restaurants overlooking the old square, poring over the plan and trying to locate my mother's former home, but were unable to identify the street. We resolved to ask about the address the next day at the Town Hall, and it took a long time for me to fall asleep that night, so excited was I at the thought of what I was about to see.

We were standing outside the Town Hall at 9.00 am sharp. I was taken to a small office and introduced to a woman who spoke German, and after some discussion she advised me that 45 Lobenstein was not in fact a street name but a small village now called Uvalno, and that there were no street names, simply house numbers which would help me to identify her former house. Furthermore Uvalno/Lobenstein had its own registrar and she phoned and arranged for me to visit the office that same day, told me which train to take and how to get there from the station, and within fifteen minutes we were walking down the street from the square to the railway station. I was disappointed at the delay, yet I consoled myself with the thought that my mother must have walked this same street on her way to and from the station some 50 years previously.

Uvalno was just as sleepy and deserted a village as Jesenik had been by the time we stepped off the train at around 11.15 a.m. Obviously the inhabitants in this area lived life similarly to all southern Europeans, who were active only in the cooler early mornings and evenings, and took siesta time very seriously.

Signs indicated that the Polish border was one kilometre to the north east, but we turned south west and walked in the oppressive heat for what seemed an interminable length of time. We passed a group of houses, and crossed a main road to the side of which lay a small hotel. The thought of stopping for a drink seemed inviting, but we had an appointment to keep so continued up the long road and its never-ending incline, my small trolley suitcase screeching like a truculent child as it was pulled reluctantly over the rough surface of the road, struggling and fighting my hand the whole way. My attention was eventually distracted from my suitcase to the houses we were walking past, modern looking bungalows, with smallish gardens, and some older looking barn conversions, uncannily similar to those in rural Germany. The numbers of the houses followed no chronological pattern and it occurred to me that, as there were no street names, and the numbers were the sole means of identifying an address, then the number must have been applied on each building as it was built. In which case, my mother's house must have been the forty-fifth building erected in this village.

Suddenly we passed a striking church and walled graveyard. The sun reflected blindingly off its whitewashed windowless walls, and the only adornment, a simple black cross, stood out like a black tattoo on pale skin.

I became lost in thought, imagining my mother sitting

dutifully beside her grieving father at church on a Sunday, or walking down this road, her hand in his, as he dropped her off on his way to work at the border patrol. It struck me with a frisson of exhilaration that the hotel we had just passed could have been the inn run by my great-grandmother, and the group of houses on the main road could have been Dobischwald.

The Registrar was waiting for us on the steps of a rather unusual looking round-towered medieval building which seemed smaller at the bottom than at the top, and was totally out of keeping with the style of the surrounding houses.

She smiled encouragingly and showed us into the dark interior, where we were able to relieve ourselves of our baggage, and enjoy the cooler air. Richard was asked to wait downstairs and I was taken up a round staircase to a small bare walled room furnished only with a plain wooden table and two chairs. I got the impression that these were the originals which had survived with the building. On the table was an enormous black covered ledger, and after the formal pleasantries, I was told that she had located the page where my grandfather's death was recorded. She opened the thick tome, lifted a few heavy yellowed pages, and turned the book towards me.

I felt as though my heart was being squeezed by my mother's unseen hand as I read that Rudolf Langer of 45 Lobenstein had died of heart disease in 1943, and was survived by his wife Hedwig. My mother's name was not mentioned. Tears welled in my eyes, and after I had composed myself I asked if I could take a photograph, but was informed that this was not allowed. For some reason I did not have the wherewithal to ask for a copy. I simply stared at the page and willed my brain to memorise what I could see.

Aware that our visit had encroached on the registrar's lunch hour, I asked for directions to house number 45 and whether it would be acceptable to leave our luggage while we went and looked at my mother's and grandfather's former house. I sensed some discomfort on her part at my request, and thought I had gone too far by asking to leave the bags. But it seemed that the bags were not the problem; rather that her reluctance was in supplying me directions.

I briefly remembered an article I had read regarding the increasing number of displaced persons making restitution claims on former properties once the iron curtain had come down. I quickly assured her I only wanted to view the property and did not wish to disturb those that were now resident there. After all, my mother had said the house had been partially destroyed during the war and I had no intention of claiming what someone else had taken time and money to restore. I merely wanted to see the location as part of my quest to understand my heritage.

The house was located further up the hill, but the road became tree-lined and shaded, and the walk was not as arduous as before. We found number 45, a pink-washed bungalow, and I was surprised at how small the garden was. Surely this was not the land bordering the house described by my mother, on which had been reared pigs and on which great trees had produced an abundance of fruit to be gathered and preserved every year? The numbers of those houses on either side were of course out of sync, and I wondered if they had been built on the land once belonging to the bungalow. Perhaps the bungalow in front of us was not the original building.

I realised what Brigitte had said was true – her home as she knew it had been destroyed as a result of the war. And with that thought I remembered another conversation, and her telling me how glad she had been her father had died before the Russians came and the aftermath had begun.

When we returned to the Registry office it was still shut for lunch, so we walked to the black and white church which we had noticed before. We found it locked but thought we might wander around the graveyard, again looking for any stones displaying the name Langer. We cooled off momentarily in the shade of the lush green cypress trees shading the front and sides of the building, before following the neatly tended path to the rear. We were amazed to find that only the far end of the flat hectare of land was dotted with stones. It was as though the dead were banished as far away from the embrace of the church as possible. We trawled through the unadorned bereft stones but very few had legible engravings, and all those I could read had Czech names on them and had died within the last fifty years. What had happened to the graves of those prior to the war years? Had there been extensive bombing which had desecrated this hallowed ground?

We returned to the registry office and waited until a man came and unlocked the door. There was no sign of the lady I had spoken to earlier, and it turned out that the man could speak no German, so I could not ask about the graveyard. On our way to the train station, we stopped at the inn we had passed earlier for a quick refreshing beer. The place was deserted and we didn't think we would have time to order and wait for something to eat before the train was due. The young girl serving us had no German, so I could not ask about the history of the inn. It was blandly white walled and unadorned inside, and I got the feeling the original building had probably been rebuilt or at least modernised recently.

As I sat on the train heading for Opova and watched my mother's home town disappear into the distance, I felt a mixture of emotions. I had been moved by the inscription in the ledger, but other than that I had not really found anything that made the place appeal to me. I was merely left with a general feeling of unease at the woman's pan-faced reaction to our visit, so different to the enthusiasm of the hotel keeper the night before. It was almost as though we were not welcome.

Chapter 30   Seek And Find 2002

On returning from my trip to Prague and Krnov, I located my mother's garnet brooch and took the train into Glasgow to find a jeweller who might be able to give me a value for insurance purposes. During the hour long trip I reflected on its history.

It probably originated in the early eighteen hundreds and may well have been crafted by the hands of a master jeweller in the town of Jagerndorf. I had been told it had been bought for my great-great grandmother's wedding trousseau. It could have been worn on a high collared silk evening dress at a visit to a concert in the town hall we had visited, for the middle class Langer family had obviously enjoyed the prosperity of this industrialised town under the Habsburg dynasty. It was probably bestowed on her only daughter on coming out into society. In due course it would have been gifted to her only son, my grandfather Rudolf, who gave it to his bride Paula in 1912. She would surely have worn it at the christening of their daughter Brigitte. Were my mother's sky blue eyes drawn to the blood red shape glinting on her mother's breast?

It might have been hidden away as a safety precaution against envious eyes, after WW1 left the town ravaged by political dissension and inflation following the collapse of the Habsburg Empire, or it might have been carefully wrapped in tissue paper in sorrow after Paula died from Spanish Flu in 1918. Was it unwrapped once more and given to Hedwig on Rudolf's second wedding day? Or did he gift it to his daughter as a memoir of the much missed mother whose face she no longer could recall, during those awful years her stepmother ruled the household with a fist of iron?

And after my mother finally fled the nest at seventeen to work as a governess in Vienna, did it sit proudly on her collar, shining at the passers-by as she sat at opulent café tables, eating strudel on her days off? Did it glower darkly on the day my mother returned back home, summoned to help look after her father who had suffered a stroke?

Did it feel impending doom as my mother sewed it into her coat lining while Nazi boots marched through Krnov? How long did it remain hidden under the fur collar, centimetres from the papers which now had to be carried in my mother's coat to show on demand, identifying her as a Mischling? Did it listen to her sobs as her life degenerated into a round of work, sleep, hunger, and despair? When did they both see the light of hope again?

As I travelled the brooch's journey in my imagination, I realised I had come a long way since that day it had been gifted to me. Five Generations of history sat in my handbag, and I felt immensely proud.

I found a jeweller who bought and sold antique jewellery, and walked into the shop. Hinting only at the age of the brooch, I asked the young man behind the counter if it could be valued. He looked at the two hundred year old item through his loupe, and hummed and hawed. Eventually he said that the garnets were most likely fake – they were much too similar in size and cut to be real, and besides, they would have been set in gold if they were valuable. He would not be interested in buying such a worthless piece.

I thanked him politely, grabbed it out of his hand, and walked out of the shop. The thought 'pearls before swine' popped into my head, but as I tenderly rubbed the dimpled coldness, and looked once more at the engraved initials on the back, I chided myself. After all, what did he know?

A few days later I found several exciting emails waiting for me on return from work. Prior to our trip I had stumbled across an online community forum which helped with genealogical research and had posted a query on the message board. I was advised that I could search for my father's name on ships' manifests, leaving from Hamburg, the port most used for refugee transports in 1953.

The Mormons now had an online database, which I searched, but discovered no reference to a Kaluba Oldrich. I had a brainwave and did an online search on the US phone directory and found seven Oldrichs, four of which were in New York, not too far from Pittsburgh. I got as far as lifting the receiver and dialling, when the absurdity and cruelty of that approach hit me. What would I say? I am looking for my father - are you related?

I envisaged taking a flight and appearing in the neighbourhood, not saying who I was, just standing in the shadows watching those who walked in and out of the building that housed my possible family, to see if I could catch a glimpse of a likeness. I laughed out loud at my reverie - it was such a ridiculous idea, apart from the fact that I could not afford it. I concentrated on finding proof.

I began an online correspondence with a South African gentleman who had traced his family back to the seventeenth century, and gathered a wealth of information on generations spread across the globe. I wrote him my story, and he offered his knowledge as a gift to me, and started researching on my behalf.

A few weeks later I got a response to my posted online query from a gentleman in the Czech Republic, who told me I had made a terrible mistake.

Oldrich was a Christian name, and Kaluba, a name of Polish origin, was a surname. I had been looking for someone who did not exist!

I checked the baptismal certificate and looked at the name again. Oldrich Kaluba. But how could the name Karl fit into this configuration. Reality suddenly touched me with slow cold fingers. Had I subliminally transposed the name simply to make the name of Karl fit into the equation? Could my mother have been involved with two people at the time of my conception and simply got confused in the telling? It made sense. She had said that she had not known that she was pregnant until she was four months gone – presumably when the symptoms of pregnancy would be well enough advanced that she could feel me moving in her womb - she had had a baby before so she would have recognised those butterfly flutterings. Was she unsure who the father had been? Was it only later, when I was four, and she could see a likeness, that she had known once and for all who the father had been and felt obliged by the duty of conscience to her Catholic faith, to supply his name for the baptismal certificate?

I envisaged her visiting me in the orphanage every Sunday, searching my changing features for a glimpse of Karl or Oldrich, and my agony deepened.

Suddenly I felt that old wound in my heart, gouged out by my mother's secrets, healed with time and counselling, starting to rip open.

I could not sleep that night. I could not concentrate on work the next day. I became unaware of my surroundings, sat and stared at the PC instead of answering mails and preparing for meetings. That evening, as I sat on the couch, the TV screen a blur in front of me, I started rocking.

I saw the concern in Richard's watchful eyes as he put out a hand to stop me. I suddenly realised that for the first time I was not alone whenever anguish caught me by the throat. I did not need to call Jacqui for support. I had Richard to talk to, not to say how I felt – I still suffered from emotional dyslexia - but I could talk through what was going on in my head.

I opened up to him, and this simple act of telling him what had been spinning around my head, gave me immediate relief and solace. I cried and, like a needy child, I was held in his arms and comforted.

When the adult in me returned, we made a plan. We consulted the US Telephone Directory and found seven listed numbers with the surname of Kaluba. We drafted an opening phrase which would help me get a conversation started, without hopefully doing too much harm.

It still took me a few days to gather the courage to take the list of names and pick up the phone. In the end I did it when I returned from work one day, before Richard got home, and my sons were out. Somehow I needed to do this alone. I sat down on the floor in the hallway, back to the wall, knees drawn up, as small as I could make myself, as I took the first and largest mental step towards forever establishing my future status – family member or orphan.

The first number rang out.

The second number went to answer machine. I had not anticipated this so stumbled a bit before I launched into my routine.

"Er. Hello. My name is Saskia. I'm calling from Scotland. I am doing some research into my family history, and looking for an Oldrich Kaluba. Do you have any objection to me asking you a few questions?" Now what? I had to improvise. "I will call back tomorrow in the hope of finding you in. Thank you for your time".

I felt like a cold calling salesman. I took a deep breath and dialled again. The third number answered. In my best American accent I reread my script. I held my breath as I waited for the reply.

"Oh, how interesting!" The voice was that of a young woman. "No, not at all – no objection, though I don't know of any Oldrich in my family. But why don't you ask my mom. She might know. I can give you her number..." My fear dissipated as I marvelled at this good hearted response and inwardly thanked the Americans for being a nation so openly warm and polite. The number she quoted was one I already had on my list. I thanked her, and dialled.

"Hello, my name is Saskia and I'm calling from Scotland. I'm doing some research into my family history and am just off the phone to your daughter who recommended that I call you. Do you have any objection to answering a few questions?"

"Oh, can you please call me back in about 20 minutes; it's not convenient at this time." I rang off politely, unsure if I was being given the cold shoulder or not. I checked my watch and sat on for a few minutes, marvelling at how easily my worst fear had been overcome, and then got up to relieve the numbness in my posterior, and started making preparations for dinner.

Richard arrived home and I told him of my calls. We sat together on the couch as I called back exactly 20 minutes after my last call.

"Ah, yes. My daughter phoned me and asked if you had

called. How can I help?"

"I'm searching for a man called Oldrich Kaluba, who left Germany in 1953 and emigrated to the States."

"Oh, our family emigrated from Poland after the first world war. I'm not aware of any member of the extended family living in Germany."

"Well, Oldrich was actually Czech as far as I'm aware – a refugee from WW2 who ended up in a DP Camp in Nurnberg. Did your family have any connection to Czechoslovakia?"

"I'm afraid I am not aware of anyone. But, you know, Kaluba is a relatively rare name. We are the only Kaluba family in the States. All the names in the phone listing – we're all related. Are you sure he emigrated to the States?"

"No, well, perhaps he moved back, or he may be dead, he would probably be in his seventies by now. Well, thank you very much for your help."

"Not at all. You're very welcome. Oh, I'd be very interested to know if you find him. Would you call me back and let me know?"

I looked at Richard as I put down the receiver, and then at the computer. I powered it on. I never even got to search the German Telephone Directory. My South African correspondent was already one step ahead of me. AOL's "You have mail" prompt led me to open a message from him, detailing the German address and phone number of Oldrich Kaluba.

The needle had been sticking out of the haystack all along, sharp and glinting with truth, but I had not been able to see it for the dull sheen my mother's secret had painted over my perceptions.

Chapter 31   Are You My Father?

"Hello Herr Kaluba. I'm doing some research on people who lived in the Valka Camp outside Nurnberg around 1953. I wonder if you can spare me some time to answer a few questions." I deliberately did not mention my name. I had planned this call very carefully and did not want to give too much away at the outset. I don't know why, but I felt that I needed to play him like a trout – taunt him with a titbit until he was committed to the bite, and then draw him in. It was as though I sensed there might be an undercurrent of resistance.

"Yes... I lived in the Camp. How can I help?" I heard surprise, interest and uncertainty in his gritty and tremulous voice. He sounded old and frail. Suddenly my tactic seemed hard and cruel. I had to be careful. I did not want to put him into a state of shock that might cause him harm.

"I live in Scotland and am doing research on my family. I'm looking for anyone who might have known Brigitte Langer".

A pause.

"How did you get my name?" His voice was careful now, suspicious.

"I found it amongst some of my mother's papers."

"I can't help you." He hung up. So much for my fishing skills, I thought.

I discussed the call with Richard, and we considered if I should ring him back, but decided correspondence might be less confrontational. So I spent the next few days preparing a letter in German in which I apologised for my rudeness at calling him and interrupting his peace and quiet. I introduced myself, provided a little of my background, and requested if he could let me know what he thought of the baptismal certificate I had found after my mother's death in which he is named as my father. I photocopied the certificate and an identity card dated 1953 with a photograph of my mother attached, in order to jog his memory, and, just before I sealed the envelope, decided on a whim to insert a photograph of me and my two sons, which had been taken at a wedding just a few months previously.

I waited three protracted weeks for an answer, before I called him again.

"Herr Kaluba. This is Saskia. I hope you received my letter. I appreciate the information I sent you must have been a shock, but I hope you understand my need to get some clarification." I was unsure what his reaction would be and steeled myself for some verbal abuse.

"Yes, it was a shock. I did remember your good mother after I saw the photograph. It was a long time ago, and there are a lot of bad memories from that time which one likes to forget, so it took me a while to remember. Yes, I knew her for a few months, but I don't know anything about a baby. It's a mystery to me why my name is on the certificate."

I felt disappointment but also hope. Disappointment that he had not acknowledged paternity, but his conciliatory tone meant at least he might be willing to stay on the phone this time and talk about the possibility. "Would it upset you if we talk a little about the Camp?"

"No, it's alright. Go ahead, ask your questions."

"Was she living at the Camp when you met her?"

"No, she wasn't in the Camp. She lived nearby."

"Where were you from originally?"

"Plzen, in Czechoslovakia. I got out before the Communists made it impossible."

I realised I had just heard a deviation from my mother's story. Plzen was south of Prague – my mother had said Karl came from near her village which was north east of Prague.

He continued filling me in with a few personal details. He had left in 1947, leaving his parents behind – they had told him to get out and make a life in the west, to head for the American Sector. He had been able to keep in touch with them, but it was only after the Velvet Revolution in 1986 when the Soviets left Czechoslovakia that he was able to return and visit his mother a couple of times before she died.

Since becoming a pensioner, the state paid for his yearly retreat to Karlsbad, which was his only link with his home country now.

There was an awkward moment, the same as there would have been making polite conversation with any stranger. I asked him if he kept well. This question was important for me – for I knew that most children die of inherited diseases, and I was suddenly faced with an opportunity to find out if there was cancer or heart disease in the family. He said he was in good health, considering his age (he was 75) and that since his partner's death nine years previously he led a quiet life, but tried to keep active by going ballroom dancing three evenings a week; although he did go to the doctor every other Wednesday afternoon to get his blood checked. Despite my best efforts I could not figure out what the condition was that he was being treated for, but I did make a quick calculation that he must have been eleven years younger than my mother when he had known her.

I was surprised by his next comment.

"When I was visiting the doctor I told him about your call and letter. He said paternity tests are relatively easily available now. If you wish to pay for one I will be willing to take it."

"I think that is a little way off yet. Can we just get to know each other a little better first?"

A pause.

"If you wish, but I really don't see the point, as you live in Scotland and I live in Germany."

He agreed to my calling him again, stating that writing was a problem for him. I asked if he could send me a photograph.

He sent more than one. He mailed me about a half dozen – although the images they portrayed did not look like those of a 75 year old man. The content of the photos gave a rough indication of their age. The oldest, in black and white, showed a man in patterned swimming trunks standing leaning against a fence, his feet in sand. It was difficult to put an age to his features, not only because of his baldness, but also because of his distance from the camera, although I was struck by the shapeliness of his legs which looked very similar to those of my younger son. My older son had skinny legs with bony knees like his father's.

None of the shots supplied very good facial close ups, apart from two colour photos. In one, his shiny round head was dominated by a somewhat large nose protruding over a grey closely cropped beard. His eyes looked brown rather than blue. He was smiling at the dark haired woman sitting beside him. I guessed from her hairstyle and dress the photo had been taken in the Eighties, possibly on holiday as both of them had good tans. In another photo he was sitting on a flower covered balcony with a different woman, younger than in the previous, his face in profile, his nose not as hooked as I had first surmised, his face clean shaven this time. I noticed his neat ears with small lobes, like mine.

Richard looked at the photos and commented on how Oldrich seemed to enjoy the company of pretty younger women. I smiled as I gently commented that any opportunity for an older man to sit next to a young good looking woman would probably be exactly the sort of occasion where photographs would be taken.

I called him a couple of times more before I made arrangements to visit.

Chapter 32   The Visit

In August 2002, 35 years after I had attended Jeff and Florentine's wedding in Belgium, Richard and I witnessed the marriage ceremony of their only daughter, Greet. It was wonderful to once again see my "Belgian family" - a term adopted by Jeff over the years. Of all those I had stayed with during my childhood trips, I still kept regular contact with Jeff. His daughter Greet, and Katy, Maria's daughter, had been over to Scotland to visit me in 1988. I had in turn visited Jeff and Mama Yvonne with my family, usually on our way to or from France during our annual holidays. Sadly, Mama Yvonne's heart finally gave out in 1990.

Greet wanted our presence to be a surprise for her father, so it was agreed I would pretend to Jeff that we would be unable to attend. Apart from anticipating the look of surprise on Jeff's face, I was also looking forward to introducing Richard for the first time. But I hoped the climax of this trip would be a face to face meeting with Oldrich in his home, which would somehow allow me to get a sense of the man, and permit that gut feeling which had so often in the past been my guide, to confirm to me whether he was indeed my father.

We flew to Charleroi in Belgium and hired a car. Our plan was to spend a couple of days visiting in Bornem after the ceremony, and then to drive to Germany to visit Oldrich. When I had called to advise him of our plan to visit, his response had been positive and encouraging.

We reached Aachen at noon and, having located the suburb in which he lived and then booked into a nearby hotel, made our way to his apartment.

My heart fluttered like a fledgling on its maiden flight as we drove along the winding road past several blocks of grey albeit well maintained concrete apartments, their drabness cheered up by splashes of intense colour from the hanging baskets and window boxes adorning the balconies.

Richard parked the car and we walked along the neatly bordered path to the entrance of Block E. I felt as excited as a child about to attend its first birthday party. Richard squeezed my hand in encouragement and I pressed the button beside Oldrich's name on the intercom. The door buzzed open and as we climbed up two flights of stairs I wondered how a 75 year old would manage these stairs on a regular basis.

Oldrich opened the door just as we were peering at the name plate. He was taller than I had imagined, slightly older and more distinguished looking than in the photos. His smile was welcoming as he formally proffered his hand, but I impetuously put my arms around him and hugged him. He didn't exactly draw back but I could feel his rigid deportment. I urged myself to take things slowly.

He showed us into his apartment and we walked through a dark lobby to a living room. I introduced Richard and as they made small talk about the journey and the weather, I studied him. I noticed that his eyes were, after all, hazel and almond shaped, like mine. His nose was as imposing as in the photos. He was well turned out, wearing a classy lightly patterned silk shirt, and well cut beige trousers. He bore himself erect, like a dancer, and I was impressed by his natural grace as he walked into the kitchen to get us a cool drink. I imagined him sweeping a woman across the dance floor, suavely gliding like Fred Astaire or Gene Kelly.

I inspected the sitting room. The carpet was threadbare, as was the little sofa and mismatched armchair. There were handmade doilies on the two occasional tables at either end of the sofa, on top of which sat little knickknacks indicating past trips to Turkey or Greece. The place was spotlessly clean, but I could see it needed refurbishment.

My eyes were drawn to a portrait resembling the same attractive woman with the eighties' hairdo in his photo. It looked as though it was painted while they were on holiday, no doubt by some bushy haired, leather skinned artist sitting at his easel in the shade of an olive tree, baiting passing tourists with an array of sketches leaning against the white washed wall behind his lair.

When Oldrich reappeared he confirmed this was indeed a portrait of Andrea, the woman who had been his partner for nineteen years, and had died of cancer nine years previously. I found it touching that he still had her portrait hanging in memoriam on the wall above the old fashioned sideboard.

As I raised the glass of coke to my lips and sipped the cold liquid my throat was momentarily choked. I could not believe I was finally sitting in his presence, in his sitting room, drinking from a glass which must have touched his lips a thousand times before mine. Judging by the age of the furniture and the way he had taken care of his home, the glass was probably older than the decade I had spent dreaming of finding him.

We went out for lunch – to a local Chinese restaurant he recommended. He told us if we hurried we would still get there in time to take advantage of the lunch-time special. Later I could not remember what I had eaten; I was too absorbed in watching him.

He seemed to relax, talking about his childhood in pre-war Czechoslovakia and how he had survived after the war. He had taken part in the building of the new Germany, working cash in hand at labouring jobs, and moving between the various displaced persons camps dotted around the country, following job opportunities. He described how his plans to emigrate to the States were gradually abandoned as stories came back that the roads in God blessed America were not after all paved with gold; how he drifted until he finally met Andrea and settled down in this northern city; how he spent his retirement - ball room dancing, doing crossword puzzles and entering competitions - and occasionally winning big prizes like the microwave sitting pristine and unused in his kitchen. He didn't much care for modern contraptions.

Once the coffee was served, I finally found the opportunity to ask the question that had been tying my tongue in knots for the last hour. "You told me only briefly before on the phone, please can you tell me in some more detail how you knew my mother?"

I sensed a slight change in his manner, spied a tiny

contraction of the muscles around his eyes. He took a sip of his coffee before he answered. "I thought about that very thing after your first phone call. Trying to recall what one did 50 years ago is not easy. Anyway, I seem to remember meeting her when she was working in the haberdashery department in a large store in Nurnberg, I cannot recall the name. Any way we started up a conversation and it turned out she was living in a boarding house not far from the Valka Camp. When I realised we were compatriots, I asked her to join me for a cup of coffee. We saw each other for a few months. We took pleasure in our shared backgrounds, talking of home, surrounded as we were by so many strangers from so many countries."

"Did you know she was Jewish?"

He seemed genuinely taken aback. "Your good mother never told me that, Saskia. No, I did not know."

I digested this new piece of information. So my mother had not divulged this part of her history to him, just as she had chosen not to disclose it to anyone else later in life. Had she felt so ashamed of that particular label?

"Not that I had anything against the Jews. I remember one of my friends at school was Jewish, although I don't know what happened to him after Jews were stopped from attending school. I don't know whether his family emigrated or if he was taken away, but I never saw him again."

I had always felt uncomfortable with the way some people had to justify themselves – almost as if they were protesting their innocence, trying to reassure me that they were prejudice free, whenever the subject of the holocaust was brought up.

"Brigitte was not Jewish in the true sense. She came from a mixed marriage. She was designated Jewish Mischling of the first degree."

Ah, yes" he acknowledged. "Unfortunately the war brought out the worst in people, Saskia, but it also brought out the best."

I recalled the many times my mother had echoed these same sentiments and forgot my discomfort.

"And life after the war was different too – people who had lost everything, been forcibly relocated or had no homes to go back to, found themselves living in worse or at best the same conditions they had endured during the war, almost a decade after the war ended! In 1953 I lived in that Camp in wooden barracks – with eight of us to a room, there was no privacy, no solitude. We were given some pocket money by the government, we worked off and on, and we lived from one day to the next in conditions worse than today's prison inmates have to endure. We had nothing other than hope for a better life that only emigration seemed to offer." He stopped and looked straight at me. "So you see, when an opportunity arose for intimacy with another person, one took it. To share some human feeling other than a need for survival made existence bearable. Do you understand?"

I thought I saw supplication in his eyes. What was he looking for? Forgiveness? There was a long, painful pause.

Richard called for the bill.

"So how long were you and Brigitte together?" I asked.

He looked away, started fumbling with his jacket. "I don't know - a few months, three or four. I can't remember exactly. I got an offer of work and moved out of the Camp. The job lasted a few months and when I came back I asked about her and heard she was with another man, another Czech. I never saw her again.

"Do you know his name?" I asked quickly.

"No, I don't."

"Did you know she was pregnant?" I knew I had asked him the question before but I wanted to see his eyes when he answered me.

"No, I didn't. And I can't believe that she would not have told me, sought me out to tell me, if, as you say, I had been the… if I had been your father."

I wasn't sure if he was telling the truth or not. There was blatant anxiety in his eyes. Then, in a lower voice he said, "What do you want from me? Money? I don't have any money. I am a poor pensioner."

Later, when I was waiting for sleep, lying clinging onto the edge of the soft bed in the airless, slightly musty smelling room of the hotel, I replayed that afternoon's meeting. I was shocked by his assumption. Did he really think I had searched for him so long in order to extort money from him - to demand reparation for not knowing I existed? It didn't make sense. I supposed there were unscrupulous people that might consider making a financial claim, a paternity suit. I had learnt online of the reparations still being paid out to Jews by the German Government. Was he simply claiming that he had not known of my existence because he was afraid I would raise a suit against him? It was a laughable thought. But his fear was an obstacle, for how would I ever know if he was telling the whole truth?

I berated myself for judging him so harshly. He had never experienced fatherhood. He had never known what it was to care for one's own flesh and blood, so how could I expect him to suddenly be overwhelmed with feelings of joy?

It was true that he had asked very little about me or my sons – his potential grandchildren. I knew I would simply have to give him more time to get used to the idea. Not many 75 year old men could take in their stride being told on the phone they had fathered a child half a century previously, and I advised myself that I should take things slowly, work towards gaining his trust, and towards building a solid relationship with him. I decided that even though we lived in two different countries, this would not be allowed to become an obstacle to my resolve.

We had arranged to pick Oldrich up at 10.00am at his apartment and he was to take us for a tour of the city. I hid my consternation behind dark glasses and tried hard to ignore the dull throbbing behind my eyes.

My spirits lifted once we were shown the quaint medieval city centre. Oldrich proved to be full of local and historical knowledge and did an admirable job of keeping us entertained as we wound our way up and down the cobbled streets. My headache gradually disappeared.

We stopped for a drink at a corner shop just off the old town square. He grumbled at two teenage skateboarders who zipped past, all baggy trousers and arms flailing. Suddenly he started a loud diatribe which took me by surprise.

"Why doesn't the government get these idiots off the streets? Get their hair cut and teach them some respect. They run about like they own the place, show no manners. No wonder there's so much unemployment, these layabouts don't want to work – they want the state to support them!" He carried on ranting in a similar vein as we walked on, and Richard and I looked at each other and grimaced.

Here was a new side of Oldrich we had not seen before - a hurdle I had not anticipated. I cringed at the thought of what he would think of my teenage sons with their fashionably long hair, grungy trousers worn at half mast, and their adolescent arrogance, although I knew they had more respect for their elders than Oldrich might be aware of. I reasoned he was just displaying the fear that accompanies the inexperienced. It was unlikely Oldrich would have had much opportunity to mix socially with the younger generation.

Richard diverted Oldrich's attention away from the cause of his antagonism by exclaiming in wonder at the medieval Town Hall we were now facing, and asking about its history and Oldrich turned back into the role of benign tour guide. Richard suggested taking a picture of Oldrich and I standing in front of the imposing entrance.

We duly posed and smiled for the camera. Then Oldrich looked at his watch and asked if we would like to meet a friend of his – a dancing partner - for lunch.

The apartment blocks we parked at this time were not adorned by gaudy hanging baskets. These residences exuded affluence by their very lack of ornamentation. We took the lift to the eighth floor and were met by a woman standing at an open door. She was in her mid sixties, elegantly blond and quite charming.

We were formally introduced to Frau Bernhardt and as I shook her hand, she exclaimed "Well, Ulli, you never told me you had such a beautiful daughter!"

We were shown into a sumptuously furnished living room and made polite conversation for a few minutes, after which we were asked to go through to the dining room and sit at the table set with white and gold matching glass and tableware. Frau Bernhardt then vivaciously served a three course meal that was so flavoursome and tastefully presented, it would have made the maitre d' of a Michelin Rosette restaurant proud.

The only thing I found disturbing was the way she treated Oldrich. I had noticed during lunch on the previous day that he suffered from slight shaking of the hands when he lifted a glass or a fork to his mouth, although it did not hinder him in any way. However, Frau Bernhardt insisted on cutting up his food, tying his serviette round his neck and feeding him like a child.

As the conversation progressed we learned that Frau Bernhardt was a widow, who had known Oldrich for a couple of years, and it was odd to listen to her chirpy lightweight comments followed by more lectures from Oldrich on the state of the nation. It was rather comical to watch her roll her eyes and try to deflect him as he grumbled about one topic after another.

Once we had moved back into the living room, Frau Bernhardt turned the conversation to me and my life, politely grilling me for the information Oldrich had never seemed to want to know.

I liked her directness. It gave me an opportunity to say why I had been looking for my father, to explain my need for roots. I thought I saw understanding in her eyes.

She looked at my father as she said "I think it's wonderful that you've found each other. It won't be easy to establish a relationship living so far apart, but time will help. I think this is a good thing for you, Ulli."

Oldrich sat like a stone next to me sullen and distant. I asked where the bathroom was to give myself some time out. Looking in the mirror I wondered if an observer could guess at the turmoil that rocked inside from my impassive face. Was Oldrich feeling the same under his granite front?

As I washed my hands I noticed that one of the double sinks displayed several brands of aftershave.

When I returned to the living room the conversation had turned to the safer topic of how winters in Scotland compared to those in Germany. This led to Frau Bernhardt insisting on taking me to her bedroom to show me a rather bright yellow cashmere pullover she had bought for Ulli the previous Christmas, complaining that it continued to sit unworn in her wardrobe, and stating she could not understand why he did not like it. I decided that Ulli might be rather more than a mere dancing partner as she opened the wardrobe to reveal several men's shirts and trousers.

As we returned to the sitting room, I was astonished to hear Ulli say that he had remembered an incident with Brigitte. I smiled encouragingly as I sat back down beside him.

"Your good mother was very sensitive to the cold - always wrapped in several layers of clothing." I grinned at the shared memory as he continued. "I remember we were sitting on her bed in her room one evening, and one thing led to another and I put my hand up her skirt. Well, you wouldn't believe it! It was lined with fur! I laughed my head off – I had never seen a fur lined skirt before!"

I gritted my teeth, determined to keep the smile pasted on my face, but inside I was falling apart. I remembered a fur lined coat - not a skirt. The coat my mother had owned for as long as I could remember, and guarded until the fur had ripped and perished, the coat she had used as an extra layer on her bed at night during those long freezing winters when she could not afford to heat the numerous flats through which she had passed, rootless and searching for the warmth of hope.

Chapter 33   Loose Ends

Later when we dropped Oldrich off at his apartment before heading back to the hotel, I thanked him for letting us visit. We were due to leave the following morning.

He said we were welcome to come back anytime, and it was up to me if I wanted to organise a paternity test. As he waved goodbye, and I returned the gesture, I felt my heart was so listless, the blood in my veins must have slowed to a trickle.

I ran the day's scenes through my head during the interminable night that followed. My instinct was that he was my biological father, yet I could not find myself drawn to the man as a person. I could not but help wonder, if I had been introduced to this man socially, would I have wanted to establish a friendship with him? Sadly, my gut response to that question was 'no'.

I knew that I normally would give people the benefit of the doubt when it came to first impressions – was I being too sensitive because of who he was and the subconscious image I had nurtured of what my father should be? Had my expectations been impossible to fulfil and was this the reason for my disappointment in him?

I wondered at his relationship with Frau Bernhardt. It had surprised me – this mother/child/lover/gigolo liaison – had she seen something in him that I could not see? Was I prepared to go through the strain of trying to work at this relationship in the hope of one day seeing in him qualities that I could admire?

The minutes turned to hours and sleep continued to evade me. My thoughts revolved as in a centrifuge, and the single thought that kept separating itself from the rest was the discrepancy between my mother's description of their relationship and his version of the story.

For him the relationship had obviously been a brief union between lost souls needing human contact.

For her the relationship had been one of love, had consisted of a planned future together that due to circumstances beyond their control was doomed to failure. I recalled very clearly her description of him, and there were simply too many inconsistencies. She said Karl had come from near her home town and their fathers had known each other. Oldrich came from a totally different part of the country and never indicated that there had been any family connections. Karl had been a promising concert violinist; Oldrich did not play any musical instrument, let alone a violin.

I could only conclude two possible scenarios.

Either there had been two men that could have fathered me. The first was a fleeting affair, the second the love of her life, who may not have been the physical father of her child, but had become the designated father of her child because it was what she would have wished.

Or, the alternative was that there had never really been a Karl. She had simply invented him, a romantic lie, in order to hide her shame at the sordidness of the truth.

I wiped the involuntary tears away with the back of my hand, and hoped my muted sobs would not wake Richard.

As the light of dawn wound its tentacles through the cracks in the curtains, it occurred to me that I was in a position to make a choice, and that it should be made now, to avoid further anguish.

I wondered at myself, my hardness. If I made the decision not to see him again I would be denying my children their grandfather. Why after all the time I had spent searching should I give up on him so easily? I told myself it was because I could not face up to the ordeal of having to gain this man's trust. I looked to the future and I could not see myself visiting him again, or taking my sons to visit him, translating, playing the go between, covering up his and their prejudices to make everything seem as it should be. I was not sure I could mentally bear the emotional trauma.

It hit me that the choice I was agonising over was probably the same one my mother had faced over half a century earlier. She chose to deny me my father. What had made her choose not to keep contact with Oldrich?

My last thought as I slipped into a restless doze was that although there had been a physical bond between Oldrich and my mother, there had been no love to sustain it.

When we returned to Scotland I had our photos developed. I showed them to my sons and the friends whom I had told of my search and find.

Some marvelled at the resemblance, others could not see any. My sons looked curiously at the image of the old man and then expectantly at me.

I chose one picture and got it framed and it now hangs in my bedroom like a trophy - confirmation that I have a father. But whenever I look at the two of us posing falsely together, smiling happily for the camera, all I can remember is the confusion and hurt I felt, and I am glad I made the decision that I did.

In the end I was just like my mother. I tied a big knot in the loose ends of my personal history and moved on.

Neither of us has been in contact since.

Saskia with Oldrich in Aachen, Germany 2002

Chapter 34   Karl

And so my story was finally concluded. I had gone as far as I could. Or so I thought.

In 2006 Richard heard that the national Radio Station, BBC Scotland, was going to run a feature the aim of which was to encourage people to write. "Write Here, Write Now" was to last for the month of February and subscribers would get encouraging emails to help them reach their target of 1000 words of creative writing per day for the month.

Richard encouraged me to join up. I agreed that it would be cathartic and give me an opportunity to leave a written memoir for my children. By the end of the month I had the best part of my childhood memories completed. Of course I had to delve into the box of secrets again to confirm dates, and I also had to look for the folder my mother had created which contained various newspaper clippings. I wanted to get my facts straight regarding Mr Moss' funeral which had been reported in the local paper.

It had been stored along with some other magazines in the carved chest he had bequeathed to her. As I rifled through the contents I came across a hand written notebook that I had never noticed before. It contained medical phrases and notations, and words rewritten over and over in an attempt to learn their spelling. The writing was my mother's. I concluded she had kept it from her time at Papworth.

Inside the notebook I discovered two hand written letters written in Czech, dated September and November, 1954. I could hardly make out the writing but I could see that they were signed "Karel". Not the spelling I had used, but I had assumed a German version of the name.

In a frenzy of excitement I had to endure a week's waiting as they were being translated. Would these be two of the letters written during the time my mother said they had corresponded? Would I find declarations of love, or a response to her letter advising him that we would not be joining him?

This is what I finally read:

Translator's note:
As the letters are hand-written in a colloquial style and misspelt in places, the names may not be accurate (not easy to read);
also, Mr Továrník can in fact mean a "factory owner".

Letter 1

Landshošt, 2.9.54

Dear Brigitte,

First of all – lots of greetings and memories of you and Saskia.

Many thanks for the letters you have sent me; this one is in reply to your last, received today. You are very good to ask about me in spite of my not writing to you lately. But please understand that nasty and vindictive letters do not deserve a reply. Brigitte, I don't know what you have negotiated with Mr Továrník (?) but I don't think I can represent a company here in Germany when I don't speak German.

You also mention that you are coming to Landshošt on Saturday. I have no objections to your coming as I should like to see you after such a long time. I think, however, that it will cost you a lot of money which I would have thought you badly need just now, and am not sure whether the trip is going to be worth it.

Greeting and kisses to you both,
Yours Karel.

P.S. Do squeeze the little Indian for me until she squeels and tell her that's for me.

Letter 2

Landshošt, 2.11.54

Dear Brigitte,

I cannot imagine why you are not writing at all. I understand that when you did not arrive on Thursday last month, it could not have been your fault but you could have written straight away what had happened? I expect a message from you daily but in vain. Don't you have 20 pf for a letter? So that I don't worry what has happened to you? It is irresponsible on your part to let me wait so.

It does not really matter that you did not come last Thursday as a journey to Munich would have been useless in any case, as the lady from Munich came to see me on Wednesday, a day before we wanted to go and see her. From what she said here, it would make no sense to travel in the matter on behalf of Miss Nicolo (?). I shall tell you all about it when we speak.

I would much appreciate it if you could get Mr Aurich (?) to confirm that he would employ me, perhaps from 15.11. or 1.12. I need a confirmation for those in Munich (for Miss Nicolo), I shall certainly get something as the lady said when she came here, she is called Mencik (?) , she is a clerk in Miss Nicolo's office. So please get it for me immediately and I shall fix the rest myself.

Please give my regards to Mr Továrník's family and give him my sincere thanks, I hope he will do that for me.

Greetings and kisses for you and the little one.

Yours,
Karel

And so, again, I was left with more questions than answers. The only difference is that fourteen years had passed since my mother died, and I had become accustomed to the frenzied highs and cavernous disappointments.

Turning once more to the internet, I tried to locate "Landshošt" but failed. The handwriting was so poor that it was actually difficult to make out the exact spelling. I had lost my connection with my previous correspondents, having bought a new pc and changed internet service provider, so no longer had their email addresses and previous mails. I couldn't relocate the web site – perhaps it no longer existed.

And yet, it no longer mattered as much. Was it because I was ultimately happier since I had come to terms with my mother' life, had met my father, visited my mother's homeland and achieved the closure that Jacqui had talked about? I was now married to Richard, we had moved and set up a new home together, and I had a secure job. The boys were making their way in the world. I realised I had never been so content.

I put the letters back in the notebook and placed it into my mother's box of secrets, as I now called that old attaché case which had somehow played a major role in my life. It still sat in my spare bedroom, ready for me to delve into as and when I needed information, as I continued writing my story.

But one day, when I was looking through the family photos my mother had kept with her in order to scan them for inclusion into the manuscript, I came across the picture of a man standing at the edge of a road, with nothing on the back other than the year of the photograph, 1955.

I allowed myself to wonder. There were a few photos of people I did not know. I had always assumed this particular photo was of a long lost friend, but now I asked myself, if this was taken in 1955, knowing that he was not in the States after all, could it have been "Karel"?

I will never know.

It is one of two loose ends that, despite my best efforts, still continue to prick at my consciousness.

Is this Karl 1955?

Chapter 35   The Aftermath

Occasionally, when I told people old enough to remember the war that my mother had lived in the Sudetenland, comments were made regarding the suffering of the inhabitants of that area, and how unfairly they had been treated, but I never really took on board what they were referring to, mentally lumping this together with the general mistreatment meted out during the Holocaust.

Again, it was the Internet that supplied me with the opportunity to make discoveries. Four years after my visit to Jesenik, I serendipitously input the right search criteria, followed the correct links, and discovered the final part of the story of the Sudeten Germans - the "aftermath" to which my mother had referred.

The Russians arrived in the region in which Jagerndorf and Freiwaldau were situated in February 1944, and were quartered there as occupation forces, supposedly to ensure peace and order. The Czechoslovak National Front coalition government was formed at Kosice in April 1945, and Czech troops moved into the area around May/June 1945, to enforce the decrees issued by that new government. These determined that all Sudeten Germans, except those who could prove their demonstrable loyalty to the Czech Republic, were deemed unwelcome and to be expelled.

German property was to be confiscated without compensation. All officials of the SdP, the Sudeten Nazis, and all members of the Nazi Security Police were to be prosecuted. Sudeten Germans were to be subjected to restrictive measures and conscripted for compulsory labour to repair war damages. A Czechoslovak administrative commission composed exclusively of Czechs was established to oversee these measures.

However, in practice an individual's political affiliation or proof of loyalty was the last thing to be taken into consideration. Personal grievances were the order of the day. Homes were looted, and inhabitants were forcibly rounded up and transported to holding camps (often former prisoner of war, labour, or concentrations camps) before being expelled from the new Czechoslovakian state. In fact, the immediate aftermath consisted of individual acts of retaliation which matched the inhumane degradation and bestiality of the holocaust.

The measures enforced by the government decreed that Sudeten Germans were to wear the letter "N", for Nazi, sewn onto their jackets, were forbidden to use the pavements or trains, were allowed to go shopping at specific times only, and had an 8.00 pm curfew imposed on them. The resemblance to the earlier treatment received by the Jews is obvious, and the above measures are probably understandable as a means of retribution. It seems, however, that other more lawless activities were often endorsed, probably because people had the ability to act out their grudges without interference by the law. There are reports of soldiers from the occupation forces raping women and girls, while their relatives were made to watch. Further reports tell of victims that were beaten and murdered in the streets and later in the camps.

Official figures state that some half a million people were forcibly resettled in the spring and summer of 1945, and during this time it was estimated around 24,000 known deaths occurred, although unofficially relatives claimed twice that number. Cause of death was quoted as being murder, suicide and death from disease or malnutrition.

In July, Czechoslovak representatives were called to address the Potsdam Conference initiated by the United States, Britain, and the Soviet Union, and to present plans for a more humane and orderly transfer of the Sudeten German population. The resulting Potsdam Agreement provided for the resettlement of Sudeten Germans to Germany. The transfer began in January 1946. By the end of the year, some 1.7 million Germans had been resettled in the American Zone and 750,000 in the Soviet Zone. Approximately 225,000 Germans remained in Czechoslovakia, of whom 50,000 emigrated or were expelled soon after.

I discovered that Jesenik District had four camps established where expellees were interred prior to transportation, Jauernig, Adelsorf, and Thomasdorf for men, and Biberteich near Freiwaldau for women. The camps were run by the gendarmerie or police, but the guards were Czech and Russian partisans who had fought with the Soviet advance. I read online reports of the harsh treatment endured in the men's Camps. None of the reports I found mentioned conditions in Biberteich. I knew from the sites I read that they were probably prejudiced towards the Sudeten Germans whose experiences were being described, and I had to take a reality check when I was reading the more lurid accounts, yet I think it is more than likely that my mother was mistreated, starved and possibly raped during her two post war years in Freiwaldau. I recalled how she had told me that the Russians were worse than the Germans, "taking" a woman several times a night. I can only guess at what that comment meant for her, and hope that whatever choices she was forced to make helped her and her baby to stay alive.

I have concluded that the baby was probably not strong enough to survive this particularly bloody and shameful episode in the aftermath of the war in Europe. I recalled the strange evasiveness of the woman in Jesenik town hall, the lack of any Germanic names on any gravestone, and the recalcitrant reaction of the registrar in Lobenstein, and suddenly it all made sense. I wondered how many more relatives have come looking for traces of family members killed in this now forgotten national cleansing and found no trace of any grave.

Finally I understand the reason why my mother did not tell me about the baby. Surely this trauma, this brutal experience, this abasement, this despair and hopelessness, this fight for survival for herself and for her baby, was what she would have wanted to forget more than any of her previous experiences. During her time of forced labour under the Nazis she was at least still working in an office, useful to some degree. She had escaped and thought she had survived a fate of which she had only heard rumours. The war was coming to an end, and the Allies were coming to rescue them, to put an end to the Nazi terror. There was hope. And then, by a strange twist of fate, her Sudeten German identity meant she had to endure persecution a second time.

I now comprehend her bitterness and angry cries of frustration at the cruel fate life had meted out to her in such abundance. But even if I had understood as a child what I understand now, I could never have comforted her. What words of solace could I possibly have given her?

I can finally acknowledge it was best she kept her secret firmly locked in her heart.

The End

Author's Note

There have been numerous books and studies on the long-term effects of the Holocaust on the children of survivors (also known as Second Generation Survivors, Second Gens, or 2G). Indeed, they have a "psychological profile," because their parents' experiences shaped not only their upbringing but personal relationships and perspective on life.

According to an article by Lisa Katz, http://judaism.about.com/od/holocaust/a/hol_gens.htm entitled The Effects of the Holocaust on the Children of Survivors, psychologist Eva Fogelman, who treats Holocaust survivors and their children, proposed a second generation 'complex' affecting identity, self-esteem, interpersonal interactions and worldview.

Studies have shown that survivor-parents often tend to be involved in their children's lives, to the point of suffocation. The reason for this over-involvement is probably the survivors' feeling that their children exist to replace what was so traumatically lost. This over-involvement may exhibit itself in feeling overly sensitive and anxious about their children's behaviour, forcing their children to fulfil certain roles or pushing their children to be high achievers.

Another possible characteristic of Second Gens is difficulty with psychological "separation-individuation" from their parents. A higher frequency of separation anxiety and guilt was found in children of survivors than in other children. Many children of survivors have an intense need to act as protectors of their parents.

Some survivors did not talk to their children about their Holocaust experiences. Others talked a great deal to their children. In both cases, secondary traumatization may have occurred in Second Gens as a result of exposure to their traumatised parents.

According to the American Academy of Experts in Traumatic Stress, children of Holocaust survivors may be at higher risk for psychiatric symptoms including depression, anxiety and PTSD (Post-traumatic Stress Disorder) due to this secondary traumatization.

I had heard that holocaust survivors often had psychological issues coming to terms with what happened to them. The term PTSD did not exist until after the first Iraq war. Since then it has become a recognised fact that people suffering a traumatic event do suffer psychological and physical aftereffects.

I understood that my mother's lack of desire to talk about the war was her way of coping with the trauma she must have experienced. As I have shown, I knew that I was the apple of her eye and she had high hopes for me. I felt as though she wanted me to become what she never could. I knew that I tried to keep her happy, subsuming my desires for hers. I knew that I did not want to disappoint her, because I feared losing her. I felt guilty when I left home. I felt guilty when she died.

I felt distraught when I discovered her secrets after she died. Discovering those secrets was my undoing. I had lived my whole life in the shadow of that guilt, and two years later I suffered a mental breakdown.

So, I am indeed a Second Gen. And I never even knew it.

No, scratch that.

I didn't know I knew it. But I did. The proof? I wrote it all down in this book, eight years ago.

If you have any questions or would like to learn more, you can contact me via email:

survivingbrigitte@gmail.com

or visit my blog:
http://survivingbrigittessecrets.blogspot.co.uk/

Acknowledgements

This memoir would not have been published without the encouragement of many individuals, who believed this story needed to be published.

Thanks to my early readers and supporters – Anne Rowen, Marian Weir, May Mitchell, Margaret Baldwin, Caroline Atkin, Clarabel and Jim Tepe, Ailie Scullion, Frances Gilmour, Kenneth MacDougall, Anne McKinnon, Ann McLaren, Chris Ravenhall, Lynn Henderson and Catriona Malan.

My gratitude also extends to my editor, Margot Aked and members of both Helensburgh Writer's Workshop and Strathkelvin Writers Group, who helped me to hone my writing skills, and The Scottish Association of Writers for providing me with competitions to enter at their annual Conference, and whose adjudicators, in particular Janet Paisley and Mary Edward, allowed me to believe in my writing capabilities. Thanks too to Nalini Chetty whose kind comments put me back on the search for publication after countless rejections.

I would also like to thank Pamela Templeton for her interest and enthusiasm, as well as countless other friends and work colleagues, who continued to listen to the saga of my struggle for publication. I am sure your ears are enjoying the rest.

Special recognition and thanks are also due to Gerry and Elaine Mann, of independent publishers Authorway Ltd, without whose help and advice this manuscript would still be sleeping on my pc.

I must also mention the support of Glasgow Caledonian University's staff, especially Diane Joyce and Jill Watt, for organizing the competition amongst its Graphic Design students, which allowed me to discover Kevin Hickey's talents, and resulted in the cover for my book.

I will be forever in debt for the opportunities provided by the Gathering the Voices Association, especially my personal angel, Angela Shapiro. The group's work towards the success of the worthwhile project www.gatheringthevoices.com is immeasurable. Conceived to gather and record oral testimony from men and women who sought sanctuary in Scotland to escape the racism of Nazi-dominated Europe, it proved to be the means for me to record my mother's story for history, and rekindled my need to get the written version published. I am proud to be able to help this project in its future endeavours.

My never-ending admiration and love go to my patient and wonderful husband Richard, who had to suffer many hours being ignored by his distracted wife. I promise to make it up to you.

And finally, Scott and Drew, much love and special thanks for being there for me when times were hard. This book is for you.

About Author Way Limited

Author Way provides a broad range of good quality, previously unpublished works and makes them available to the public on multiple formats.

We have a fast growing number of authors who have completed or are in the process of completing their books and preparing them for publication and these will shortly be available.

Please keep checking our website to hear about the latest developments.

Author Way Limited

6226527R00151

Printed in Great Britain
by Amazon.co.uk, Ltd.,
Marston Gate.